CW01018477

BEST
PRACTICES
for MANAGERS
and EXPATRIATES

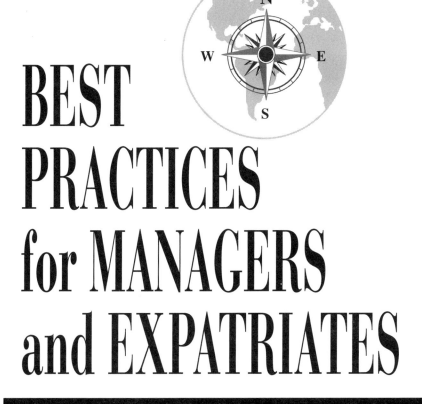

BEST PRACTICES
for MANAGERS
and EXPATRIATES

A Guide on Selection, Hiring, and Compensation

STAN LOMAX

JOHN WILEY & SONS, INC.

New York • Chichester • Weinheim • Brisbane • Singapore • Toronto

Published by John Wiley & Sons, Inc.
Published simultaneously in Canada.

This publication is designed to provide accurate and authoritative information in regard to the subject matter covered. It is sold with the understanding that the publisher is not engaged in rendering professional services. If professional advice or other expert assistance is required, the services of a competent professional person should be sought.

Illustrations by Liz Lomax.

Library of Congress Cataloging-in-Publication Data:

Lomax, Stan, 1937–
    Best practices for managers and expatriates : a guide on selection, hiring, and compensation / Stan Lomax.
        p.   cm.
    Includes index.
    ISBN 0-471-39206-5 (cloth : alk. paper)
    1. International business enterprises—Employees.   2. Career development.
3. Executives—Employment.   4. Employment in foreign countries.   I. Title.
HF5549.5.E45 L658   2001
658.3—dc21   2001026115

Printed in the United States of America.

10 9 8 7 6 5 4 3 2 1

For Elizabeth and Charlotte Lomax

Acknowledgments

Michael Brookes
Mary Cass Bing
Thomas Cook
Michael Hamilton
Elizabeth Lomax
Gilbert Parker
Marianne Ruggiero
William Sheridan
John Stern
William Twinn
Dr. Hoyt Wheeler
Many thanks—your help was invaluable.

Contents

Preface   xi

Chapter 1   What Is the Global Demand for Expatriates?   1

Chapter 2   What Are the Profiles of Today's Expatriates?   29

Chapter 3   What Are the Purposes of Expatriate Assignments?   47

Chapter 4   What Challenges Do Expatriates and Managers Face?   79

Chapter 5   How Can Managers Identify the Best Expatriate Candidates? What Can Individuals Do to Enroll?   105

Chapter 6   How Should Managers Assess and Train the Candidates?   133

Chapter 7   How Should Managers Select the Best Candidate
             for Each Overseas Assignment?   159

Chapter 8   How Can Managers Design a Sound Expatriate
             Rewards Package?   195

Chapter 9   What Are the Issues to Consider While the
             Assignment Is in Progress?   231

Chapter 10   What Are the Issues in Adjusting the Length of the
             Assignment?   257

Chapter 11   What Are the Issues in the Next Assignment Process? 275

Chapter 12   Expatriate Assignments: Future Directions   303

Index   309

Preface

The overseas assignment experience can be wonderful yet traumatic for individual expatriates and corporate managers. The purpose of this book is to encourage both to work closely together to maximize the rewards of this experience while minimizing the difficulties that often arise.

As a human resources director, I've developed and managed expatriate programs for some of the world's leading multinational corporations. Also, I've been an expatriate myself on interesting assignments in Europe, the Middle East, Asia, and the Pacific. Having been on both sides, I've come to view the expatriate assignment as a professional relationship, a marriage of sorts, between the company and the assignee. I've learned what works and what doesn't. And I'm pleased to share with you the many experiences, innovative ideas, and best practices that you can use to achieve your goals.

Today, most multinationals move quickly to exploit competitive opportunities thousands of miles away, dispatching teams of specialists overnight to evaluate the economic potential and to close business deals. But in many cases, these same companies are unable to put the right expatriate assignment programs in place, and to manage these programs in ways that fully support their global business strategies. What are these companies doing wrong, and how can they improve their current practices?

Also, potential expatriates and those already on overseas assignments should be asking similar questions about what they can do to enhance their own careers. Many expats accept, or reject, assignments for the wrong reasons, and they often do not negotiate the best terms and conditions in such critical areas as compensation, benefits, housing, career planning, and repatriation. How then can expats better match their personal goals with their companies' business strategies?

Throughout this book, corporate managers and individual expatriates will find practical, down-to-earth answers to these and other questions. We'll walk through each step of the international assignment process and address each party's special interests and concerns. We'll discuss the global demand for expatriates and profile the characteristics of today's assignees. Strategic planning is critical in defining the purpose of every assignment as well as evaluating, training, selecting, and preparing the best candidate for it.

Individuals will learn how to sign up for overseas postings, get the training needed for success in different countries, and negotiate the most favorable assignment packages. You will also learn how to communicate effectively with home country managers, keep your career on course, and plan your next assignment or repatriation to further your personal and professional interests.

BEST PRACTICES
for MANAGERS
and EXPATRIATES

Illustration by Liz Lomax

What Is the Global Demand for Expatriates?

What Is the Global Demand for Expatriates?

"These are the times that try men's souls."
Thomas Paine, *The American Crisis*,
No. 1, Dec. 23, 1776

Thomas Paine, the passionate supporter of the American Revolution against colonial rule, would have little difficulty grasping another kind of dramatic transition: today's global business revolution and the often violent reactions to it. He would empathize with the genuine fervor of street protestors who disrupted the World Trade Organization meetings in Seattle and Prague in the year 2000. But instead of military forces pitted against each other, these present-day rebels are attacking global businesses, which they perceive as posing dangerous hazards for their countries. The protestors are well-organized groups, including environmental organizations such as Greenpeace, coalitions of national and local labor unions, and governmental antitrust regulators. They're calling for protection for the environment, human rights, free trade, job security, and other socioeconomic issues.

Consider the startling street violence in Prague, where more than 100 individuals were injured, 400 protestors jailed, and extensive damage done to Mercedes-Benz showrooms and Kentucky Fried Chicken (KFC) restaurants, among other global targets. *The Village Voice* of October 18, 2000, reported:

"The 12,000 activists who flooded the streets of Prague weren't the only ones targeting the titans of global capital last week. In addition to the militants hurling molotovs and bricks at the police and financiers during the annual meeting of the International Monetary Fund and the World Bank, thousands of other protestors waged war on line by squatting the two organizations' web sites."[1]

Isn't it ironic that the antiglobalization forces are now appropriating the computer-based tools of modern technology that the multinationals themselves are employing so successfully? *The Village Voice* ran eye-catching headlines: "Couldn't Get to the Protests in Prague? Thousands Threw Virtual Stones Instead" and "Hactivists Chat Up the World Bank."

There is little doubt that the antiglobalization crusade has the organization, power, and publicity to pose a serious threat to globalization. Indeed, the globalization process has been relentlessly carried on in office meetings, cross-border communications, and most importantly, by means of an estimated half million employees sent abroad from their companies' home country headquarters. These peaceful invaders are expatriates. This new kind of army generates no violence and little publicity.

Which movement—globalization or antiglobalization—will prevail? Whether you're a manager for a multinational organization, an expatriate on assignment, or a person seriously considering the opportunity to work overseas, you have a vested interest in the ongoing conflict. If globalization is slowed or stymied by the protesters, your overseas aspirations might be dashed.

This scenario, however, is highly unlikely. Whether multinationals are attacked visibly on the street or assaulted, unseen, through the Internet, they have progressed so far along the road to globalization that no forces, whether governments, unions, or protesters, have the power to restrain them. Today's frenzied pace of cross-border mergers, acquisitions, and joint ventures is testament to the lack of effective restraining forces.

How are governments reacting to the force of globalization?

Instead of trying to seal off their borders, government officials are accepting the movement as part of their own transitions to compete in the worldwide marketplace. Many nations, such as China, Russia, and the Asian "tigers," are dismantling the economic controls and liberalizing the economies that had been restraining their efforts to attract foreign investments and export more goods and services. It's been a difficult process.

Western-style governments are also speedily embracing the globalization concept. The European Union's antitrust commission rejected only 13 major mergers outright over the entire past decade, with proposals averaging about 300 per year.[2] Indeed, the U.S. picture appears to be fully consistent with Europe's. Thomas Friedman, the foreign affairs correspondent for *The New York Times*, wrote: "But what happens to democracies when companies grow to size extra-extra large in order to compete globally, but democratic institutions—like the antitrust division of the Justice Department—remain a size small?"[3]

Can unions and environmental groups fare any better?

Most unlikely. Let's listen to the head of the AFL-CIO, John J. Sweeney, who recently stated: "Globalization is happening one way or another and it can't be stopped."[4] *New York Times* columnist Joseph Kahn adds: "It's probably a mistake to think that globalization isn't threatened. On the contrary, the unions and environmental groups that assail the World Trade Organization seem on the whole to prefer that nations become more like one another faster—and in a great variety of ways. They are not so much trying to block globalization as to hitch a ride."[5]

So the global companies, without the traditional fanfare of fifes and drums, continue to cross national frontiers with the avowed purpose of expanding market penetration. As these corporate monetary investments into new territories escalate, their need for quality employees to manage those investments will soar. And as globalization continues, more expatriates will be required to maximize efficient management of current investments and to explore further opportunities in these new territories.

In short, expatriate activities will continue to thrive in the future. But there will be some changes in the kinds of assignments; and hopefully, there will be sufficient manager interest to reform the overseas assignment process.

This book addresses the two audiences who must work together to make expatriate assignments successful: the managers of the process and the expatriates themselves. After more than 30 years as a manager of the process, both sending out and receiving expatriates, as well as being an expatriate, I've often wondered why planning and communications are so lacking throughout the entire assignment and return process. Managers and expatriates should literally be reading from the same page, in this case the same book. Why the literature in this field is written for one party but not the other is puzzling. If each party to the expatriate contract were more fully aware of all the relevant factors affecting the other party's thinking, there would be far fewer failed assignments, early terminations, and "brownouts." These issues continue to plague both managers and expatriates, with no discernible trends for improvement on the horizon.

Our purpose is to examine each step of the expatriate assignment process, and to furnish practical guidelines and best practices for both the expatriates and the managers of the overseas posting process. We'll view the evidence of current assignment practices in major corporations and explore their ramifications. This research includes a variety of sources: managers, search people, former expats, expatriate case studies, newspaper and magazine articles, survey findings, and other recent books focusing on this dynamic field.

Each global corporation designs its own approach to expatriate programs, and no two have identical programs. To be really effective, these programs must be customized to each company, its industry and business, its stage of global growth, its financial well-being, and its management styles. We'll observe the interplay of these factors at work as we discuss what the multinationals are doing for their expats today. Those practices impact on the expats and their families. Given the expatriate tendency to be outspoken, we'll have little trouble gauging their reactions to those policies. As we proceed we'll make some constructive recommendations for both the expatriate and the managers of the expatriate programs. In addition, we'll have ideas for individuals considering an overseas assignment as well as those who are managing expats.

We'll examine the major global competitors. They vary by how far they have progressed toward true globalization; that stage of transition can have a great impact on the nature and importance of the expatriate workforce.

In this regard, they can be likened to surfers at the beach. As each organization sees the rising wave of globalization, each has to decide, recognizing its own strengths and aspirations, how to ride that surge to its fullest—or in some cases, whether to dive below the breaker and take a chance on the next wave. For those of you who have enjoyed the experience of body surfing, you appreciate the need to furiously swim in advance of the crest in order to catch the surge and be propelled by it—a truly joyous experience as you ride to shore. Carrying on this analogy, those companies that are thoroughly committed to riding the globalization wave must have trained, energetic expatriates to accelerate the firm's growth pace to catch the wave and capitalize on its momentum.

Conversely, if your present organization has elected to avoid all that extra exertion by diving underneath the breaker (remaining domestic), there is every possibility that some unlikely global giant from somewhere may be a "Jaws," looking for some lunch—your company.

As a manager or a current or potential expatriate, you need to assess what stage of the globalization transition your own organization has reached. If senior management has not directly communicated the facts of its global development efforts to its employees, you can often pry those facts out of the annual report. In a similar vein, management usually communicates its business strategy, if not verbally, at least by deeds. Your unclouded understanding of your company's position will enable you to view more clearly how the overseas assignments are perceived by senior management, and whether they are esteemed well enough for you to take the plunge in trying for such an assignment now—or should you wait for the next stage of global growth?

Indeed, many of today's more advanced global competitors have endured painful learning experiences on the progressive path to globalization that demonstrated the need to change their approaches to the overseas marketplace, both for customers and expatriates. From their histories we can draw some understanding that can be put to work for us. Let's explore recent experiences of Procter & Gamble and Coca-Cola.

Procter & Gamble

This leading consumer products company had to learn about globalization the hard way: by trial and error. *Fortune* magazine ranked this company among the 10 most admired organizations for eight consecutive years in the 1990s. However, P&G's poor performance in Japan in the 1980s serves as an illustration for managers and expatriates alike that its successful U.S. marketing should have been modified to succeed in Japan.

Procter & Gamble had long been a world-class manufacturer and marketer of a wide variety of consumer branded products when it first entered the Japanese market in 1972; but it suffered more than $250 million of operating losses by 1983. The company's soap and detergent products, enormously popular in the United States, were being passed over by Japanese consumers for two local brands. To solve this problem, P&G senior management gave the new U.S. expatriate country manager a dire ultimatum: either make the business profitable or shut it down.

As a Harvard Business School case summarized, "Procter & Gamble charged into Osaka with marketing strategies that played so well in Ohio. The results were disastrous. They didn't listen to anybody."[6] Indeed, the company was proudly following its traditional "The Procter Way" approach to marketing, which emphasized the advantages of selling standardized products everywhere, products that were thought to be superior. The P&G Japan operation, staffed with U.S. expatriates in senior roles, had been unable to figure out why their products were performing so badly among Japanese consumers.

After viewing operations, the new U.S. expatriate country manager determined that the company had not thoroughly researched Japanese consumer preferences; he also found that certain soaps and detergents did not suds up properly in the hard mineral water. P&G's research and development group swung into action, reformulating and testing new products while conducting consumer satisfaction surveys. P&G's new country manager went to the extent of appearing on Tokyo television to humbly make a formal apology to local consumers, admitting that the company had not carefully evaluated the local needs and wants of the marketplace. The new P&G in Japan proceeded to shift its emphasis in hiring, focusing on attracting and retaining more Japanese nationals to staff more responsible and career-track positions. And the company promised to listen to these people.

In the human resources area, the company's policies reflected strong centralized management, with the Cincinnati, Ohio, headquarters controlling worldwide operations. Local Japanese managers had previously received little encouragement for career growth within the company. Further, P&G management had insisted that they be proficient in English. However, given more decision-making authority, the new U.S. expatriate country manager elevated the roles of the Japanese managers from being order takers to being customer service representatives. Thus, P&G staged a remarkable comeback in Japan by empowering Japanese staff to better serve local consumer needs.

Although this case is taught in connection with sales/marketing strategies, it also shows how expatriate performance can make or break an overseas operation. Expatriates who become thoroughly knowledgeable about the host country are valuable assets to their companies, especially when they are given substantial autonomy in developing and implementing sound business plans. In a very real sense, management's universal responsibility is to see to it that highly qualified employees are selected and trained for their expatriate assignments, and given a reasonable measure of independence in setting direction and policy for the company to take in the host country.

In sum, the P&G Japan experience shows that even the most highly regarded of global players can stumble in a foreign market and that recognition of mistakes is critical for long-term global survival. As long as managers understand the nature of the problem and are strong enough to take risks in fixing it, overseas expansion, and with it the need for solid expatriate representatives, will continue to flourish.

Coca-Cola

This leading beverage and food company has savored a traditional centralized management philosophy that stressed decision-making and technology improvements that emanated from its Atlanta headquarters. The company has preferred to keep its soft drink taste relatively standardized throughout the world, and has long been known for its pride in maintaining its original formula. We are all familiar with its attempt to drop that traditional taste from the market shelves, and the U.S. public's clamor for Coke Classic to be restored. The company duly bowed to its clients' tastes and brought back the original to the market. But Coca-Cola's financial problems have not been limited to the fall and rise of Coke Classic in the United States. Of the company's $20 billion in worldwide revenues reported in 1999, it recorded only $2.4 billion in profits, down a full 31 percent from 1998. The firm was heading in the wrong direction and needed some global expertise in a hurry.

In February 2000, the company surprisingly selected Douglas Daft, an Australian national with more than 30 years of Asian regional postings, to be its new worldwide chief executive officer. This choice broke a long tradition of promotions from within the Atlanta headquarters. Mr. Daft had no Atlanta headquarters experience, but did come to the CEO post with several years of hands-on market exposure to the Asian marketplaces. He had implemented product modifications there that were working. Further, he presented credentials of an executive who knew how to observe, listen, and then make decisions about how to accommodate local tastes. Clearly the Coca-Cola board had to be expanding its horizons in seeking out a more global perspective for the firm from its corporate leader. Six years of falling profits at Coke were enough for its board.

Indeed, Douglas Daft was virtually a stranger in Atlanta because of his overseas postings and constant travel, "in just a few weeks he has turned the world of Coca-Cola upside down."[7] In an interview, Daft said that his restructuring of the company will "let local managers make decisions about products, advertising, and other functions that were previously controlled from Atlanta. It's something I've always lived by."[8]

Incidentally, one of the major results of pushing downward the empowerment was a layoff plan involving 6,000 employees, almost half of whom were Atlanta-based. As a telling sign of headquarters' lack of confidence in its expats, the Atlanta headquarters had maintained a roster backups for expatriates in case of failures. In fact, these corporate staffers were constantly monitoring the overseas people and checking on information about them on a continuing basis. Daft was not slow to recognize that this "shadowing" practice depressed overseas morale. By illustration, when a manager wanted to shift advertising dollars among brands, he or she had to wait for approval from Atlanta before being able to implement such a change.

Stephen C. Jones, who was the number two executive in Japan, stated that Daft is "very careful about delineating his point of view, but at the end of the day it's: You live here, you're accountable, you make the decision."[9] There's a quote that ought to please you expats on assignment—that golden delegation of real responsibility, essentially the same tactic that had been used so successfully in Japan by P&G more than 10 years earlier.

Daft had taken overseas postings in Indonesia, originally for one year (extended to five), Hong Kong, Singapore for three years, and back to Hong Kong for a four-year stint. What does a successful expatriate carry away from a succession of diverse postings?

"In China, I really learned the value of relationships and understanding political agendas, and there was a real need to understand that you sold and marketed to consumers on a local basis. In a country that large, with that many people, you would really miss a lot if you tried to generalize," Daft said in February 2000.[10]

Do you have any doubt, as manager or expatriate, about Coca-Cola's new expatriate philosophy? Let the empowerment begin!

The global transition process—that traditional tug-of-war between central corporate power retainers versus expanding overseas autonomy—remains a critical strategic struggle for every company considering competing in the global market today. Here we've seen how two respected and successful giants have become even more successful overseas by thinking small, permitting their expatriates on the scene to manage their operations. These two brief histories ought to pose an attractive challenge for you expatriates seeking opportunities to develop your own expertise in an autonomous managerial environment. That's really surfing the globalization wave.

DaimlerChrysler

Here is another recent corporate case study centering on how different managements perceive the expanding global markets and fashion their staffing strategies overseas accordingly. But in this case we can learn from a huge merger between global giants that had sharply contrasting approaches to expatriate programs. This merger was at first allegedly to be a marriage of equals, but it rapidly evolved into a combination of oil and water, culminating in a power struggle that put an abrupt finish to the "equals" publicity. What could go wrong with this largest of all mergers?

"In truth it was a marriage of opposites, a highly diversified German conglomerate getting hitched to a streamlined American car manufacturer," note Bill Vlasic and Bradley Stertz in their book *Taken for a Ride: How Daimler-Benz Drove Off with Chrysler.*[11] "Daimler and Chrysler didn't develop, manufacture, market, or sell cars the same way. Daimler executives had larger staffs and fatter expense accounts. Chrysler officers had broader responsibilities and bigger salaries and homes. Virtually all the German executives spoke English. None of the Americans, with the exception of Lutz [Chrysler's president] spoke German."

Another illustration of the disparities between the corporate parties was reflected in the fact that the Daimler-Benz chairman, Juergen Schremmp, had extensive expatriate experience. Indeed, at the time of the merger (1998), Daimler had more than 1,500 expatriates on assignment, while Chrysler, with a total employee head count of more than 121,000 people, had only 300 posted abroad, a clear sign that it put less value on cross-border postings as stepping-stones than did its new German partner.[12]

Nine months after the 1998 merger date, both companies agreed that it would be mutually beneficial for the new organization if a small group of promising executives could be expatriated to the other headquarters for purely developmental assignments. The avowed purpose was to enable each of the transferees to better understand the other company's business methodology and culture. As expected, the call for selected volunteers drew an enthusiastic response from Daimler managers, who voiced little concern over having to adjust to their new host country location, Auburn Hills, Michigan. German nationals who clearly had recognized an invaluable developmental overseas posting when they saw it immediately filled the Daimler quota of 40 expats.

Chrysler, perhaps having anticipated possible employee reluctance, emphasized the richness of the expat packages that would be given for employees taking their developmental postings in Stuttgart. The company offered the following rewards package for its 40 expatriates:

- **Compensation.** U.S. expatriates are to stay on their U.S. payrolls and be paid in U.S. dollars.
- **Housing.** Daimler pays expats' housing costs in Stuttgart *and* for upkeep of their existing homes, including snow removal and lawn care services.
- **Vacation.** U.S. expats are to receive 25 days of paid vacation each year *and* one round-trip airfare for the expat family unit.
- **Family Assistance.** The company pays up to $5,000 per year for activities that help an expat's spouse enter the German job market; the company also pays tuition and school expenses abroad for the expat's children.
- **Employee cars.** U.S. employees in Germany may get Mercedes vehicles at German employee rates.

Chapter 8, describing expatriate packages, will further review the elements that must be included in competitive reward systems today, but suffice it to say here that the Daimler package was generous to an extreme—indeed, far more lavish than the package that had been offered to the Daimler expat candidates.

Surprisingly, only about one-half of the allocated assignments were volunteered for by the selected pool of Chrysler employees. Many explained that living in Stuttgart would be too uncomfortable for them—less space, different food, new schools, and, of course, the language and German customs.

The substantial group of rejections is troubling. This opportunity was a once-in-a-lifetime event. At this initial stage of the merger, there would have to arise a considerable need for both companies to have on staff people who are experienced in understanding the differences in business philosophies and styles as well as the cultural influences that affect the way each managed their operations. This kind of unique cross-corporate experience would be invaluable for the merger and ongoing operations. While there is little question that the upheaval caused by transferring overseas always represents a trauma for the entire expatriate family unit, there is little doubt, in today's world of accelerating globalization, that most employees would have gained a distinct advantage in competing for top corporate positions through their understanding of how the other corporate partner actually operates. This would have been especially enlightening for the Chrysler expats; Daimler had prospered overseas while Chrysler had not.

So it is difficult to understand the reticence of so many of the eligible Chrysler employees in rejecting the transfers, a truly developmental opportunity, to Stuttgart. Did Chrysler management adequately portray the benefits involved? Were some of the U.S. nationals so homegrown that a two- or three-year overseas assignment was really too difficult for them to adjust to? Had they reached age levels that produced too many family ties and responsibilities to balance against further career opportunities?

As an update to the "marriage," by November 2000, most of the top U.S. executives had left the old Chrysler organization, and Dieter Zetsche, the son of a German expatriate born in Turkey, with expatriate assignments in Brazil and Portland, Oregon, in his record, was named to head the Chrysler unit, replacing a U.S. national, James Holden. Indeed, the press concluded, "Most of Chrysler's top executives have either quit or been pushed out."[13]

How do you think all those Chrysler expat candidates who rejected those developmental assignments would look back at their decisions today? Would they have been better positioned in the staff realignment? While there must have been a percentage of the Chrysler candidates who had thoroughly valid reasons for some of the turndowns, it is highly unlikely that one-half of all those receiving the offers actually had such reasons.

Why, then, was there this strong reluctance on the part of these U.S. nationals to be an expatriate for a few years?

The answer should exclude two major concerns that usually govern assignment rejections: the nature of the assignment itself and the size of the expatriate package. In the Chrysler case, the company constructed these two items as very attractive features. The assignment was for developmental purposes, a splendid opportunity for an employee's career advancement. Further, the package being offered for it was far richer than most current expatriate packages.

The reasons that the Chrysler people gave were generally vague. One would expect an outpouring of physical problems or spouses with employment issues or children with school difficulties. These were not generally offered. Rather, there seemed to be a perceived issue with the smallness of housing, adaptation challenges to the German culture, and having to leave their large, comfortable homes in such pleasant suburbs.

We can extract some useful learning points from the failure of this well-intended program. All overseas assignments carry real trepidation for the entire expatriate family. They will not look forward to having to pull up stakes from a community that they have been comfortable with for years. The spouse will more often than not be currently employed, accompanied by his or her own long-term career aspirations. Consequently the spouse will not be comfortable putting his or her career on hold while leaving for some strange place that many not be able to offer a suitable substitute. Schooling may be a serious concern for the children.

All of these are serious concerns, and we will analyze each of those factors in Chapter 4. But for now we need to focus on why U.S. nationals seem to have such difficulty in making that fateful decision to try an overseas posting. I'll submit that this general American reluctance to work abroad will sharply decline as the differences in lifestyles among countries narrow and the use of younger expats who have traveled more extensively than their parents did when they were young grows.

These two trends will take some time to play out, but in the interim, the globalization wave is still swelling. That means smart employees will want to capitalize on this window of opportunity, while there are still many good potential candidates out there who are leery of the process, even in the face of the career advancements that such assignments might bring.

I've had the pleasure of instructing at the New York State School of Industrial and Labor Relations at Cornell University and the University of South Carolina, and explored what these human resources students thought about the Chrysler rejections. Ironically, students at both schools were unanimous in indicating their own willingness to take such developmental assignments, even in the face of family disruptions. They fully recognize that globalization spells out a requirement to develop expatriate experience or, at the least, exposure to one of the non-U.S. organizations doing business here. We'll present lists of the biggest players (surfers) in each category further on, after covering one more aspect of overseas assignment that does not receive much attention from the press or other authors: the sheer enjoyment and learning benefits that can be had from these overseas postings.

First, as to the expatriate positions themselves, those that are ongoing staff or line jobs that are needed to do the company's business on a regular basis tend to be broader than those back at the U.S. headquarters or other domestic operations. One finds the need to act as a jack-of-all-trades, which is for most humans more fulfilling than doing the same narrow tasks repetitively. Along with breadth of job scope is increased autonomy. The separation by space and time zones gives rise to more decision making rather than advice and consent taking that often governs headquarters and domestic U.S. operations. For an employee desiring to develop managerial skills, these positions often offer the challenge of working with local staff employees, whose culture must be learned and appreciated in achieving their fullest cooperation. Increased patience and the sharpening of listening skills are just a few of the major attributes that can be stimulated by the expatriate assignment.

There is also the unique knowledge that the overseas assignee acquires that can be put to work in coordinating efforts with other corporate functions as potential projects. Or, upon repatriation, there will be the need to fully debrief a cross section of headquarters functions as to the host operation. There will also be training and mentoring opportunities that should be explored upon return. Another fact: Overseas experience is in great demand on the job market. There just may be a better opportunity for you repatriates with another company than putting up with a make-do job back in your home country.

All of these career paths open in some form to repatriates.

As for the remainder of the expatriate family unit, the experience of living within another culture can and should be a fascinating albeit challenging experience. Youngsters often find where they stand in the spectrum of global living conditions, especially if they have been reared in suburban communities or pockets of wealthy neighborhoods within U.S. cities. This can be an enlightening experience for them, and they may gain an appreciation of what they have taken for granted so long as the normal lifestyle. Exposures to more extreme cultures of wealth and poverty are worth lots of sociology classes.

This experience of exchanging values with new neighbors should provide real insights into what really makes for a target for life's pursuits. In fact, the children of expatriates seem to make excellent expatriate candidates. Perhaps once the mind is opened to new sets of foreign concepts it eagerly pushes on for more such exposures. We will see in a Chapter 2 expatriate stories that reflect feelings of enjoyment even in the remotest and most savage of physical and social climates. These assignments, in addition to all the other benefits we'll describe, can also be the most rewarding and enjoyable work and cultural experiences you may ever encounter.

So I've hoped to arouse enough interest in those still deciding about expat careers, and for you present expats and managers, I hope I did the process justice.

Let's see which multinationals are the biggest of the behemoths. For those of you perusing the field of target employers, the lists of the largest organizations, both U.S. and non-U.S.-based, make for a good start in looking over the types of businesses that are crossing borders today. First we will set out the 25 largest U.S. organizations doing business overseas (see Table 1.1). These firms, unfortunately, do not break out expatriate totals; consequently these head counts include those working within the United States and those working beyond its borders.

The remaining 75 largest U.S. multinationals were listed in the *Forbes*, July 24, 2000, issue.[14] Additional statistics showing the employee head counts were published in the *Fortune* issue of July 24, 2000. There the largest 500 global firms were listed.[15]

Both lists ought to afford valuable guidance for those of you searching for a new corporate home overseas. While there may be no direct correlation between the percentage of revenues being made overseas and the overall employee populations, you can gain a feel from these two statistics as to the volume of overseas positions that represent that company abroad. There should be some relevance for the two statistics in providing some guidance as to the volume of overseas opportunities that may be available at that company.

Table 1.1 Largest U.S. Organizations Doing Business Overseas

Company	Foreign Revenues ($ U.S. millions) 1999	Foreign Revenues as Percent of Total Revenues	Percent Change from 1998	Number of Employees
Exxon Mobil	$115,464	71.8%	8.5%	106,000
IBM	$50,377	57.2%	8.7%	307,401
Ford Motor	$50,138	30.8%	14.4%	364,550
General Motors	$46,485	26.3%	−6.6%	214,613
General Electric	$35,350	31.7%	13.0%	340,000
Texaco	$32,700	77.1%	14.8%	18,363
Citigroup	$28,749	35.1%	9.4%	176,900
Hewlett-Packard	$23,398	55.2%	8.7%	84,400
Wal-Mart	$22,728	13.8%	85.6%	1,140,000
Compaq	$21,174	55.0%	23.2%	76,100
AIG	$20,311	13.8%	13.8%	55,000
Chevron	$20,020	50.0%	23.5%	36,480
Philip Morris	$19,670	44.3%	−0.7%	137,000
Procter & Gamble	$18,351	48.1%	2.4%	110,000
Motorola	$17,760	57.4%	26.9%	121,000
Intel	$16,694	56.7%	14.0%	70,200
DuPont	$13,262	49.3%	13.4%	94,000
Xerox	$12,687	54.9%	−0.3%	94,600
Lucent	$12,187	31.8%	47.0%	153,000
Coca-Cola	$12,124	61.2%	3.4%	37,400
Johnson & Johnson	$12,086	44.0%	8.4%	97,800
Dow Chemical	$11,446	60.5%	3.8%	39,200
Ingram Micro	$11,255	27.4%	47.5%	15,376
Pfizer	$10,740	38.9%	13.9%	51,000
Halliburton	$10,117	67.9%	−9.8%	103,000

Data Source: Forbes, July 24, 2000, and Fortune, July 24, 2000.

There are some surprising numbers here for those who may not have been monitoring the extent to which U.S. companies have crossed national borders in the quest of greater revenues. Since most of these U.S.-based organizations continue to staff their overseas operations with U.S. expatriates, it stands to reason that there are significant numbers of overseas postings at all the organizations listed here, as well as the rest of the companies set forth in the *Fortune* and *Forbes* tables. So we are looking at thousands of expatriate opportunities; the glass is half full if you have the desire and the talent to find an appropriate one, and the glass is half empty if you choose not to sample the global wave. You may find yourself competing for a "domestic" promotion against a repatriate, whose broader background could well be the decision-making factor.

As increasing numbers of expatriates return to their companies or enter the open job market, they will represent formidable competition for job seekers here, especially for openings at those multinational firms that need to put the overseas experience to work, either here or back at a host location. This may mean that you should consider getting your expat ticket punched even if you are not deliriously happy about leaving your U.S. domicile.

There are some observations worth noting about these annual corporate listings. It comes as no surprise that in 1999, when technology was riding its own wave of investor popularity, that several technology organizations such as Lucent and Ingram reported overseas revenue increases of 40 percent or more; this was astounding growth then, but would that surge be perpetuated?

No. The fall of 2000 brought more than chilly weather. It also brought a severe decline in the once high-riding tech and dot-com stocks. But whether that means these companies are no longer desirable entrance points to the world of expatriate assignments is still unclear. You'll need to monitor these organizations very carefully if you are thinking about that type of overseas career.

There is another trend from the *Forbes* report worth considering. Only 15 percent of the 100 companies reported declines in their revenues from overseas operations, and most of those were negligible drops. Many were attributable to the sharp decline of the euro, which lost more than 14 percent against the dollar that year.

Unfortunately, no one seems to know for sure how many expatriates are on assignment today. The size, globally, of the cross-border businesses may be gleaned from a United Nations report that estimates there are 53,000 companies operating as multinationals through 450,000 affiliates worldwide. So if we can't isolate absolute numbers, let's turn to the world of surveys to at least get a feeling for whether the overseas employment trends are continuing to increase, commensurate with the money invested, or whether there has been some leveling off in expatriate employment.

We'll refer to a widely cited annual survey: the May 1999 *Global Relocation Trends, 1999 Survey Report*, which was sponsored by Windham International (consultants advising multinationals), the National Foreign Trade Council, Inc. (a nonprofit organization whose prime objective is the promotion of the open trading system, with over 700 member companies), and the Institute for International Human Resources (which provides a forum for 5,200 professionals in the international human resources field with members in over 80 countries). We note the origin of this study because the sponsors do not have a specific agenda that might color the structure of the results. Consequently we will refer to this project, which was participated in by 264 companies with a worldwide expatriate population of 74,709. The study crosses industry lines and has been considered a reliable benchmark for human resource planners throughout its six years. We'll refer to the most recent survey as the 1999 NFTC survey in future citations.

That survey asked the participating firms whether their U.S. expatriates and third-country national (TCN) populations had increased, remained level, or decreased over 1998. The majority of the companies, some 52 percent, reported an increase, 28 percent indicated that the head count had leveled, and 20 percent reported a decrease in the overseas assignee head count.[16] The increase at 52 percent represented a drop from the prior year's report, when 66 percent of the respondents had indicated that their overseas assignments had increased. When asked for their estimates for year 2000 assignments, 66 percent expected to increase their number of expatriates, while 22 percent thought there would be no change, and only 12 percent estimated there would be a reduction in the expatriate head count.

When we visit some of the expatriate challenges in Chapter 4, we'll examine the cost factor that has been so widely written of as spelling the death knell of overseas postings. It appears from the 1999 NFTC survey that such a trend has not materialized as yet.

The balance between expatriate achievements against their costs and the use of local staff or third-country nationals will have to be remeasured by each company on a regular basis to determine staffing levels for the future. For the present, it would appear that the 1999 NFTC survey prognostications by international human resources professionals will continue to indicate that more rather than fewer expatriates will be sent out in the near future by the majority of U.S. global competitors.

For those of you potential expatriates who are seriously considering the U.S. company marketplace, there is another useful magazine article at your disposal; this one a *Fortune* table listing the 500 largest corporations by revenues, profits, assets and stockholders' equity.[17] This listing can be especially timesaving in that it gives a corporate headquarters breakout by state, providing the headquarters contact points, both for the web and telephone.

Thus far we have considered the U.S. global corporations. As you see every day from advertising in this country, or when you turn on your Sony headset, television set, or CD player, or drive your Honda to your corner gas station to fill up with Shell or BP Amoco in order to shop at your nearby Royal Ahold supermarket, there is an invasion of non-U.S. companies competing for ever greater shares of the U.S. marketplace. And this highly visible penetration of the local marketplace ought to give even the most domestically oriented of employee career aspirants an ominous hint to the effect that avoiding expatriate exposures will be all but impossible over the next few years. You could be working for a purely domestic little U.S.-owned organization one day and wake up the next to discover that a non-U.S. global giant has decided to acquired your employer—and you! As the initial trauma fades, you'll appreciate that you've just been exposed to the world of expatriate assignments; only this time, you are the local staff.

For those individuals who really do not want to try the expatriate path now but recognize the need to become globalized now, there is another alternative for you to explore: work for a non-U.S.–owned company here. So if you've always had a hankering to work in France, but your daughter is entering her senior year of high school and would not accompany you if you had such an assignment, why not hedge your longer-term expatriate assignment to Paris with a position working for a French-owned organization doing business here? You will encounter many of the cultural issues that would confront you on the potential Paris job without having to leave your home and being distracted by settling issues that invariably present themselves at the initial stages of a foreign relocation. Additionally, most foreign-owned subsidiaries doing business here will eventually have opportunities back at the home country headquarters, especially for those employees already employed in the corporate family. They already have knowledge of the corporate culture and possibly the language. Such jobs here also present a testing opportunity to see if you really enjoy working with that corporate and national culture.

Executive search people have recognized this possible employment avenue and are beginning to seek out attractive candidates for the foreign subsidiaries, knowing that some of these candidates may want to consider expatriate assignments seriously further along in their careers, and they will have an inside track, whether it is with their own subsidiary now or some other foreign-owned company. Indeed, Thomas Cook, a managing director of DHR International, an executive search firm that has grown a niche for international positions, can attest to the value of a candidate's experience with a foreign-owned subsidiary here, not only from the headhunter's viewpoint but also because of more than five years of serving as human resources director at Daiwa Securities America, a New York–based subsidiary of one of Japan's enormous brokerage firms. Tom had this to say about the value of expatriate or foreign subsidiary exposures:

"Whether an individual gains cross-cultural experience while on an overseas posting or as an employee of a foreign-owned company here, those exposures are highly valued assets in today's competitive candidate market. I've found that those candidates bring flexibility and a measure of self-confidence that give them a distinct advantage over candidates who come to the interview room with no foreign exposure, whether the position in play is located overseas or in the United States for a non-U.S. organization. At Daiwa's New York operation, there were all the issues of Japanese and local U.S. staff coordination challenges that one could ever find in Tokyo."[18]

For those of you potential expatriates who are seriously targeting foreign-owned subsidiaries as a first step to taking the big plunge into that globalizing wave, there is another useful article for you: this one a *Forbes* table of information setting out the 500 largest organizations in the world, appearing in the July 24, 2000, issue.[19] It is from this table that we will set forth the 25 non-U.S. companies producing the largest amounts of revenue in this country (see Table 1.2).

As we saw in the listing for U.S. corporate revenues generated from overseas, there is a broad spectrum of industries represented here. While the focal point for this chart is the size of firms' business results and their global head counts, you may proceed to assume that some proportional consistency would affect their local staff employment of U.S. nationals. And once again, the signs of dynamic revenue growth are starkly captured in the

Table 1.2   Non-U.S. Companies Producing Largest U.S. Revenues

Company	U.S. Revenues ($ in Millions)	Percent Change from 1998	Number of Employees (Global Total)	Industry or U.S. Affiliate
DaimlerChrysler	$88,071	3.5%	466,938	Autos, Chrysler
BP Amoco	$51,841	22.3%	80,400	Energy, ARCO, Amoco
Royal Ahold	$25,542	N/A	96,000	Supermarkets
Sony	$21,117	13.0%	188,700	Music, film, consumer products
Royal Dutch/Shell	$18,438	12.5%	96,000	Energy, chemicals
Toyota	$17,863	16.0%	214,631	Autos
Diageo	$17,539	−2.7%	66,045	Wines, Burger King, Pillsbury
ING Groep N.V.	$14,997	10.7%	86,040	Insurance, financial services
Deutsche Bank	$14,500	29.7%	93,232	Banking, Alex. Brown
Tyco International	$14,409	82.7%	182,000	Manufacturing
Siemens AG	$14,350	14.1%	443,000	Electronics
Vodafone AirTouch	$14,000	128.2%	29,485	Telecoms, Verizon
AXA Group	$13,371	11.3%	92,008	Financial services
Petróleos de Venezuela	$13,317	27.2%	47,360	Energy, Citgo
Honda	$13,100	12.4%	112,000	Autos
Nestlé	$12,799	0.4%	230,929	Food, cosmetics
Nortel Networks	$12,758	26.3%	80,627	Telecoms
Delhaize "Le Lion"	$11,194	8.6%	124,933	Supermarkets
E.On	$11,083	20.3%	131,602	Chemicals, VEBA
AEGON NV	$11,083	27.4%	24,316	Insurance, AEGON USA
Zurich	$11,075	2.2%	68,785	Insurance, Kemper
ABN Amro	$10,965	13.4%	109,938	Banking, European American Bank
Prudential Corp., Plc	$10,619	25.4%	22,372	Insurance, Jackson National Life
News Corp.	$10,193	5.5%	50,000	Media, News America Holdings, Inc.
Tengelmann Group	$9,993	−0.3%	52,585	Supermarkets, A&P

Data Source: Forbes, July 24, 2000.

percentage gains from 1999 over 1998. Consider that only two of these 25 lost revenue ground. Also indicated in that *Forbes* report was the fact that foreign companies spent a record $238 billion here in 1999, a whopping 31 percent increase over expenditures in 1998.

So deep runs the non-U.S.–owned entry into the American pastime that not only has baseball been touched by the many outstanding non-U.S. players from around the Caribbean, Australia, Japan, and Korea, but globalization has even reached the hallowed environment of Boston's Fenway Park, where the huge Citgo electrical sign has been a venerable Boston landmark just outside and over the famous left-field wall. How many of those staunchly loyal Red Sox fans know that the company's parental identity is really the Venezuelan energy giant Petróleos de Venezuela? Globalization has really landed in Boston! Bostonians, surf's up!

And the pace of takeovers is accelerating. Consider the recent acquisition of Atlantic Richfield (ARCO) by newly merged Amoco. The year 1999 also witnessed the Giant Food company, the Dutch supermarket giant, acquire Giant Food here, at about the same time Group Carso was acquiring Compaq. Indeed, wasn't it just a few years ago that Compaq had acquired Digital Equipment Corporation (DEC) in what was seen by many as a way to protect against the very takeover that just occurred?

The pace of acquisitions continued unabated in 2000, with the purchase of the spirits giant Seagram (which also owned Universal Studios and Polygram) by the French company Vivendi. Also in that year, the venerable investment adviser Alliance Capital, still another huge financial services organization, purchased Sanford C. Bernstein; but Alliance is indirectly owned by AXA, the French insurance behemoth. Certainly as these non-U.S. business managers continue to invest here, they will need dependable, bright local U.S. nationals to help them to do that professionally.

To help you view this terrain, let's take a look at how some major non-U.S. companies doing business here have fared in terms of their employment histories in this country. We'll view two Japanese global giants, Sony and Nomura Securities. These two highly successful firms, domestically, approached the U.S. labor market (and other markets around the world) very differently. It may surprise some that there could be marked contrasts between Japanese overseas management styles, but stereotyping any group of companies as diversified as the Japanese organizations doing business in the

United States is hazardous at best. This will become apparent at the outset of our descriptions of how each approached the U.S. marketplace, in terms of both business and employee relations results. Obviously both organizations could be viewed as final employers of U.S. nationals here, or in the future, potential employers for U.S. nationals overseas in their other offshore locations or home headquarters, Tokyo.

Sony

This modern-day global power grew out of the ashes of Tokyo in 1946 as an engineering firm. The power behind the development was the late Akio Morita, an independent and progressive thinker. His book, *Made in Japan*, was a worldwide best-seller and promoted much discussion among corporate students as to whether this approach, the Sony way, could be a feasible model for companies around the globe. As a human resources person, I found the following excerpt of particular value, and for you managers and potential expats, it should be the kind of policy you ought to be searching for:

"We have a policy that wherever we are in the world we deal with our employees as members of the Sony family, as valued colleagues, and that is why, even before we opened our U.K. factory, we brought management people, including engineers, to Tokyo and let them work with us and trained them and treated them just like members of the family."[20]

That was written in 1988 at the time when Japanese organizations were vigorously pursuing global expansion almost everywhere, often using the traditional Japanese corporate techniques that had worked so well in Japan. So what has happened since that time, given the Japanese economy's substantial downturn in the 1990s? What did Sony actually do here as an employer of U.S. nationals? Did its original policy of equitable treatment continue and keep pace with its highly successful innovations in electronics, motion pictures, and entertainment, or were adjustments made to that policy?

We asked those questions in September 2000, to John Stern, who was executive vice president, human resources, for Sony Electronics for the United States for 15 years, from 1979 through 1994. Here are his comments:

"Sony's culture is highly localized. Local nationals can aspire to the highest jobs in the United States and even to become directors of Sony's parent corporation in Tokyo. In the United States, Sony targets the top business schools for candidates for global assignments. Those candidates are asked if they would feel comfortable being assigned overseas.

"As for current local staff employees [U.S. nationals], they are encouraged to indicate that they would desire an overseas posting. Sony will listen to them and will try to accommodate those career aspirations where the circumstances, skills, and openings permit. The company prefers that qualified, bright U.S. employees spend time in Tokyo in developmental roles lasting about six months prior to their next assignments, which could be another expatriate posting or a repatriation back to the United States."[21]

John, recently retired from his post at the Darla Moore Graduate School of Business, University of South Carolina, summed up the four traits that Sony management was looking for when identifying potential candidates for overseas assignments:

1. Willingness to relocate.
2. Flexibility in dealing with cultural differences.
3. Language skills.
4. The proven ability to work hard and succeed.

According to Stern, Sony continually provides for specific training in each of the various functions, especially where new technology needs to be mastered. John himself had been sent to the Harvard Business School for nearly six months of advanced executive training. Here is the story of a company taking its direction from the chief executive and following through with policies and procedures that should be attractive for those of you considering the expatriate or foreign subsidiary career paths.

Nomura Securities International

This is the U.S. subsidiary of the Nomura Securities Company, the world's largest securities firm in terms of assets held. In Tokyo, this firm dates back to its founding in 1927, and notwithstanding severe economic recessions and the war, it not only proved resilient enough to survive, it prospered in the Tokyo retail market as the most powerful of Japan's four major securities giants, garnering almost one-third of the entire nation's shareholder market.

In the 1980s the parent firm took on global proportions when it set up subsidiaries in New York, London, Hong Kong, and a dozen more major offices sprinkled through Europe, Asia, and the United States. The company needed to look for a market niche in each of its overseas locations. In New York it concentrated on the institutional, fixed-income business (trading bonds with other companies), a new line of business for the firm. Unlike Sony, which was positioned in industries that stressed technological skills as entry points into the U.S. market, Nomura would have to rely on the expertise of experienced U.S. professionals who could leverage the firm's giant capital into positions that would make trading bonds and stocks profitable ventures for the parent.

By 1986, when I joined the firm in New York as their director of human resources, the firm had approximately 200 employees and was led by two senior expatriates who had successfully split the leadership role into inside management and outside business and public relations. There was a sprinkling of U.S. local managers, but the majority of managers were expats from Tokyo on three-year terms. This was the standard structure of most Japanese-owned subsidiaries in the United States.

The firm needed two kinds of U.S. nationals—experienced Wall Street veterans who could immediately start up their divisions, and junior individuals, U.S. nationals fresh out of college.

This college recruiting program was a classic example of how to construct an appealing orientation for a new person coming to the securities industry. The program proved highly successful because it was structured to provide a blend of formal instruction with learn-on-your-own processes. The program called for a formal three months' classroom training session at the parent headquarters in Tokyo, where the New York hirees attended basic sessions with Oxbridge people from London, and all kinds of recent graduates from Nomura offices around the world.

After the first three months' orientation at the Tokyo headquarters, the program called for three separate training exposures back in New York. Each of these rotations—equities, fixed income, and investment banking—featured desk training, a process of observation of a bond trader trading, the opportunity to ask questions, and then the ability to assist. After the full year of those four experiences, both the recent graduates and the division heads made preference lists as to who wanted what, and those assignments were made following those mutual priorities. This kind of program, with substantial opportunities to test the water and mix with the professionals while on the job (rather than in a formal classroom setting), proved to be highly sought by the top students at the top schools. If you happen to be still at school while pondering where to enter the global marketplace, that sort of program can produce ultimately solid job opportunities for those who have the patience to proceed through the 12-month program period. This kind of rotational program continues in many organizations, although Nomura decided to discontinue it for its U.S. operations.

The program effectively encouraged non-Japanese nationals to pursue careers with the firm, including expatriate assignments to Tokyo, London, and Hong Kong. The training target was clearly to build a global workforce, producing individuals who understood all four operation centers and their distinctive cultures. This was consistent with what the parent firm's then CEO, Yoshihisa Tabuchi, had stated at the annual Tokyo headquarters conference in 1986: "I will be the last in this position who has not worked outside Japan and cannot speak English." Indeed, at that meeting, there were encouraging reports from all overseas locations regarding expansion plans, and in the case of London, significant results as well. Authentic globalization of the company appeared to be just on the horizon. Has it become a reality?

As to the campaign to lure Wall Street veterans, the firm encountered some difficulties, not exclusively a Nomura challenge in that tight labor market, but a learning point for those of you evaluating foreign-owned subsidiaries as your career targets at this time. Let's turn to an objective perspective as to what actually happened. Professor Samuel Hayes III of the Harvard Business School collaborated with Phillip Hubbard in 1989 on a book entitled *Investment Banking: A Tale of Three Cities*, in which they draw the following conclusion:

"Nomura's role as a truly global investment bank has depended not only on its success in Tokyo, but also on its activities in London and New York. . . . The key to developing these areas [sales and trading of corporate bonds and equities] is recruiting and retention of skilled professionals, particularly Americans. Nomura has made an effort to differentiate its personnel practices in America from those in Japan. However, without an American at the helm, it seems likely that a number of talented individuals will shy away from a firm that could be viewed as heavily directed from Tokyo."[22]

Nomura eventually did appoint an American cochairman and grew its U.S. workforce to 1,200 employees, but it has not achieved leadership status among its Wall Street competitors. Mr. Tabuchi's prediction that he would be succeeded by an English-speaking person with extensive expatriate experience was nearly borne out; his successor's successor, Junichi Ujiie, currently heads the firm, after extended expatriate assignments in Switzerland and New York.

Let's wrap up our two cases' analysis with a quote from the venerable Japanese consultant Kenichi Ohmae, who concluded that the general failure of the Japanese subsidiaries derived "from their failure to fully empower their native talent—always reserving key decision-making authority for native Japanese."[23] Clearly Mr. Ohmae was referring to the more traditional-thinking of Japanese firms doing business here; there are certainly more exceptions to his general rule than Sony. And, to be fair, that conclusion was rendered more than a decade ago. Many of the non-U.S. firms doing business in the United States have adopted more progressive management approaches here. Each of these companies is torn between its own unique culture, originating in some form from its home-country culture, and the need to effectively adapt to the U.S. business cultures.

You, as a job candidate, or as a U.S. national working for a non-U.S.–owned subsidiary, need to consider the relative autonomy we've been describing here. Sometimes this empowerment springs from a change of expatriate or parental leadership, and these accidents of personal philosophy are a continuing concern, since the tendency of most foreign subsidiaries, regardless of nationality, is to replace these people at regular intervals. So you must make careful probings as to your target company's current philosophy toward bona fide delegation of decision-making authority, and where that direction emanates from.

Whichever career path you choose, international work should be a continuing goal.

Notes

1. "Pecked to Death by a Duck," Sarah Ferguson, *Village Voice*, Oct. 18, 2000, p. 50.
2. "Why U.S. Giants Are Crying Uncle," Edmund L. Andrews, *New York Times*, Oct. 12, 2000, p. W2.
3. "Corporations on Steroids," Thomas Friedman, *New York Times*, Feb. 4, 2000.
4. "Globalization: If You Can't Beat It, Reshape It," Joseph Kahn, *New York Times*, March 9, 2000.

5. Ibid.
6. "Procter & Gamble Japan (A)," Harvard Business School, R-391-003, Revised Jan. 30, 1992.
7. "Learning to Think Small," Constance L. Hays, *New York Times*, Feb. 6, 2000, Sec. 3, p. 1.
8. Ibid., p. 5
9. Ibid.
10. Ibid.
11. *Taken for a Ride: How Daimler-Benz Drove Off with Chrysler*, Bill Vlasic and Bradley A. Stertz, New York: HarperCollins, 2000, p. 249.
12. Ibid.
13. "DaimlerChrysler's Transfer Woes," Jeffrey Ball, *Wall Street Journal*, Aug. 24, 1999, p. 1.
14. "Global Giants: The Largest 100 U.S. Multinationals," Brian Zodiac, *Forbes*, July 24, 2000, p. 335.
15. "The World's Largest Corporations," Jeremy Kahn, *Fortune*, July 24, 2000, p. 232.
16. *Global Relocation Trends, 1999 Survey Report*, Windham International, National Foreign Trade Council, and Institute for International Human Resources, May 9, 1999, p. 6.
17. "The 500 Largest U.S. Corporations," *Fortune*, April 17, 2000, pp. F-1–F-54.
18. Statement of Thomas Cook, Nov. 12, New York, NY.
19. "The International 500," *Forbes*, July 24, 2000, pp. 342–347.
20. *Made in Japan: Akio Morita and Sony*, Akio Morita, New York: E.P. Dutton, 1988, p. 143.
21. Statement of John Stern, Sept. 18, 2000, Columbia, SC.
22. *Investment Banking: A Tale of Three Cities*, Samuel B. Hayes III and Philip M. Hubbard, Boston: Harvard Business School Press, 1989, p. 292.
23. *Beyond National Borders, Reflections on Japan and the World*, Kenichi Ohmae, Homewood, IL: Dow Jones Irwin, 1987.

Illustration by Liz Lomax

What Are the Profiles of Today's Expatriates?

What Are the Profiles
of Today's Expatriates?

"I am not an Athenian or a Greek, but a citizen of the world."
Socrates (496–399 B.C.)

A s we profile the spectrum of individuals who compose today's thousands of expatriates, we should keep in mind that they differ sharply in skill sets, but the successful ones all must have in common a genuine appreciation for work overseas. If that base of genuine cultural curiosity is not flourishing inside the overseas assignee, he or she may have a difficult time in successfully completing the assignment regardless of the technical skill required to perform the job. To a large extent job skills can be developed and finely honed through training, but the will to live comfortably within a different culture seems to be inbred in our individual character.

At a U.S. Army camp near Tonq du Chon-ni, Korea, I observed that many of my fellow 7th Infantry Division companions were oblivious of the ancient Korean culture, visible from across the camp's wire boundary. Harvest and funeral processions, Buddhist temples, and Korean traditional family dinners were all within easy access for cultural explorations but were often shunned in favor of evenings inside the camp's clubs that offered nostalgic, down-home Johnny Cash songs and familiar American food and drink.

For whatever reasons in their upbringings, these men were simply not curious about their new cultural surroundings; they were more concerned with crossing off another day on their "short-timers" calendar.

They were missing an opportunity to view a culture more than three thousand years old, and a chance to learn about the values of a very strong, proud people that were not anchored in western materialistic perspectives. That education was available—indeed far more practical than much of their formal academic exposures—yet the critical curiosity factor was simply not there. Perhaps with maturity those soldiers will appreciate subsequent culture explorations.

Some individuals develop this cultural curiosity over time, "stoking the fire inside," especially when they had not recognized their own problems in the process of adapting to other cultures. Again, self-recognition is fundamental to developing ways of thinking and behaviors that will make the whole culture integration process work.

Consider the lessons from the classic 1950s film *Zorba the Greek*. You may recall that a bright but socially naive British teacher, played by Alan Bates, travels to Crete in order to inspect a tin mine that he has inherited. On the way there he encounters Zorba, played by Anthony Quinn, who promises to guide him through the Cretan culture. After a series of vivid encounters with the best and worst of the Cretan life, the teacher watches in horror as the mine project is ruined by collapsing overhead lines—completely destroying his property.

The teacher turns to his Greek mentor, Zorba, at the film's conclusion on the beach and says, "Zorba, teach me to dance"—a symbolic request that shows how the teacher has finally come to understand and adapted to the Cretan culture's way of showing heartfelt emotions.

Indeed, the teacher's mental transitioning—through the help of Zorba—was clearly portrayed in Nikos Kazantzakis' novel on which the film was based. In the book, the teacher writes in his diary, "My life with Zorba had enlarged my heart."[1] The film closes with Zorba and the teacher dancing the traditional Greek dance arm-in-arm on the deserted beach. To some extent, all expatriates start their overseas assignments in the mode of the teacher and need a facilitator such as Zorba to guide them through the cultural adaptation process that causes so many assignments to fail. Company managers can provide effective facilitators, and good expats will learn from the adaptation process.

It boggles the mind how many employees there are working in nations that are not their own countries of origin. Entire regions, such as the Middle East, have imported thousands of workers from outside their borders to do everything from performing the most difficult of technology tasks to staffing their armed forces to doing the manual labor that few home country nationals want to perform. Adam Smith's natural forces of supply and demand are operating today with little effective hindrance from border patrols. If the jobs are there, willing workers will come to those jobs, even if they have to cross national borders illegally to do them.

As only a small fraction of these massive movements of expatriates around the globe, the U.S.-based multinational firms have created their own classifications of the kinds of people they want to do this work. These human profiles start with the types of overseas job assignments they have been selected to perform.

The 1999 NFTC survey[2] for the first time, asked the 264 multinational organizations about the purposes of their expatriate assignments. Table 2.1 reviews the survey results that asked the companies to rate each of five categories, from 1 as the least common to 5 as the most common assignment objective. (I've taken the liberty of adding what I've seen as general age profiles for each of these categories.)

The ages are offered as general estimates. Corporate philosophies can, and often do, reflect the particular age/experience perspective of the CEO, which would mean that each company has its own selection pattern when it comes to age groups. Clearly the Age Discrimination in Employment Act (ADEA), the federal law that bars discrimination against an employee because of age, must be considered when making the selections. After all, it is usually the experience, or lack of it, that is going to be a major factor, along

Table 2.1   Assignment Objectives Ranked by Frequency of Use

Assignment Objective	Rank from 1 to 5	Age
Fill skills gap	3.2	30s
Launch new endeavor	3.0	30s–40s
Transfer technology	2.6	20s–30s
Build management experience	2.2	20s for orientation 30s–40s for development
Transfer corporate culture	1.8	40s–50s

Data Source: Global Relocation Trends, 1999 Survey Report, Windham/NFTC/IIHR, p. 9.

with developmental potential, that drives the decision as to who gets the particular kind of overseas assignment.

Earlier we asserted that all expatriates have to possess two key abilities: the strength of character to uproot their families from a comfortable environment and then sufficient skill to successfully cope with the challenges inherent in moving into a different culture. When individuals and their family units demonstrate both abilities, they evolve into prized corporate assets. In Chapter 4, focusing on major assignment challenges, we'll see how often the selected expatriates possess both fundamental skills.

Their proven cultural adaptability is accountable for the fact that 44 percent of the expatriate population in the 1999 NFTC survey have previous expatriate experience, and, very significantly, 18 percent of all current expatriates obtained that experience with another company. These significant statistics suggest that managers are regularly selecting proven overseas assignment veterans over potential first-timers and that this meaningful preference extends beyond the company's own expatriate candidate pool (if, in the rare case, it actually has one) to find the right candidate from the labor market at large.

You can verify this preference yourself by logging on to any major job postings site. Just look at the listed minimum experience required section. Further, if the overseas opportunity never makes it onto the site because managers believe that an outside search firm would be a more effective conduit, then actual overseas experience assumes an even greater role in final selection. Search people tend to be extremely wary of loading up their final slate with untried candidates. Company managers could have taken those kinds of risks themselves; they want proven technical and cultural skills sets.

Where Do Today's Expatriates Come From?

Geographically and by industry, expatriates are emerging from all over the United States and from virtually every one of this country's industries that has even a remote connection to cross-border business. If we trace back the history of expatriate employment from the end of World War II, we'll learn that it wasn't always that way. In fact, the growth patterns from those days up through the present are worthy of your consideration because some fragments of overseas assignment development have survived to this day. They affect current expatriate practices and are worth your understanding.

The modern era for U.S. expatriate assignment growth started after World War II, when the major U.S. oil companies began to expand their exploration, extraction, and refining processes around the globe. The first set of expats constituted a mixed bag of white males. There were some managers and facilities people who were going to stay for years, ensuring that all who followed would be properly managed and cared for. Then there were the oil patch workers, "hands," who worked the rigs or platforms in the drilling process—strenuous physical work performed over long stretches of hours. This work and the remote locations where it was being performed gave rise to a rotation system of 28 days on and 28 days off the company-built compounds. Oil company profit margins being what they were, the compensation policies were generous and geared to the short term. Many of these rig workers hailed from the Southwest. They had little contact with the local culture since they were isolated from it by the company compounds. Whenever the 28-day respite came they were only too happy to board the first plane headed home. These expats gave new dimensions to the term "mercenary." They often changed company alliances, and their lack of concern for the local nationals or culture was hardly ever concealed.

In many oil-producing countries this legacy is still difficult for today's expats to overcome. In many of those nations, the local national perceptions (a mixture of envy and resentment) of expatriates are still somewhat influenced by that history. Then managers from other industries decided to adopt many of the premiums, bonuses, and allowances that the oil management had installed to try to retain those free spirits of the rigs.

The third group of pioneer expats who also had been sent over by the major oil companies, but whose assignments were for fixed terms of years, included geologists; engineers; drilling, extraction, and refining technical people; and a host of support services—financial, research, human resources, and government relations people—all of whom also received the high levels of compensation, the various premiums, bonuses, and allowances that have survived through today. The employee compounds needed all kinds of support services for these expatriates, including sound schools, since these people had their wives and children accompany them. The home leave concept began to flourish with these individuals; their lives in the compounds were comfortable but restricted.

As overseas manufacturing and sales functions began to flourish, the mix of U.S.-based expats broadened to include veteran employees from all over the United States, most on the three-year term that was the assignment average for almost three decades. The combination of more universal backgrounds and the longer assignment durations required the sending companies to commit time and money for appropriate training. The new expats were not isolated in oil patch compounds; they were living in local neighborhoods and had to acclimate to the local culture at close quarters. The white male profile was expanding to include females and a variety of ethnic backgrounds.

In that transformation of expatriate requirements, managers found that there was a general reluctance on the part of many potential U.S. expatriates to take the assignments. We don't have statistics on rejected offers, but suffice it to say that before the highly publicized advent of globalization, employees were not stampeding to the HR office to get overseas jobs.

Many of those expats of the 1960 and 1970s obtained their assignments as rewards for some project or because they were friendly with a senior executive. Those jobs could be doled out because there really wasn't in place a set of career paths that would be propelled by a completed assignment overseas. The assignments were fragmented and not always carefully managed; home headquarters often did not value the work performed then as a major contributor to the corporation's success. The domestic U.S. market was still the focal point. This led to the selection of some people who were not truly motivated for a career as long as the location was good for their experience.

Such expats could become somewhat brash. In the mid-1970s I recall attempting to describe the machinations of the balance sheet approach to an NBC news correspondent in Paris. She was genuinely shocked that the company would decrease the foreign service premium for living there, reminding me how truly difficult Paris can be for a non-French-speaker. One could only ponder how much more difficult other assignments, such as Beirut or Calcutta were for the correspondents there. (As a sidelight, this was the only person I encountered in 30 years of this work who objected to the term "expatriate." She asserted that it reminded her friends of the Hemingway bistro-oriented lifestyle and wanted the company to substitute a more professional title. I'm still searching—any suggestions?)

There is another source of expatriates that bears our review—the third-country nationals (TCNs). These individuals, employed by a company headquartered in country A, are assigned to work in country B, and they are nationals of a third country, country C. For U.S.-based multinational firms, the TCNs offer some distinct advantages over sending out an expatriate from the home country headquarters. First, many third-country nationals hail from neighboring countries in the same region as the host country. Their upbringing in close proximity to the host country enables them to possess a greater understanding of the host country culture than many first-time U.S. expats would bring.

Managers see reduced costs as a second advantage for employment of TCNs. Their expatriate reward packages are often structured on their home country or host country national staff levels. There has been some movement to modify the TCN programs; in fact, some consultants are providing separate compensation matrices for them. From a manager's standpoint, however, there is an unfair element in the relationship when two expatriates working side by side in the host location receive sharply disparate compensation treatment based solely on whether they are nationals from headquarters or another nation. For that reason many multinationals treat TCNs in exactly the same fashion as company home-country nationals.

At NBC during the 1970s, we found that there was a floating population of experienced TCNs, usually as camera or sound crew, who would work for any of the U.S. networks in countries with armed conflicts without seeming fazed by the potential dangers of the News Division jobs. They reminded me of the hardened sergeants of the U.S. Army's 7th Division in Korea; they simply had developed tough enough skin through years of undergoing stress to weather hardship situations. In those days, management set up a middle tier of compensation levels, between the expatriates on the full balance sheet program administered out of New York and the local national staff rates that were managed locally.

How far has this utilization of TCNs advanced? The 1999 NFTC survey reports that the TCN workforce has reached 30 percent of the total expatriate population, a figure that is slightly up from 29 percent reported in 1998. That large percentage, nearly a third of all U.S. company expatriates coming from outside these shores, has to indicate the development of what could be called a truly global workforce; individuals regardless of nationality able to help the highest bidder wherever that help is needed. As a result, the profiles of expats continue to broaden out to include increasing numbers of nonwhite males. The only reservation I've encountered with the expanding TCN workforce, given the apparent U.S. reluctance to move abroad, is that these employees need to establish links with the headquarters operation to begin to be familiar with what strategies and plans they ought to know about. They need to appreciate and contribute to what the U.S. headquarters wants to do in the host country and how that approach fits into the bigger strategic plan. It makes sense for management to bring them back to corporate headquarters periodically for strategic reorientation, given the tendency of companies to shift gears rapidly in today's competitive global jungle.

How Are Today's Expatriate Programs Doing in Terms of Diversity?

The 1999 NFTC survey shows that 13 percent of the current expatriate population is women.[3] This figure is down from 15 percent reported in the prior year. Given that women make up nearly one-half of the workforce in the United States, what are the factors that might account for the significantly smaller percentage of them working overseas? Is there a case to be made for that same "glass ceiling" condition that has prevented qualified women from being promoted in the United States is also preventing them from being selected for overseas work?

I can offer no survey data as to why this is occurring. It is a puzzling situation, especially given that from 1994 to 1997 the percentage of females in the entire U.S. expatriate population had reached 20 percent. The survey sponsors offered the thought that women, according to the U.S. Bureau of Labor Statistics, account for only 29 percent of U.S. computer professionals. They suggest that since there was a hefty increase in the high-tech firms in their survey, this factor might have influenced the substantial drop in women expatriate percentages. Perhaps there is still interplay between some cultures (particularly in the Middle East and parts of Africa and Asia) wherein the role of the female as an accepted business associate is still emerging, especially for host country women. Additionally there are social mores of some host cultures and security concerns that women potential expats and human resources ought to review, locality by locality.

Godfrey Golzen, with the perceptions of a British national, offers some troublesome conclusions about global organizations' current approach to diversity in the workforce. In conducting a Global HR Leaders' Agenda Survey in the spring of 2000, he comments on the management committees of today's global giants and is particularly objective in terms of his view of U.S. companies:

"Such bodies are overwhelmingly mono-cultural, mono-national (that is, home country constituted), mono-ethnic, and mono-gender. Several do have some degree of diversity, but they are in a minority. We have not come across any company where the management board significantly represents the diverse composition of its workforce."[4]

In most cases, HR leaders say this will have to change and they are working on it. Others defend their position on the grounds that U.S. companies make few concessions to diversity at senior level, but are nonetheless very successful. True enough, but will this work as a long-term strategy in a global economy?

The demographics suggest it won't work. According to a survey produced by the Cranfield University School of Management, one of Europe's leading business schools, by 2010 only 45 percent of the U.S. workforce will be white males. Furthermore, the 1996 U.S. *Digest of Education Statistics* shows half the degrees in management, accounting, and law are now being awarded to women. These graduates ought to be able to qualify for expatriate assignment considerations, especially as the career prospects brighten for those who finish up their assignments successfully.

Diversity of age, gender, and race in the workplace mirrors the marketplace and also the global environment. In fact, we're not certain that there are credible statistics on age or race of expatriates. Many serious marketing mistakes have arisen out of a failure to understand customers on a geographical, age, or gender-related basis.

Consider the P&G situation in Japan. Expatriate managers were apparently unaware that the hard Tokyo water was not appropriate for making their soap effective—a basic understanding that the two local companies were capitalizing upon, manufacturing the kinds of soap that would maximize the effectiveness of the washing combination for the local consumers. Likewise, would those same managers have understood how inappropriate their standard U.S. diapers sizes were for the typical Japanese infant?

But there have been, and will be, fine examples of women managing to land expatriate assignments and then succeeding in them. In my expatriate travels in the 1970s and 1980s there were very few women on assignments in Asia, Africa, and South America that I encountered. One of them, Marianne Ruggiero, was one of the pathfinders, having worked in Singapore's

American Express operation going as far back as the 1970s. Here is her account as to how she landed the expatriate assignment:

"The Asia-Pacific group for Amex was interested in having a full-time trainer in the field. The hiring manager was based in Singapore and was Indian, most recently living in Malaysia and then Singapore. The prospective candidates were all men. I went to my boss and said, 'When the guys all turn the job down, let me know. I've already traveled in Asia and I don't need a fam [family] tour to get to know the area. I'm willing to move to Singapore sight unseen. I've studied Chinese and Asian history. I also happen to be a qualified candidate for the job.'

"As I predicted, every guy turned the job down. . . . Eventually I was interviewed, and the hiring manager said that I would have to take a six-week business trip, and if I passed the test, he would offer the job to me. . . . Lucky for me I got the job! . . . The experience was exciting and challenging as I had expected. . . . Managers took me seriously and looked to me for more expertise than I really had to offer. People were focused on growth—their national economies, their businesses, themselves, their people—and me, too. I left entitlement back in New York [the global headquarters of American Express]. Being a pioneer, an adventurer, was fun and rewarding."[5]

Marianne moved on to become the top human resources executive for the U.S. headquarters of ING-Barings, for J. Crew, and for other companies. Her experience performing an expatriate function genuinely stretched her skill levels, as is often the case for individuals who have become adjusted to the more narrowly constructed jobs of corporate headquarters. This facet of overseas work should provide a strong motivation for those of you who have not been exposed to the wider scope of expatriate demands. With all of the gender issues against her (think of what would have happened had one of "the guys" wanted that Singapore job!) she had one advantage over her potential male competitors: She had no spouse or family at that time and could move without further issues relating to a trailing spouse or children.

How Many of the Expatriates Have Families?

The 1999 NFTC survey shows a distinct trend toward a smaller percentage of the expatriate population being married.[6]

1993, 1994   Married expats: 78%

1998   Married expats: 74%

1999   Married expats: 69%

What could account for the almost 10 percent decline in married expats in five years?

The U.S. Bureau of Labor Statistics has indicated that 43 percent of all families in the United States have dual careers; it is entirely feasible that this factor has played a role in the selection process, whether it is a self-select or a decision by the company that a single-status person would be more appropriate for a particular assignment. The prospect of one's spouse not only moving to a new culture but giving up a career as well could well combine to be such substantial negatives for the expatriate to decline the overseas posting.

Table 2.2 reflects the family status of all 74,709 expatriates on assignment who were reported in the survey just cited. Note that "significant others," while legally not "family members," have been identified as a separate category for the first time in the history of this survey.[7]

An interesting note from these statistics, in addition to the relatively few women on expatriate assignments, is the proportion of married males to single males—a ratio of about three to one. This is a strikingly different picture from the female statistics, which turn out to show populations nearly even (5 percent for married females, compared with 7 percent for single women). It should be kept in mind that these are legal-status statistics and, with the exception of the significant others, do not represent whether the spouse has elected to accompany the expatriate to the host country for the assignment (once termed "trailing spouse").

Table 2.2 Family Status of Expatriates

Status of Expatriate	Percent of Total Expatriates
Married males	64%
Married females	5%
Unmarried males	21%
Unmarried females	7%
Males with significant others	2%
Females with significant others	1%

Data Source: Global Relocation Trends, 1999 Survey Report, Windham/NFTC/IIHR, p. 13.

Whether to accompany the expatriate or not? This is proving to be a more difficult dilemma to answer today than it was more than a decade ago when chances were that the spouse did not have a career of his or her own. The numbers in Table 2.3 set forth what percentages of the spouses are actually accompanying their spouses to the host countries for the assignment.[8]

The volatility reflected in the survey statistics is difficult to interpret. Why should there be such wide fluctuations in a series of decisions by expatriate family units that are based on almost identical circumstances from year to year? I can only hazard a guess that the 1998 massive street violence in Indonesia, the random bombings of U.S. targets over the past two years, together with the 1997 economic crash involving many of the formerly Asian "tigers," may have combined to produce enough angst within expatriate family units to convince them that they should ride out overseas assignments separately. Whatever the motivators for these variances, we are left with the knowledge that almost one-fourth of the married expatriates have not been accompanied by their spouses, a practice that, when we review current challenges to the overseas posting process, can readily spawn serious issues, both for the expatriates and for the manager.

Another dimension of the family profile of current expatriates concerns their children. Children on an assignment often prove to be completely delightful; they are flexible enough to learn new languages, adjust to customs, make a variety of friends, and very often serve as a conduit to other expatriate families working for other companies at the host location—in addition to the pleasure of helping and observing children develop anywhere. An overseas environment can provide strong stimulus for further learning about other cultures, and the children of veteran expatriates seem to be especially independent and interested youngsters. Albeit they may lose some academic advantages had they stayed at home, the trade-off in learning sociology firsthand is an invaluable lesson in real life.

Table 2.3   Expatriates with/without Accompanying Spouses

Survey Year	Percent with Spouse	Percent without Spouse	Percent with Spouse Change
1995	69%	31%	—
1997	89%	11%	20%
1999	77%	23%	–12%

Data Source: Global Relocation Trends, 1999 Survey Report, Windham/NFTC/IIHR, p. 14.

Before we review the current trends for bringing the children along, let's take a look at a pertinent case history of some expatriate neighbors we met in Dubai, in my opinion proving a point of the benefits of bringing along the children on overseas assignments.

GLOBAL CHILDREN—A CASE STUDY

Our next-door neighbors in Jumeirah, near Dubai, were veteran expatriates who had been through a series of challenging oil patch postings. That family stands out as an example of how globalized youngsters can become when exposed to a series of expatriate postings. Trevor, a jovial, wiry Australian (indeed, one needs that sense of humor when exposed to the horrific heat of Saudi's desert) had an equally pleasant Latvian wife, Krista, and twin daughters, Kaili and Tiiu, who were barely teenagers when we met them in the small backyard we shared. Then, in the early 1980s, Dubai was still a place with few creature comforts, perennial 100 percent humidity, and 100 degrees plus draining heat every day in the summer.

The family had not been to Trevor's home back in Australia for many, many years, Trevor having held a succession of CalTex expatriate assignments all over the globe. Spouse Krista and daughters had accompanied Trevor through all his postings, becoming familiar with a host of languages and cultures along the way. When one conversed with any member of the family, but particularly the daughters, one became aware that they were immediately comfortable wherever they happened to be, and seemed to have no real ties to any single "home." They were eager to learn about the customs, languages, and history of Dubai, and never seemed to be in any way bothered by the climate or the conservative mores that many of the Dubai people had toward non-Islamic women. When we left them late in 1983, they were still ever-smiling. We've been in annual contact with them every year since, following their continuous movements from country to country until just a year ago, when Trevor finally returned to the small Australian town of Thirimere on the edge of the outback in New South Wales.

The daughters have continued to thrive as citizens of the world. Tiiu, after a series of expatriate assignments, now works in Oman, in a truly remote camp in the desert there, where she is the only female employee in a camp of 500 men and thoroughly enjoys the life. The other daughter, Kaili, has worked in three countries, including the United States; she left here only recently to work in human resources in Australia where she hopes to find another expatriate assignment.

Apparently something about these overseas assignments can get into people's blood, and that rich variety of life is what they have enjoyed, and what they want and need. There are probably many families similar to our example family out there now. For you human resources people looking for expatriate potential, here's a category of individuals who possess the proven experiences to all but guarantee successfully coping with the cultural readjustment that forms the foundation for competently completing overseas postings.

Another ideal background as a potential candidate pool would be the sons and daughters of career military people. During my own Army assignments at four installations, the exposure to various cultures by "Army brats" had often produced culture-friendly offspring who would have relatively little difficulty in adjusting to the culture shock inherent in the typical expatriate assignment.

We have extolled the virtues of bringing the children along to the host country assignment. What has been the actual practice of today's expats? Again, the survey data provides some surprisingly low percentages of those children who do accompany the expatriates. The breakout in Table 2.4 involves those expatriates who had children at the time of the expatriate assignment and had to decide whether to bring them along.[9]

We'll venture that the major reason for not bringing the children along has to be concerns about education. These issues fall into two categories: the stage of their education and a hesitancy to try the school system at the host location.

For the first category, high school seniors and most juniors (particularly those targeting colleges) are in a precarious position regarding transferring at this late stage in their secondary school careers, a move that could all but doom hopes of being accepted by the university of their choice. Both years are witness to a lot of emotional and growth transitions by the student, and adding the complication of moving overseas while one is concentrating

Table 2.4   Expatriates with/without Accompanying Children

Survey Year	Percent Bringing Children to Host Country	Percent Leaving Children in Home Country
1994	62%	38%
1998	55%	45%
1999	61%	39%

Data Source: Global Relocation Trends, 1999 Survey Report, Windham/NFTC/IIHR, p. 15.

about the choice of universities is a tough chore for anyone, much less an emotionally challenged 17-year-old.

As for the quality of education available at the host location, you expats have at your disposal a variety of handy tools that will enable you to explore the nature of your local school candidates. The Internet, repatriates, and direct communications with the schools are as near as your computer as you wrestle with the alternatives to accompany or not. They should all be fully explored before deciding not to take the youngsters along; the chance for a really meaningful overseas exposure may not soon reappear.

After all, wouldn't it be delightful to watch a young Socrates of your own grow into a citizen of the world?

How Are Nonfamily Members Treated on Assignment?

Our time-honored view of the family concept has had to be entirely refocused in light of the rapidly changing perceptions of acceptable social pairings and the issue of whether legalizing the relationship is a necessity. Such an overhaul in thinking has been transpiring over the past two decades that expatriate assignments would sooner or later also have to examine how to deal with all the relationships that have been increasingly accepted by the U.S. legal systems as well as by the general populace.

PARTNERS

Close associations, in some states recognized as legal with or without religious approval, have become more recognized in the United States, especially in the world of corporate benefits. Here the trend has been to allow benefits coverage for the employee's partner. In Table 2.2 for family status we saw that 2 percent of U.S. expatriate men and 1 percent of U.S. expatriate women had brought along unmarried partners to the host country assignment and were with them in 1999. Those figures are likely to rise as more companies recognize that that direction is being taken by a greater number of people in U.S. society each year, and therefore this fact of life will need to be accepted by those organizations intent on sending the best employees to represent them overseas.

These observations should apply to all kinds of partners, regardless of gender, national origin, race, religion, or any other factor. The only practical difficulties lie in the acceptability of these relationships in various host countries. These are factors that need to be fully explored by both the expatriate candidate and the manager when considering a possible assignment. For the potential expatriate, there is much benefit in being direct with management about these issues; otherwise there could be truly an unpleasant host country reception. Even if you are of a pioneer mind, the least you need to know is how the host country culture is likely to view your own social arrangement. Your most effective network point for finding out the "real skinny" about local mores will be repatriates from that host country location.

ELDERS

This group of fathers, mothers, and other close relatives who need serious caring for will continue to assume an increasingly critical role in all our lives as life spans continue to extend. There will be increasing pressures applied to companies to include this group in benefit programs as a part of overseas packages. We have not seen statistics for this group—yet.

Summary of Family Profiles

Why all this concern about family profiles?

These challenges are causing more expatriate assignment rejections—or acceptances without the families accompanying the expatriates—than most companies find comfortable. Yet family issues ought to be paramount for the companies if they want to clear the decks in getting the best candidate to accept that overseas posting. The potential expatriates are concerned that dual income earners, schooling problems, and the like do not receive sufficient attention from their corporate managers; hence the rejections.

Managers simply must make the time part of their busy schedules to review these concerns as they affect their employees and how their expatriate assignments could be impacted. Quality managers of the process and the expats themselves should be encouraged to open up clear communications processes, so that when difficulties involving the family arise, those issues can be properly discussed.

Notes

1. *"Zorba the Greek,"* Nickos Kazantzakis, (New York: Simon & Schuster, 1952, p. 292.
2. *Global Relocation Trends, 1999 Survey Report,* Windham International, National Foreign Trade Council, and Institute for International Human Resources, May 9, 1999, p. 9.
3. Ibid., p. 13.
4. "Progress Report: What Are the Key Findings in the Global HR Leaders' Agenda Survey?," Godfrey Golzen, *HR World,* Jan.–Feb. 2000, p. 11.
5. Statement of Marianne Ruggiero, New York, NY, Sept. 2000.
6. *Global Relocation Trends, 1999 Survey Report,* p. 13.
7. Ibid., p. 13.
8. Ibid., p. 14.
9. Ibid., p. 15.

What Are the Purposes of Expatriate Assignments?

What Are the Purposes
of Expatriate Assignments?

"To every thing there is a season, and a time for every purpose under the heaven."
Ecclesiastes 3:1

Last chapter we presented individual profiles of expatriates. Now we shift our focus to an analysis of the skills required to perform those requirements competently.

For this analysis, we'll add an important facet of each job: For whose ultimate benefit does this particular overseas posting exist? What is the end purpose of the assignment? The answers should govern the level of compensation, the length of the assignment, and the positioning of the job for a career path among other variables. So let's follow this avenue to examine expatriate work.

Professor Vladimir Pucik has been teaching international human resources courses at the best of universities in both the United States (including Cornell and Michigan) and Europe. Currently teaching at the International Institute for Management Development in Lausanne, Professor Pucik writes that managers should view their overseas jobs as either "demand driven"—that is, where the main focal point of the job is for the expat to perform a function for the primary benefit for the company—or "learning driven," where that focus shifts to the expat. For the latter class of positions, the manager's intent is to develop that expat through the overseas exposure so that he or she can further and more effectively contribute to the company in the future.[1]

In the last chapter we set out the NFTC's job breakout along with our own estimates of the age brackets that would be appropriate to consider the most effective incumbents. Now, we'll use that same NFTC job listing, by functional objective, and add to it Professor Pucik's perspective that who derives the major benefit from this job is also a logical way to gauge each expat job. So, permit me once again to estimate what Professor Pucik's classifications would look like when overlaid on the NFTC matrix.

The 1999 NFTC survey offered a breakout of five different assignment objectives, and their frequency of use is set forth in Table 3.1, with a ranking of 1 to 5, 5 being the most common objective for the assignments.[2] To the right of the ranking column is our evaluation of how demand driven or learning driven (or both) would apply to each of the five assignments.

What can we deduce from the combined matrix?

The first take-away should come as no surprise; managers need to keep the business going through the demand-driven regular staff jobs by filling skills gaps. Filling a perceived skills gap continues to dominate the reasons why expatriates are assigned. Multinationals need to be assured that the day-to-day operations continue to be efficiently managed. Second, launching new endeavors is primarily demand driven, but in the process of breaking new ground, those expats in charge will be gaining valuable information that can be applied again, key information enough to be a significant development factor in their careers. Third, technology transfers are all about one-way streets. The expat knows information that the host operation doesn't have, and the only real learning for the expat is found in the process of exploring

Table 3.1   Assignment Objectives Ranked by Frequency of Use

Assignment Objective	Rank from 1 to 5	Demand or Learning Driven
Fill skills gap	3.2	Demand
Launch new endeavor	3.0	Demand and learning
Transfer technology	2.6	Demand
Build management experience	2.2	Learning
Transfer corporate culture	1.8	Demand and learning

Data Source: Global Relocation Trends, 1999 Survey Report, Windham/NFTC/IIHR.

the host's current technology as a learning starter for other assignments, not really secondary enough learning to move it into the learning box.

The next NFTC category is clear-cut. Developmental assignments are primarily to build knowledge for the expat, but if it happens that the expat can contribute at the same time, that is a value-added factor, but not usually expected by management.

The final category, conveying corporate culture, is another demand-driven function, but in that process, expats often learn enough about the host location culture for positioning appropriate mixes.

We can see that the NFTC breakout can lead to multiple classifications for the same assignment (as we will see later in a case study) but the responses generally show that more assignments are skill driven than developmental, and that technology transfers have developed into a significant assignment factor today. Certainly the enormous advances being made in technology offer the multinationals improved tools to deploy in meeting objectives. Since the 1999 survey was the first to report the assignment objectives, it should be interesting to see how this category grows in popularity, considering the global needs for advanced technology. An additional factor at work here is the probable decline of the skills-filling assignments as more knowledge is transferred to local staff so that they can begin to perform the work formerly done by expatriates. Let's take the best of both breakouts and analyze assignments from the two basic Pucik categories. We'll proceed to delineate the demand-driven further into operating staff jobs (replacements) and special project-driven tasks (with three subclassifications). We will then briefly describe the learning-driven expatriate positions (breaking that group into two subclassifications).

Demand-Driven Assignments

REGULAR OPERATIONAL FUNCTIONS

This has been the most common form of expatriate assignment for many years, but it may be losing ground to shorter assignments that are often perceived as cost savers. Today, less than one-quarter of expatriate assignments are for more than three years. In 1993 the average was three years, but by 1996 that three-year assignment average had declined to 32 percent.[3] That statistic, as well as the assignment durations in Table 3.2, includes all kinds of assignments, even project and developmental assignments, which tend to be shorter in duration than refilling an operating staff position. Table 3.2 shows the NFTC survey results reporting current durations of expatriate postings.[4]

The replacement expatriate position is generally a permanent job within a line or staff organization at the host country location and is essential to maintain the ongoing operations of that business. All the traditional management functions are involved—marketing, sales, manufacturing, finance, human resources, public relations, systems, engineering, research, and so on. Historically, the home country headquarters believed that filling these ongoing functions with employees who were thoroughly familiar with what headquarters wanted from the host location amounted to the most secure way of maintaining close control over the host location's operations. Managers often believed, in the 1960s and 1970s, that there were not sufficient local staff people who possessed technical skills or headquarters experience for serious consideration as candidates for overseas postings.

The duration for these assignments was generally about three years, usually dependent on how difficult the host location environment was deemed to be. This was consistent with the U.S. Army's designation of difficult or dangerous nations as 12 or 13 months' hardship assignments against the normal three-year hitch associated with the more "comfortable" nonhazardous duty or nonhardship locations.

Generally there is an expatriate incumbent in the operating position who must be replaced. These kinds of jobs tend to be well defined. There is usually a job summary of some sort that makes recruitment of an expatriate successor a more refined task than guessing what the real functions would be from a job title only (too often the case with many newer organizations that have not had the time or desire to finish that basic homework).

Table 3.2   Assignment Durations

Duration of Assignment	Percent of Assignments
Under one year	8%
One year to two years	30%
Two years to three years	39%
Three years or more	23%

Data Source: Global Relocation Trends, 1999 Survey Report, Windham/NFTC/IIHR, p. 36

The basic starting points—the salary range, the overseas premiums, allowances, and benefits in addition to the basic functions and objectives of the job—are generally so well entrenched that the replacement expatriate will usually be viewing an employment opportunity that is well defined in the eyes of management and only needs to be clearly spelled out in the employment agreement for the incoming expatriate. The one drawback here is that many managers, at both the home and host locations, may not have kept current with the evolving changes to the job since the last time it was filled; hence there is always a duty for management to update the job summary, with the help of the incumbent, so that all the changes are sufficiently incorporated into a revised description.

The next element in the expatriate replacement structure is the new employment agreement for the successful candidate to consider, negotiate if necessary, and execute. These agreements have become so standard boilerplate that in many companies they are reduced to general language that could apply to any kind of job anywhere, with just a few blanks to complete to do the deal. Such standardized approaches do management and the expatriate an injustice, since they do not zero in on what the function really requires or what it is specifically asked to produce in terms of targets. These crucial essentials are generally left for a verbal review with the host country manager, and as we are all so aware, verbal agreements are essentially worth the paper they're not written on. Both managers and potential expatriates are hereby cautioned to take the time to spell out the major job requirements and goals in the written agreement. It can prevent misunderstandings that may creep into the assignment while it is underway. This matter of the employment agreement is of sufficient value to provide you with some general recommendations. We'll refer to a book by Bill Twinn and Patrick Burns, both veteran expatriates as human resources professionals. They would argue, persuasively, to draft a complete agreement as possible—and for the two decades I've known these professionals, I don't believe they would risk verbal commitments for any assignment.

In *The Expatriate's Handbook*, published in London in 1998,[5] these practitioners write: "For the first-time expatriate, obtaining your contract for Timbuktu or Billings, Montana, is an exciting moment. In terms of signing on the dotted line and returning it to Head Office, it is probably the most dangerous moment of the assignment. Once signed, the contract will shape your job conditions for many years to come. Because of this, the contract ought to be treated with a great deal of respect."

What are the terms of a model expatriate agreement?

EMPLOYMENT CONTRACTS

All of the following points pertain to both demand-driven and developmental-driven postings. In the case of developmental postings, professional care must be given to the customizing of the usual "boilerplate" to this assignee.

Job Location and Duration

The title of the job, both functional (describing what area it is responsible for and the corporate structural level, such as Director, Marketing, France, X Corp.) and legal title (as often required in order to bind the company, as a lawful agent, e.g., Vice President, Marketing, X Corp., France). The former should be crafted to open business doors or to make clients, customers, or company representatives aware of what it is you do and your relative level of importance in your organization. The legal title can come into play when signing contracts with customers, suppliers, and others, and needs to be substantiated if ever challenged in the host country. Here is the legal delegation of powers to act on the corporation's behalf; frequently the functional title will be an inflated rank utilized as a "door opener."

The major job functions and objectives can be attached and included legally by reference. The more completely this description is fashioned, the more likely it will help if issues arise as to what the job's scope actually was agreed to be. Significant changes in the position can then be agreed upon as an amendment to the position agreement. This focus on the parameters helps both the manager and the expatriate when questions arise as to authority to perform some activities at the host country site. The scope of many expatriate responsibilities is stretched far enough not to have worries creep in regarding authority to take action.

The duration of the assignment should be set forth along with a clause that by mutual agreement that period can be lengthened or shortened. Both the expatriate and the company should sign any such alteration, in the form of a letter agreement. There are many extensions and contractions of assignments today, so both parties should not be in doubt as to what the last verbal modification of the contract term was.

Compensation and Payment Method

This provision in the contract details how much, and when, and where each of the pieces of compensation (base pay, premiums, allowances, bonuses, etc.) will be paid to the expatriate. It will also detail in which countries those payments will be made, if there is a split-payroll program. The agreement should spell out when performance reviews will be conducted and who will do the ratings. This clause ought to cover merit increase and bonus review dates. If the company is using a balance sheet method of host country allowances, there should be reference made to when those adjustments to allowances are expected (often every quarter or semiannually).

The contract should detail the conditions of the completion bonus. Generally the location of the payment, for those companies that provide for it, is not set forth in the contract. This can produce serious tax consequences for the expatriate and the company, and should be fully explored before deciding when and where that bonus will be paid.

Relocation Arrangements

Who is going to pay what regarding the many costs involved in wrapping up the gritty details of leaving one household and transporting all that household furniture to the host country? These conditions are usually set forth in the company's relocation policy, and if it agreed to control your move, then that fact needs to be inserted in the agreement, again by way of incorporating a reference to that policy.

But both expatriate and manager need to ensure that all the unique conditions applying to this move are negotiated in or out of the company's financial obligations package. For example, what about that boat you would like to ship over for holidays on the Seine? Virtually all companies will leave that cost to you. And how about your pets? Will the company pay for the transport of your beloved pooch Fang? You'll need to check the pet policy; not all companies appreciate your family's tie to a dog or cat and will coldly insist that you pay the pet's transportation costs. All these items should be spelled out in the overseas manual.

The relocation section boils down to the obligation of the expatriate family unit to take total inventory of what needs to go versus what should be stored or otherwise disposed of, and to find out how the company's policy treats those transactions. Far too often expatriate families assume that the company will do reasonable reimbursements for items such as social or health club forfeitures, inability to sell furnishings, inability to find a buyer or renter, and so on. Many companies today provide a one month's base pay lump-sum payment, often called a "miscellaneous allowance," designed to cover the many expenditures that go into pulling up stakes.

The list of agreed-upon reimbursements or other company obligations, such as real estate services, also ought to be provided for in the agreement. If it isn't there, and the company's policy does not specifically include that kind of payment, you expatriates should ask for those reimbursements, or you will have to pay out of pocket.

Housing

This subject has two pieces. Many companies use consultant relocation services that will provide the moving expatriate family unit help with disposing by sale or rental of their property. If so, does the expatriate get to select which provider? Will there be payments for security and maintenance while the residence is put up for sale or rent?

Next, the housing provisions at the host country should be spelled out in the company overseas manual, and if so, again the best approach is to reference that part of the policy in the contract. Suppose, for example, that you have another child overseas. That addition to family calls for a restructuring of many of the allowances, most notably the size of the housing entitlement. In cases where there are no housing tables used by the company, there should be specific ranges of housing expenditures that will be assumed by the company during the assignment.

Allowances and Premiums

Again the policy manual may provide specific ground rules as to how the company will structure your overseas package. Each of these items should be spelled out in the agreement, particularly for the employee's protection. Suppose management decides to eliminate or reduce the overseas premium or the hardship premium while you are toiling at an oil rig under the hot desert sun or cruising down the Seine under a Paris moon? Whether there should be premiums just to go overseas, and then to fix hardships on one location versus another, have been traditional sore points between companies and their expatriates for many, many years. But the "need" issue will be bypassed if the particular premium is set forth in the agreement.

And this is an example of the advantage you expats will have in being able partly to control the changes that may come up requiring adjustments to the contract. If a particular condition is left to the overseas manual, the company will occasionally change a provision in that binder. You may or may not receive serious attention if you don't go along with that change. But if you have your own agreement in hand, managers have to secure your signature on an amendment to it in order to implement the change.

Schooling, Car, and Club

These essentials—even the club membership in many locations—all deserve elaboration in the employment agreement. The potential issues:

What happens if the school turns out to be inadequate?

Who pays for a boarding school alternative?

What are the size and cost limitations on auto purchase or rental?

Are there choices for the expatriate in terms of health or social clubs?

Vacation and Home Leave

These time-off provisions require close examination. They are usually set forth in the company's overseas manual, but they bear scrutiny if the expatriate wants to use the reimbursement amounts of the home leave entitlement to run in the streets of Pamplona with enervating company rather than to return to the placid halls of home headquarters.

Must the expatriate return to the home headquarters on home leave?

Can the expatriate convert the home leave air ticket value to cash?

Is transportation for expatriate and family in business or economy class?

Can unused home leaves or vacations be accumulated and carried over from year to year?

If business dictates the forfeiture of either home leave or vacation, then can those days be carried over or paid out?

Health and Pension Benefits and Social Security Programs

Here are three subjects that require customized treatment, based on each host location. There is no way that a boilerplate agreement can adequately handle all the problems of the cost and eligibility for the French social security program as opposed to the issues created by having no local plan whatsoever.

Let's start with the basic health insurance program applicable to you at the host location. How does that coverage apply? Who pays for it? What happens to your health plan coverage in your home country?

Next, what is the impact of your moving offshore on your company pension? Will you continue to vest if you can no longer contribute to it? And what about continuation of your 401(k)? Can you contribute? Can your company contribute or match?

If you are required to contribute to the host country pension or social security system, will you ever be able to pull out your contributions to it?

The benefits provisions are so important that you would be well advised doing some research with your home country benefits department (if staffers are knowledgeable about the host country's programs) or otherwise you'll need to apply some individual research, perhaps through repatriates, as to how the programs actually operate in the host country. That knowledge will equip you with some real bargaining power at the time of discussion with the manager (usually a human resources representative) so you can judge the impact of your host country's programs upon your entire family. Then you'll need to decide what steps you would like the company to take to provide you with fair coverage at fair cost.

Taxes

If you have sweated over what were deemed complicated tax forms in the United States and its state or city accomplices in mysterious forms, there will be another tier of sheer trauma when it comes around to filing both your home country returns and the host country returns, which will be at least the case in the first and last years of assignment. Companies are fully aware of the time-consuming and thought-diverting nature of the tax issues and have tried to solve them in two ways.

First, most of the companies offer the help of a local tax consulting firm to guide you through the nightmarish forms, say of Tokyo, where, similar to the United States and most states and some cities, there are three layers of tax-collecting forms of government. If your company at the host location does not provide this service, you need to find out why. Also, who pays for that service?

The second form of help that most companies provide is a method of removing some of the burdens of owing different sets of taxes for the same taxable period. We will review each of the major concepts—tax equalization and tax protection—later in our detailing of how the packages work in practice (Chapter 8).

Training and Preparation

Why make a differentiation between these two? Because training should be geared toward developing the employee's general or technical skill growth, and ideally, in the most enlightened of corporate worlds, it should be a continuous process, customized to the employee's need. As such, it ought to have preceded the potential expatriate's actual selection and needs to be taken up again in the host country and on all subsequent assignments. If there are training sessions that the expatriate candidate would like to be considered for, the time of the contract negotiation presents a marvelous opportunity to make those desires known, since he or she has some genuine bargaining leverage. After all, he or she has already been deemed worthy of a huge corporate investment in time, in money, and in responsibility. All the candidate is doing, therefore, is adding more value of the company investment.

The second term, preparation, is more specifically directed toward the nature of the assignment at hand, and should include the entire family unit, as they need to gain the knowledge necessary to appreciate the new culture they are about to encounter. Many larger organizations have in-house training staffs, but unless we're dealing with a host location that is so popular that the firm has developed a host country cultural expertise, the wiser decision is for the company to reach out to one of the many consultants in this field. Managers and candidates should discuss the selection of a preparation professional. Will it be someone from the in-house training staff? Will it be a consultant? Which consultant? These items should be matters for inclusion in the contract. Ideally, preparation should continue in the form of further cross-cultural training at the host location, and if this can be negotiated in the contract as well, it will be money and time well spent.

Next Assignment

This provision is difficult to obtain full company agreement on, because it calls for such long-term projections that most company representatives will hardly be inclined to include this section. But they can and should. A potential expat should start the process prior to departure. Now is the best opportunity to draw out from the manager information as to where this position fits within the corporation's planning and overall strategy. Where would the expat be assigned after returning? Even if there is no formal succession planning function or even an organization design person to review the future prospects with, a potential expatriate is well advised to start the planning for his or her career path at this stage of the expatriate process. Once the expatriate has left the home headquarters building, there will be considerably less attention paid to this planning need until the assignment has expired; then the hasty retreat to the human resources organization chart begins, usually to find that the only current vacancy may not really be a good fit for the returning repatriate.

The place to start for the expatriate is to look around at other promising positions in the home country, and gather as much information about them as possible prior to departure. Would any of these make sense for you on return, building on the maturity and exposures gained during the overseas assignment? Or does the company have some alternative positions in mind? If so, could they be included in this contract as possible, not guaranteed, alternatives? And at a minimum, is there a possible guarantee of home employment at a minimum organizational and compensation level?

Another viable approach is to agree to a deadline at which active discussions about the next assignment must commence. This contractual trigger will be more positive than a series of pleading communiqués from the expatriate beseeching the manager for access to an appropriate manager to review the next assignment options. Incidentally, I've found that this kind of expatriate insistence has the by-product of impressing most managers as to the seriousness of the company-oriented career aspirations of the expatriate. At the time these planning requests are made, we HR people can be overheard grumbling about this stickler of a candidate, but that petty annoyance is nothing compared to the possible benefits to you from directing management's attention to your career planning needs now, a refreshing change from the many expatriates who quit either on assignment or shortly after returning to the home country.

For you managers, the negotiation presents ample opportunity to obtain senior management's input as to what career paths within the company are deemed appropriate for this potential expatriate. Human resources people, in particular, need to be far more proactive in this regard. It would be refreshing for them not to rush around at the last minute before the repatriation gathering management input that could have been obtained long before the overseas assignment ended.

Termination

This may strike you as a strange subject to put into a contract, carrying with it such a negative connotation that it might put off the manager, the expatriate, or both. But the reality of the expatriate employment scene is that such a clause in the contract will prove beneficial to both parties if and when a parting of the ways is mandated by the company or by the expatriate's own desire to walk.

As with just about every other facet of the overseas posting, a central issue is the enormous costs involved with the ending of the employment relationship through the expenditures of returning home or proceeding elsewhere for the ex-employee. In fact, William Sheridan, Director, International Compensation of the National Foreign Trade Council, in chairing a symposium of expatriate programs, concluded that an overseas assignment averages around a $1 million investment by the company.[6] Indeed, none of the 80 human resources, consultant, and expatriate attendees challenged that assessment.

The costs of transporting the ex-employee and family unit; the housing, car, and club forfeitures; the time and effort to find a suitable replacement rapidly; the need for others to leave portions of their own work to pitch in while there is no one doing that function—all add up to a tremendous loss for the host country operation to sustain. This is especially true in overseas locations where jobs tend to be stretched broadly. Consequently an unforeseen loss sends deeper vibrations throughout an overseas location than it would normally produce at a more fully staffed and much larger home or headquarters building.

From the expatriate's viewpoint, he or she needs assurance that if things don't work out on the job an involuntary termination will not leave him or her (and family) left in a country miles from home, facing enormous transportation costs, the loss of insurance protection, and the quandary as to how to restore a sane existence in the home country. For those considerations, the potential expatriate needs some protection against a forced departure. The clause ought to provide that the company will pay for all return costs and maintain medical insurance under COBRA back in the United States as an option for the ex-employee upon return there.

From the company's perspective, such costs ought to be assumed—the expatriate makes the decision to end (usually abruptly) the overseas assignment to join another company at the host location or return to the home country to take another job. Under these circumstances, managers should try to shift any relocation costs to the new employer. After all, the expatriate is technically in breach of the employment agreement. We noted earlier the current trend toward hiring expatriates from other companies; much of the pirating thrives at the host country, where another company needs to take advantage of an expatriate's knowledge of that territory. In these cases, or even where the quit is to take a position back in the home country, the company is best advised to insist that there be no obligation for it to assume any more financial liability for the expatriate going forward. This may appear to be harsh, but the likelihood is that the expatriate has already built that cost into his or her new deal with the next employer.

Mentors

A potential expatriate should pursue selecting a mentor in the home country who will be responsible for establishing and maintaining effective communication links, both in terms of expected frequency and subjects, with him or her while on assignment. By the time of negotiations over the employment agreement, the manager and the expat candidate should have found a mutually agreeable employee to be mentor. Should that mentor depart, it will be valuable to have lined up an alternative mentor who knows the departing expatriate well enough that he or she could be appointed as a successor to the first mentor. Neither the company nor the potential expatriate will likely appreciate how valuable this arrangement is for the expatriate until well into the assignment, when the average individual placed far from the action at company headquarters begins to wonder "What's been going on back there?" or "Does anyone back there remember that I'm still here?"

References to the International Assignment Manual

These guidelines can be anywhere from 40 to 100 pages of policies, which set out the rules governing all assignments. In the absence of an employment agreement that specifically overrides the policies, this manual can rise to the legal equivalent of a contract if the company provides you a copy, gives you a reasonable time to read it, and asks you to sign a verification that you have read it, understand it, and fully agree to its terms. If this is the case, a potential overseas assignee needs to make the time to read over every sentence carefully. These policies were drawn for general application to the entire expatriate workforce and may not cover such items as your boat, beloved pooch Fang, or your spouse's need for job-hunting assistance.

For example, if your assignment destination is a location that is still on the U.S. State Department's security risk list, you need to have full written assurance that there is a valid evacuation plan in place there and to know what the procedures are for transporting the entire expatriate family unit out of harm's way. Or consider those host countries that do not offer special schooling for a child who requires it.

It makes sense then for you managers and expat candidates to review all these possible issues to be discussed with the company overseas programs administrator before signing either the contract or the manual acknowledgment form. It is this time, prior to closing the deal, that your concerns will be most seriously addressed by the manager. The likelihood of a positive resolution of these issues diminishes after the expatriate departs; at that point in time HR people are already focusing on the next expatriate situation and will be inclined to refer your issue to your new host country manager for resolution. And that's not the way to start off with a new boss.

ROLE OF THE PRIOR INCUMBENT

While negotiations over terms are being conducted, you, as a smart potential expat, will track down the prior incumbent, whether that person is still with the company or not. Unlike the other varieties of international assignments, the replacement posting offers the luxury of being able to learn, first-hand, the job's fundamental requirements and potential pitfalls. You need to elicit information regarding questions such as the following:

Who can be counted on to offer real help?
Which of the local staff can be a valuable conduit for understanding the local culture and learning successful methods?
What are the best avenues for an effective orientation?
What projects are in progress that the new assignee needs to address now and later?
What's the boss really like?
What is the school system's record?
Are there spouse support groups?
Are the local church, temple, club, and so on, hospitable to expatriates?

The answers to these questions will provide invaluable help in planning your strategy for the assignment. The practical difficulty, however, is that the prior incumbent has all too frequently already departed the job. In that case, your best alternative is to try to establish a direct link with that former incumbent, no matter where he or she is at present (provided he or she is still an employee of your firm, but not in the case where the assignee left to join a direct competitor or client).

If there is a possibility that the incumbent can stay on the job for a time to provide some overlap, that is the ultimate of benefits for the newcomer. But even when that person is still around, it usually is for a very short time and generally he or she is so intent on the next assignment that persuading that individual to give some serious reflection time on the job will be a most difficult task indeed.

Let's suppose that the prior incumbent abruptly left the company. Here is a red flag situation: You need to know the circumstances of that termination. Was it a voluntary quit or an involuntary termination? You need, as a potential expatriate, to ask this question and pursue the details from every management representative involved in the assignment process, from the home country human resources people to the host country manager's representatives, and most important, from peers, subordinates, and any other individuals who can relate the real facts pertaining to the departure. The reason for this information-gathering necessity goes to the heart of human perspectives: We simply don't always see the same situation in a consistent manner. We need to remind ourselves that different people observing the same act will often perceive it so differently that one is left wondering what really happened. I witnessed this human phenomenon at work in first-year torts class at law school, when the professor set up an abrupt mock shooting scenario and then asked all of us 100 lawyers-to-be to describe the details of what had just transpired. We couldn't agree on such basics as what was said, what clothing was worn, or what physical motions had been involved. Now try finding out why someone abruptly left her job; it will be a process that will call for some intensive mind reading.

Management has a difficult role in these sticky situations. Where the prior assignment totally failed, how is the fault to be assessed and how should that be explained to prospective assignees? This calls for a coordinated effort between the host country management and the home country HR to review what went wrong and how to explain that to the candidates. If the reasons are not consistent during the potential expat's probe, that signals some deep lack of communication between the host and home countries that, in all probability, would be reflected in further dealings with the potential expat.

Often there is the embarrassment of disclosing personal or family conflicts that ultimately produced the issue triggering the departure. While human chemistry issues present workplace obstacles everywhere, they seem to confront expatriates at a more serious level, since there are few escape-valve opportunities at many host country locations. The same company people are likely to be socializing, working out, playing sports, shopping, or worshiping at the same places at the host location. Expatriate community life often resembles the old oil company camps, only without the fences. Their clustered neighborhoods mean constant expat company.

The candidate must put together the pieces of the termination puzzle and try to determine whether he or she would be comfortable given those circumstances. He or she will recognize that human chemistry issues will not be identical, given the potential expat's own personality and psychological makeup. If there were clear-cut management issues, there is a need to find out what the company intends to do about those problems.

On the brighter side of the picture, replacement positions offer the potential advantage of locating the prior incumbent's spouse and children, who tend to be excellent reference points for finding out about the basics of the host location. In addition, host country HR should provide additional recommendations as to who might be the best contacts for information on schools, shopping, transportation, and background as to the dos and don'ts of cross-cultural behavior at the host location. If the incumbent has departed the location, the host country HR should contact other expatriate family units to see if they would be interested in meeting with the prospective expatriate family and providing them with an informal orientation.

This facet of the HR job is akin to the role of cruise host, the line's employee who enforces comprehensive socializing by warmly introducing everybody to everybody else and then continuously follows up to ensure that all are in fact happily mixing.

ROTATIONAL ASSIGNMENTS

Managers are well aware that conditions such as aging parents, spousal careers, and educational issues are prompting more overseas candidates than ever to turn down expatriate assignments. Some companies are opting to split up what would have been a normal two- or three-year term assignment into segments of three to six months each, assigning people who, for whatever reason, would not have been able to accept a full-term posting.

These rotational programs offer some solid advantages and some serious drawbacks to both managers and expatriates. For the expats, these postings represent that golden opportunity to gain overseas exposures. The knowledge gained should be broadening and should produce a more valued employee into the bargain. Many of these assignments house the expat in a furnished corporate setting, in a rental at a hotel, or, best of all, with coworkers in their homes, which would maximize the culture immersion process.

What are the drawbacks to rotational postings? Tom Peiffer, consultant of principal accounts for Runzheimer International, sees one in particular: "Peiffer, whose firm found that 44 percent of companies expect an increase in employee resistance to moves, is concerned that rotational assignments may actually be somewhat self-defeating in that employees are brought home just as they are getting up to speed in their assigned position."[7]

For you managers there is another problem engendered by rotations: the lack of continuity. The host country staff must acclimatize to new expats in successive, short periods of time. That means new personalities to work with, breaking in the new expat regarding basic customs, and investing substantial time in briefing the newcomer as to the background of the status of the work.

Still another managerial concern ought to be the structure of the expatriate job itself. If a company is going to mandate a time restriction as short as three months, won't that condition convert what should have been a bona fide team effort participation by the expat into a consultant-like role, in which he or she winds up observing and advising rather than doing? It is simply human nature for a group smoothly working together to accept the help of a newcomer only if that group can first test the abilities of that new person. That testing will further reduce the time given to the rotational expat to get directly into the work process.

Rotational assignments work best in hardship areas. Consider, for example, that Chevron has 700 expats, worldwide, on a rotational system that calls for 28 days on the work site and 28 days back at the home country. These schedules have been operating for up to 40 years in places such as Nigeria and Angola. Occupational categories that are involved in the program include petroleum engineers, pipe fitters, geologists, finance, HR, information technology (IT), and business analysts. These assignments are on a single basis, and the expats stay in Chevron compounds.

If you are evaluating multiple rotations, be aware that there may be serious tax consequences regarding host country tax liabilities. Check with your company's tax department.

There could well be increased use of rotational expatriate assignments as managers try to cope with the increasing reject rate trends that are facing the global competitors today.

PROJECT ASSIGNMENTS

Technical Transfers

Unlike the regular staff expatriate position, the special project assignment has no prior incumbent to replace. Rather, it calls for a first-time completion of a specified task, usually with no hard deadline. The duration is generally fixed to the project completion date, unless the project is of such a long-term nature that it will be turned over to a local staff person prior to its completion. Most of these kinds of assignments are for less than two years. These assignments are generally performed by technicians who must construct or repair systems required by the host location. These are jobs that are also capable of being categorized as filling skills gaps at the overseas post.

Frequently these expatriates are called upon to train local staff into stages of development where they can begin to assume responsibility for the systems left in place. There is a troubleshooting aspect of these positions that can extend their scope to any host country function that is suffering. There could be finance, marketing, or sales issues that require extensive help.

For project expatriates, the brief assignment duration offers fine career opportunities. The exposure, often to many cultures through several projects, provides the global experiences that grow into upgraded marketability, whether within the present company or out in the open marketplace. For family members, a mixed blessing arises from these assignments. While there is the emotional drain of the expat's departure, the remainder of the family is spared the trauma of multiple uprootings. The spouse can continue pursuing career interests and the children can continue their educational programs without discomforting transitions to new schools. A completed project, or better yet a series of successes, offers a wonderful chance to debrief both host and home country senior management. Project assignments also serve as effective litmus tests as to whether a fixed-term operational job overseas would be appropriate for the project expat.

You expats will have to weigh that nasty matter of being away from your family for extended periods of time. This dark side to project assignments, especially when they begin to drag out to six months or more, needs to be addressed through company-provided return trips or family visitations. These concerns, similar to the other conditions spelled out in the employment agreement for the operational assignee, compel an employment agreement for overseas project work.

That contract needs to detail the work that is required to be performed to complete the project and the time frame for completion. Terms for extensions, which always seem to be the case overseas, should be worked out. If an extension is required, should there be a conversion to a full expatriate package? Should the hotel arrangement be switched to regular expat housing? The contract needs to spell out what kinds of support, in terms of people and equipment, are to be furnished to the project expatriate.

Another item for the contract is the matter of reporting. How often are status reports required, to whom should they be addressed, and what kinds of meetings, conversations, and so forth about the project in progress will be expected? Importantly, who is to judge the performance of the project person, and how will that evaluation be conveyed? Will there be a performance bonus? And what about the next job? Will it be another project or a more permanent staff position, back at home or at a new host county location?

Corporate Structure Reproducer Assignments

These expatriate assignments, fewer than the other demand-driven ones, can arise in a few different ways. Let's review each.

Where managers are planning a merger or acquisition, experienced headquarters managers people need to analyze what elements of the other company must be restructured in a manner that the home country headquarters wants.

If there is a new organization to be structured, the home country management requires people who can implement that kind of structuring the way that senior management believes is appropriate.

These assignments call for experienced employees who are mature enough to understand the rationale for what the headquarters does and why it does it, and then couple that knowledge with the savvy to evaluate what portions of home country business and employee approaches would make sense at this host location.

The durations of these assignments vary all over the lot. So much depends on the particular circumstances of the two entities that hazarding a guess as to an average would be a waste of time. Just think about what the Chrysler people could have learned from their Daimler hosts and vice versa. The transfer of knowledge could take years. Should a formal report be rendered? To whom? Is there a bonus associated with successfully completing the "restructuring"? Who judges the success of that effort? These are all to be answered in the assignment agreement, again, which should follow the outline listed for the operations assignment.

Establishing New Branch Operations

These expatriate assignments are carried out by teams, usually with one representative of each major function, charged with finding host country nationals who could be potential employees, and making contacts with local search firms, the local universities, potential suppliers, the real estate people to help with locating an appropriate site, and others.

These are particularly rewarding assignments because they start at ground zero, and every day you see some growth or development that was not there the day before. These postings contrast with regular staff or line functions, also demand driven, where the expert's contribution is often difficult to quantify. But experts building an organization are fulfilling responsibilities that stretch the limits of one's capabilities. You're in a new country trying to see what pieces of the company's normal structure and philosophy would work there. The other part of the challenge is to glean all the information possible to learn what sorts of modifications would make sense in the business and cultural setting. These are challenges in which you can see the results of your work effort; hiring people, finding a suitable work site, and so on can be rewarding, particularly if senior management has given the team a substantial degree of freedom in dealing with local issues.

An actual case history—Schlumberger's establishment of a Far Eastern regional headquarters in Tokyo in the early 1980s—will enable you to see how these unique assignments can work, if you are in the fortunate position to be offered a similar task.

CASE HISTORY: SCHLUMBERGER'S
NEW REGIONAL HEADQUARTERS IN TOKYO

If ever there were a demand-driven expat assignment where the expats learned quantums of knowledge about a culture, it would be Schlumberger's installation in Tokyo of a Far Eastern regional headquarters for all Asian operations.

Here was a classic illustration of a project team trying to build a headquarters staff, an operations and research center with no prior exposure or experience with the host country market, Japan. In the early 1980s, Schlumberger was the world's largest oil service company, doing business in over 100 nations, with an overall employee population exceeding 100,000—a truly global organization, but without a beachhead in the important Japanese economy. Schlumberger's process for tackling the headquarters can serve as an example of an expatriate team's coordinated efforts to complete a major project.

The initial step for the corporate headquarters was to select a core team of experienced international staff who would ultimately be responsible for assembling teams of Japanese nationals for each of their respective disciplines: operations, finance, human resources, research, and technical support. Heading this core team was a veteran country manager, a German national with prior country manager experience throughout Europe, but who was new to the Far East. In a corporate coordination role, I was sent from New York headquarters to try to connect with the better of the Tokyo search firms, the faculty at the prestigious University of Tokyo (our engineer recruiting target), and other major (and successful) non-Japanese companies already there (IBM and American Express being particularly good best-practice models).

All three avenues had to be fully pursued if we were going to achieve success in a brand-new marketplace for us. The French HR national, the Dutch finance individual, the American research head, and the French operations person all had extensive experience with the company, but none in Asia. They would be responsible for their functions for approximately three years, and were charged with building local staffs who could quickly begin to be productive; this was a daunting task considering the difficult Japanese labor market, still following the traditional lifetime employment philosophy so prevalent among top Japanese companies in those days.

The team's strengths proved to be in their extensive technical experience and managing skills. All had more than 10 years' experience with the company, in a variety of different host nations. The major weakness of the group, however, was inexperience with the Japanese labor marketplace—knowledge that would have to be acquired quickly in order to begin the hiring of quality local nationals.

The challenge for the team: How can you find good candidates and attract them to a company with no track record in Japan?

Each functional member of the team had direct access to his or her respective functional corporate heads. They each had specific targets, and status reports were shared by the team on a weekly basis. The common challenge, where to find good people, was eventually addressed by using experienced search firms to locate recent retirees for the senior levels of the new organization, and by utilizing university professors for bright engineering graduates for the lower levels of the new company's structure. Both solutions required trial-and-error processes.

University professors needed to be in the process because they were looked upon by recent graduates as godfathers, respected individuals they could turn to for career advice, often long after graduation. The difficulty for us was they had no knowledge of the Schlumberger techniques in the wire line process, the leading edge in oilfield technology but little known by the Tokyo University engineering faculty. The research and technical team heads spent considerable time in showing them the latest of the techniques, while the human resources head explained the company's personnel policies. This required some sensitive explanations in light of the Japanese insistence on long-term employment commitments, not consistent with Schlumberger's acceptance of field engineer turnover averaging around the sixth year.

Meanwhile the Dutch finance head set about establishing relationships with the various local financial institutions, and a real estate representative was signed on to locate the headquarters site and the research and operations facilities. Corporate headquarters people were helpful both in providing further support from New York and Paris (the two corporate headquarters sites) and as catalysts, reminding the project team that time was critical to success; the three operations needed to be up and running as soon as possible to take advantage of the ballooning Far East market for greater oil exploration.

Fortunately, the contacts set up through IBM and American Express channels proved to be most effective in helping to select a well-regarded search firm, and a fortuitous hire of a recently retired senior human resources person began to feed the various functions with quality candidates they had been so desperately seeking. He, as a respected Japanese national from one of Tokyo's top-tier firms, was able to lend the local credibility that we had lacked while screening the first set of local staff hires, who would, in turn, be hiring their subordinates. The university recruiting program took more time to kick off successfully; those "godfathers" were still not keen on recommending employment to their former students in a corporation that did not adhere to the lifetime employment concept that was still ironclad back in the 1980s.

As the nonengineer hiring snowballed, the team could concentrate on developing the new local staff managers, lending their technical knowledge, and learning about local Japanese managerial mores—in the process instilling the company's policies and practices into the new Japanese workforce. The initial successes started in the fourth month of the project, considered a triumph by those of us exposed to all the threshold obstacles in Tokyo. By six months, the new operations were beginning to fill out with quality local staff; the pioneering stage of the new operation had been completed.

In due course, this pioneer team of expats was replaced by other international staff expatriates, but this time the newly assigned people had the benefit of their predecessors' experience and the help of local Japanese staff.

Should these projects also carry employment agreements? Of course. The contracts should, like the other projects already discussed, spell out whether the work duration is expected to be long enough to carry the full expatriate package or short enough to warrant using extended business trip guidelines. The essential point is to agree on a reasonable time frame, say six months, at which the assignment will be reevaluated for purposes of the reimbursement or package implementations.

Longer-Term Assignments

Despite the fact that the average duration of expatriate assignments is melting down to less than three years, there are still some types of postings that require more time for the assignee to become fully productive. Positions such as country manager or head of marketing, advertising, public relations, and so on require intimate knowledge of the host country and begin to yield solid dividends to the company as knowledge and contacts expand. Both Nomura and SK Group had expatriates who had logged more than 10 years in the United States to ultimately become official spokespeople for their respective communities. Likewise, many of the major U.S. banks have sent and kept successful managers on in the Far East for 10 years or so, largely for their unique contributions as well-respected, entrenched members of their communities. Special bonuses, extended home leaves, and title changes are all used to encourage the expatriate to stay on at the overseas post. In many cases, neither the management nor the expatriate had anticipated that the length of the assignment would be extended to such extremes, but every company has such people on its current staff today, and they represent both blessings and nightmares.

On the plus side, the company has gained a superlative advantage over competitors by having in place a well-respected leader who, through time, has gradually been accepted as a citizen of the host country community. In these cases, the expatriate has learned to master the language and understand the customs to such an extent that local clients, consumers, suppliers, and others have come to regard him or her as a trustworthy member of the business community.

The negative aspect of these elongated assignments is that time gradually erodes the likelihood that a repatriation to home headquarters will be feasible. Universally, headquarters people have a habit of changing the guard on a frequent basis, considerably reducing the chances that there will still be friendly allies in place upon a long-term expatriate's return home. Moreover, policies, procedures, and corporate philosophy will all have undergone the grand-scale transitions that all dynamic organizations perpetuate through the years. Upon repatriation, these long-timers can debrief management as to their host location. After the debriefing to those executives, the repatriate presents a difficult challenge for the employment people to place him or her in a position that would suitably use all the knowledge gained overseas.

Unfortunately, the ultimate end to these kinds of repatriations is usually unfavorable for both the repat and the company. Often the only place that the company can find is "by the window." (The Japanese use the same term for the same meaning—the employee should be out of the way of current operations.) The other alternative is for the long-termer to seek more challenging positions elsewhere, including the host country in which he or she has become so experienced.

For the expatriate family unit, the extended assignments produce a variety of serious issues that we will review in Chapter 8, on compensation packages. For now we'll mention that the toll on the family as to the social impact of being away from home for long periods of time, and the issues of spousal employment and educational alternatives all or separately contribute to hardships for the family.

Picture the social implications of getting used to a lifestyle replete with maids, chauffeurs, nannies, and the like upon the expectation levels of spouse and children. Once a child has grown up in a cloistered environment with all the niceties furnished by the company, his or her need to readjust those expectations emerges as a gargantuan task.

On the other hand, the Australian family in Dubai case study demonstrated that time away from home can ever so slowly erode the value of the "home" concept to the point that eventually the expatriate family unit may look for alternative places to settle down.

Developmental-Driven Assignments

These postings are designed primarily to broaden the expatriate's experience so that his or her career contributions to the company will be enhanced. Depending on the particular circumstances of the assignment, they can be combined with the operational jobs (often used by Japanese companies), or may be primarily to learn (often used by U.S. companies for their recent college hires) or to combine learning and doing (as many companies deploy their more experienced managers). Similar to demand-driven postings, these expatriate assignments are two-way streets; the expatriate is expected to deliver some information that will be helpful to the host location while obtaining information about how the host country operates. Unlike the demand-driven assignments, however, the development assignees are tasked to learn all about the business practices, policies, and procedures of the host location for career growth. Coincidentally, that developmental feature, in smaller doses, is also inherent in all demand-driven assignments, but there the clear purpose is to furnish service to the host location operation.

There are two kinds of developmental assignments—those for experienced managers who need to round out their corporate exposures with overseas credentials, and those postings that are offered as inducements to recent university graduates to join the company.

EXPERIENCED MANAGER DEVELOPMENTAL ASSIGNMENTS

Here the focus is on providing sufficient exposure to the host location operation so that the expatriate can gain a broader understanding of corporate operations on a more global basis, whether for use in another expatriate assignment overseas or for the knowledge gained there to be applied back at the home country headquarters. Either avenue can be a sizable step forward in enhancing the value of the employee who successfully completes the overseas posting. These assignments are essentially win-win situations; they emphasize the knowledge take-away without the strain of doing day-to-day transactions that often can be distracting from appreciation of the big picture at the host location.

For you potential expatriates these assignments are worth seeking out, and if such assignments do exist at your company, why not visit your manager or human resources representative to discuss this alternative?

As for you managers, these developmental assignments (usually for two years or less) can serve as effective measuring devices as to the skill sets of potentially outstanding executives. Now you can appraise his or her abilities to cope with a different culture and evaluate how that exposure has helped the individual grow. You can also apply a litmus test to the degree to which they proactively involve themselves in ongoing projects at the host country operation. While some developmental people do take a respite from ongoing chores during these assignments, the real go-getters are likely to explore all opportunities to pitch in.

There is a serious obligation on the part of managers to sequence the developmental assignment with a subsequent role for the expatriate to use what he or she has learned from the overseas exposure. Management succession people need to work out that next assignment before the expatriate leaves for the posting, so at least the alternative options can be considered while the overseas posting is in progress.

CASE HISTORY: NOMURA'S OVERSEAS DEVELOPMENTAL PROGRAMS

The Japanese approach to developmental assignments ought to provide us with some valuable insights as to how a sink-or-swim tack can produce wonderful results or a failed assignment. While sociologist Geert Hofstede would not categorize Japanese nationals as big risk takers, the Japanese managers assigned overseas are usually individuals who may not even have filled the specific assignment function previously in their careers. This creates a two-pronged challenge for the expatriate: learn the new culture and the job function simultaneously—awesomely difficult.

In New York, Nomura's operations often combined developmental assignments with the functions of ongoing operational jobs. In the mid-1980s, the firm was struggling to find a niche on Wall Street. In its search for a solid expatriate manager, the Tokyo headquarters sent Koichi Kane, a tall, nattily dressed, distinguished executive whose prior background had consisted of managing retail equities (stocks for the noncorporate clients: people). First, Mr. Kane was asked to lead the investment banking group, a new function for him; he carried that off nobly, considering he lacked the Wall Street ties that often produce success in that arena.

Then he was promoted to lead fixed income products (bonds for corporate clientele), again a new function for him in a marketplace, Wall Street, that was difficult enough for U.S. nationals to traverse, much less a recently arrived Japanese national. But Mr. Kane was clearly up to the task. He helped hire solid U.S. professionals and was able to get Tokyo to commit some credit to the expanding bond operation. The firm gained recognition as a primary dealer of U.S. treasuries and soon was becoming a real player in that lucrative market.

Mr. Kane applied himself in learning the various fixed income products and engaged the major customers socially. He grasped U.S. decision-making techniques, and often made straightforward decisions without the time-consuming process of consensus management, which had been the traditional Nomura approach before his arrival. As this department began to prosper, Mr. Kane was the first to give full credit for the successes to his staff, but in reality he had listened carefully to the individualistic local staff experts and then brought them together in a cohesive unit. He was soon promoted to chief operating officer, a departure from the age-dominated promotion pattern of traditional Japanese corporations, and once again performed his expanded role in an outstanding manner, getting the three divisions to begin to cross-fertilize clients.

Now equipped with managerial experience for three of the company's businesses, Mr. Kane was selected to manage the entire Asian region from Hong Kong, and then barely two years later was appointed to manage the European region out of London. All of these fast-track promotions were based on his ability to learn the lessons from each expatriate assignment and customize those lessons with the different marketplaces he was sent to understand and penetrate. In each post he quickly adapted to the cultures of the local workforce; he earned respect because he could listen well, make appropriate decisions, and communicate those decisions in a way that was effective given the particular environment within which he was working. When I last visited him in London, he was still the same Kane-san I had worked with in New York City, but his approach to his British workforce had clearly undergone some careful customizations that were designed to better fit the British standards of expected behavior. He was a natural student of effective cultural adaptation.

Not all of Nomura's expatriates sent to Wall Street performed so well in developing into global executives. By contrast, some of the newcomers behaved as though they were still in Tokyo, creating numerous brush fires with the local U.S. staff because they insisted on total consensus management, often in situations that called for decisive, swift action that the consensus process lacks. Some of these individuals lacked the brain-power and chemistry of Mr. Kane, but some could have profited enormously from predeparture preparation.

Employment agreements for developmental purposes need to be carefully drawn to define what goals are to be achieved by the assignment. They should also set out what the intentions of the parties are as to the subsequent assignment. Since developmental assignments appear to average under two years, both parties need to discuss fully what kinds of jobs would make sense after the expatriate assignment, and then agree to a reasonable deadline by which serious discussions as to future assignments will be undertaken.

DEVELOPMENTAL ASSIGNMENTS FOR RECENT UNIVERSITY GRADUATES

This is a pricey way to compete for the nation's student elite. Not many organizations have taken this path as yet, but when competition for talented graduates resembles a WWF (World Wrestling Federation) multiple tag team brawl, here is a technique that can be so attractive for the young graduates that it can spell the difference in multioffer situations.

Essentially the company, say a global giant such as Citigroup, works in the expatriate assignment as a learning experience, with gradual empowerment of input as the assignment proceeds. Many of these assignments are for two years or less, with the main concept being to acquaint the developing expatriate with the knowledge of how the firm works overseas and ask the expat to contribute whatever technical expertise may be appropriate to a given project.

The overseas posting is often part of a pattern of short orientation tours, wherein the expatriate, at the end of the various parts of the program, is asked to identify his or her own choices, in a priority listing, while the company's

various managers of those functions are also asked for their preferences in selecting a candidate for a full, regular assignment.

Nomura's developmental expatriate program for recent U.S. undergradu-
ates, considered a bit expensive and time-consuming in the mid-1980s, was
nevertheless highly successful in attracting topflight young graduates who
had been courted by more recognized firms such as Goldman Sachs and Salomon Brothers, firms far better positioned in the Wall Street marketplace.
But for graduates who were not sure where in the world of securities firms
they wanted to be, this developmental series of assignments was just the answer. It was a successful model then and is offered for your analysis now,
whether manager or potential expatriate.

Stage One

After a two-week initial orientation in New York, the graduates are sent to
Tokyo, the Nomura global headquarters, for a three-month orientation as to
the global marketplace and how Nomura approaches it throughout its various country operations. They are taught by managers from each of the three
major divisions, equities, fixed income, and investment banking. They visit
major retail branches and tour each area of the headquarters operation.

Stage Two

They return to New York, where in a succession of assignments they
spend three months with each of the three divisions there, working side
by side with professionals (as opposed to the largely classroom process in
Tokyo).

Stage Three

After completion of the third divisional assignment, each young grad is asked
for his or her priority of permanent assignment positions, while the division
heads are asked to prioritize their choices for permanent assignments to their
divisions. These critical decisions would be made during the better part of a
week, in which section heads as well as peer professionals are asked for their
evaluations. Meanwhile the grads are given vacations within which hopefully
they refresh themselves to return ready to tackle their new permanent tasks.

This developmental process was well received by both the participants
and the management. In the mid-1980s it was a market necessity when top
people were the hiring targets. Indeed, its expense and time consumption

were seen as drawbacks, but the results—good people in the right jobs for them—proved that such a concept had long-term value for managers and the candidates.

Today, many major banks offer two-to-three year assignments overseas for recent graduates from MBA programs, wherein they are assigned expatriate positions where they can exercise their expertise without enduring more classroom lectures and side-by-side peer instruction.

Now that we've reviewed the kinds of assignments and the people who are doing this work, let's review in the next chapter what obstacles lie on the path to success.

Notes

1. "Globalization and Human Resources Management," Vladimir Pucik, in N. Tichy and C. Barnett, eds., *Globalization Management: Creating and Leading the Competitive Organization*, New York: John Wiley & Sons, 1992.
2. "Trading Places," Julie Cook, *Human Resources Executive*, February 2000, p. 53.
3. *Global Relocation Trends, 1999 Survey Report*, Windham International, National Foreign Trade Council, and Institute for International Human Resources, May 9, 1999, p. 22.
4. Ibid., p. 36.
5. *The Expatriate's Handbook*, Bill Twinn and Patrick Burns, London: Kogan Page Ltd., 1998, p. 28.
6. "The Million Dollar Investment," William Sheridan, National Foreign Trade Council Symposium, New York, NY, March 2000.
7. "Optimizing the Expatriate Experience," Letter from Marianne Ruggiero, New York, NY, July 26, 2000.

Illustration by Liz Lomax

What Challenges Do Expatriates and Managers Face?

What Challenges Do Expatriates and Managers Face?

"Life that dares send
A challenge to his end
And when it comes,
Say, Welcome, Friend."
Richard Cranshaw, 1613–1649,
"Wishes to His Supposed Mistress"

Life would be pretty boring if there were no real challenges to overcome, and when it comes to the expatriate assignment process, there will be no boredom for either managers or expats; moreover, these same challenges have persisted for many years. This is most puzzling, since managers have been trying to find the right answers to those challenges for five decades. If it had taken senior management that long to do an acquisition or a merger, the shareholders would have been readying the tar and feathers.

Could it be that the top managers don't feel the problem is that important?

Are they aware of the expense of these programs?

Do they understand how planning could make them more effective?

Do they feel that hands-on overseas experience would be valuable in plotting global strategy?

Are these companies learning from their past poor practices and improving?

Well, those are some of these nagging questions apparently puzzling managers who have the ability to answer them and observers such as myself who wonder out loud why they don't apply more brainpower and muscle to work through the right solutions. And indeed, it is a bit easier for me to step away from the daily battles that surround expatriate assignments when no longer actively engaged as a participant. Let's try to analyze exactly what parts of the system are breaking down and see if we can come up with some reasonable ways to fix them.

For starters, every sound managerial process starts with planning. Senior managers are expected to look ahead to anticipate what the business will be like in the future, what their competitors will do, and, most important, what their own companies can do to maximize their competitive advantage. Is good management devoting enough time and brainpower today to produce the quality of planning to turn around the overseas assignment process?

We'll see, by analyzing the various practices at each step of the overseas assignment program, that most multinational firms have still not been able to plan out the process effectively. Let's start with an ironic anecdote that highlights company woes in the expatriate arena.

CASE STUDY ON PLANNING: PROCTER & GAMBLE IN GENEVA

But you ask, isn't this the same company that learned about cross-border realities in Tokyo? After its Japan country manager faced the public on television, apologizing for not carefully listening to an overseas consumer market, would it be safe to assume that P&G senior management would be supremely sensitive in its overseas planning process in order to avoid another front-page spectacle?

Apparently not.

After the Tokyo mistakes, P&G staged a remarkable recovery there, utilizing locally sensitive expats and local staff alike—a model that was applied globally until 1997. In that year the company implemented a global restructuring program. Management began to look for a city in Europe that would serve as its new regional headquarters. P&G had been operating there since 1953, and as salespeople like to say, "They knew the territory." So it began a phased-in move of the 2,000 expatriates who would be relocated there in June 2000. From this point I'll turn over the narration to Terrence Moore, the HR executive responsible for the move, as this massive expatriate relocation program was described in the *New York Times*.[1]

"I arrived here on June 6, we started the move on June 7, and by June 8, we realized we had a problem," Mr. Moore admitted. The problem was the shortage of housing, cramped spaces, and high prices. But even more importantly, management had not prepared the new expatriates for their transfers.

That lack of basic preparation caused considerable pain for the expatriates and once again, public pain for P&G management. Here is a summation of the process gone wrong:

> Housing and schooling aside (both proved to be totally inadequate for the new expatriates, both in quality and in quantity), there is an emotional factor in such relocations, Mr. Moore acknowledged. "Most of these families never expected to be transferred," he said.

Let's see what happened in the expatriate quest for good schooling.

> Local resentment flared again when many of the 300 P&G families flooded into the city's international schools, which were unprepared for them. Two new primary schools were opened, but to the dismay of parents paying $15,000 a year, some children will be schooled in makeshift structures until another campus can be built. . . . P&G, which insists that it never asked for priority for employees' children, gave the International School of Geneva $2 million. The money has yet to be spent because the school system is in a bitter dispute over how best to accommodate the increased number of students.

There were similar nightmares for those expats who had been comfortably living in their own homes and found to their great consternation that Geneva actually could offer only apartments, invariably too small, and for high prices because Geneva landlords "moved quickly to raise prices even higher to cash in on P&G's subsidized rentals."

> The language obstacle and the inability of the spouse to work, which is permitted in Switzerland only if the spouse can find a sponsoring company, has left many families feeling irked and unsettled. "It was a good idea on paper, but this move overwhelmed the infrastructure here," said one disgruntled wife, who insisted on not being identified because she feared her husband could be dismissed. "If anyone had bothered to really look, they would have predicted the problems."

How can managers prevent ugly public spectacles like that endured by P&G in Switzerland?

They must put into place reasonable procedures and then administer them professionally. P&G's procedure should have called for extensive planning at each step of the relocation process. There should be no unpleasant surprises if managers had thoroughly investigated each contingency involved in the moves. It makes an observer wonder, if a company has a two-year or more head start on a large-scale relocation project, why wouldn't the managers be able to deal with the housing, schooling, and expatriate notifications on a timely basis? Although Mr. Moore's all-too-public admissions reached all the way to the front page of the *New York Times*, the real damage here was not done to P&G's professional image; the real destruction will be evidenced in how all the dissatisfied expatriates perform or leave the company whenever a suitable opportunity arises.

Let's analyze the steps of the expatriate assignment process to determine what practices we can follow.

Offers and Candidates

Our starting point is whether the appropriate potential expatriate is being asked to consider the overseas opportunity. Although hard statistics as to the percentage of rejections of offers are basically nonexistent (who would be willing to share that corporate in-house embarrassment?), we have some survey data pertaining to the factors that are motivating refusals and resistance.

A 1994 survey sponsored by Windham International and the National Foreign Trade Council[2] set forth the percentage of participating companies reporting that these factors caused candidates to refuse or resist overseas postings. (See Table 4.1.)

Table 4.1   Factors Causing Resistance to Overseas Postings

Issue	Percent of Companies
Family Concerns	81%
Spouse's Career	53%
Assignment Location	39%
Repatriation Concerns	34%
Financial Problems	20%
Job Concerns	13%

Note: Respondents provided multiple answers.
Data Source: Global Relocation Trends Survey, 1994, Windham/NFTC, p. 6.

These corporate reports should provide some helpful pointers for managers of the overseas posting process and the potential expatriates alike. The family issues, including spousal career concerns, carry enormous importance in the offer process and need to be fully and openly discussed at the time the offer is being prepared. We're going to look at these factors in greater detail shortly.

Are the right people (including the entire family unit) being professionally evaluated? The significant role of candidate doubts about the assignment location should also merit managerial concern. What does management do to describe the benefits of the assignment to the candidate as weighed against the inconveniences of the particular expatriate destination? Should you, the candidate, do your own research on the host location? If you have access to a computer, you have no excuse not to uncover what you need to know about housing, schools, and so on at the host country location.

There were additional factors reported by the 1994 survey that bear your scrutiny, since they amount to an efficient checklist for expatriate selections for both managers and candidates:

- The job content did not sufficiently fit the employee's qualifications.
- The opportunity did not fit with the employee's long-term economic goals and expectations.
- The employee and/or management perceived the job to be an inappropriate career development step.
- The employee was not willing to give up the support of his or her social and family network in the home country.

All these factors could have been flushed out during screening and assessment programs; the assignment process steps should not have progressed all the way to the offer stage.

Screening and Selection Procedures

So let's take a step away in the procedure to examine its shortfalls. If inappropriate candidates are receiving the offers, it makes sense to trace back why these candidates were allowed to proceed to the offer stage to begin with. The serious rejection factors argue for more effective assessment and screening processes well before the assignment opportunity even arises.

Clearly, the building of a pool for expatriate assignments is preferable to the usual practice of scurrying around at the last minute to locate someone, anyone, willing to trek overseas.

WHY WORRY ABOUT THE EXPATRIATE FAMILY?

Veteran international human resources director Rick Swaak provides some HR perspectives that are all too grimly revealing:[3]

> When a company lacks a well-defined global staffing strategy that's aligned with the business plan, its decisions on using the best talent are likely to be influenced by expediency and urgency. If a top talent turns down an overseas assignment for family reasons, the company very often will turn to a second or third available candidate. As one staffing specialist at the NFTC meeting pointed out, "We just do not have the time to search for another available best candidate. We definitely do not have the opportunity nor the patience to accommodate the family, and certainly not the spouse. What management wants from me is to fill that job in Hong Kong quickly—without complications—with someone who can be coaxed into going. Whether that choice makes good business sense or not is not an issue."
>
> Another HR executive concurred: "My job is to find people in a hurry, and if they are not interested, I look for them somewhere else," she said. "It is a highly risk-oriented and unsophisticated system, which does not concern itself with the needs and wants of the contemporary family."

These views are shortsighted in the extreme. The proportion of failed assignments, whether curtailed or permitted to be completed under negative circumstances such as by expatriates who have ceased to fully perform, speaks of huge losses for companies, in terms of people and opportunities wasted, and needless and excessive financial expenditures. Until managers can concentrate on evaluating the impact of dual careers, marriage, and educational factors, this continuous swinging door of expatriates will continue to rotate. My HR associates know that "not having the time to do this properly" is, in essence, a cop-out. Planning a sound assessment system beforehand would eliminate most of the need to scurry around each time an expat quits to find a breathing body; and the state of the family is vital to the assessment process.

Consider the observations of Karen Taylor in HR World,[4] who, in an article aptly titled "The Parent Trap," asserts that "Research shows that expatriate couples are one and one-half times more likely to divorce than those that stay at home." If one contrasts that depressing statistic with the lack of serious attention being paid to screening of the candidate's family unit, one can only conclude that the managers of this process are not concerned enough to revise their procedures to evaluate the entire family unit more carefully.

The likelihood that spousal issues will continue to plague the overseas posting process was affirmed in a 1998 survey of 166 U.S. and Canadian companies sponsored by Atlas Van Lines.[5] That study, as cited by Valerie Frazee in *Global WorkForce,* found that an unhappy spouse was the number one deal-breaker. Of all the possible factors causing assignment failure, almost 20 percent of the responding survey participants listed "lack of adaptability by the employee's spouse" as the main reason behind the failed relocations. This spousal issue appears to be worsening; the same survey only two years earlier reported only 8 percent of the corporate participants having listed the spousal issue as the most important ongoing challenge to successful postings.

Managers simply must appreciate the increased likelihood that the expatriate's spouse will be in the midst of his or her own business career pursuits.

Other surveys have focused on the entire expatriate family unit, exploring which aspects of the relocation process are proving to present the greatest challenges to them. The 1998 Windham/NFTC report,[6] covering 177 U.S. companies with over 51,000 U.S. expatriates on active assignments overseas, reported data concerning the priorities of family issues confronting them. (See Table 4.2.)

These findings confirm the results of a prior Employment Relocation Council study (1997), which also reported that spouse/partner employment and concerns about the children's schooling were major concerns of U.S. expatriates working for many other U.S. global companies than those participating in the Windham/NFTC study. Taken together, these reports isolate

Table 4.2 Critical Family Challenges

Family Issue	Percent of Companies Reporting Issue as Critical
Family adjustment	68%
Children's education	67%
Spouse resistance	54%
Spouse's career	44%

Note: Some participants gave multiple answers.
Data Source: Global Relocation Trends, 1998 Survey Report, Windham/NFTC, p. 17.

the core issues troubling overseas assignments. While there may be some disagreement over the exact priorities of which concern is most important, the inescapable fact is that they are all important enough to merit attention by company managers. Given that the handwriting of major family issues warnings is on the wall, how have companies begun to respond to these clear-cut challenges? Let's turn back to the same 1998 Windham/NFTC survey report just cited.[7] (See Table 4.3.)

The stark contrast between what is perceived by the companies to be their major expatriate family unit issues and what they are actually doing about tackling those issues is particularly evident in the relatively little use of counseling programs in the face of hard evidence of the need for them, in terms of both family adjustment and spousal resistance.

The broad gap between growing expatriate family needs and slothlike company responses is also clearly visible when we turn to spouse career assistance programs, a looming demographics issue that will only continue to grow in the twenty-first century. The 1998 Windham/NFTC survey gives us the data shown in Table 4.4.

Are you surprised at the high percentage of companies that have decided not to implement any programs at all to support the spouse? There would appear to be a head-in-the-sand perspective among senior managers in those companies not recognizing the scope of the need for these programs. Are human resource managers partly at fault in not pointing out the connection between what is happening regarding working couples and the increasing difficulties in finding expatriate family units to consider the overseas relocation? Spouses are clearly having a strong impact on failed assignments, and the statistics bear this out.

There is a diabolical perception difference that continues to govern this dilemma. Managers appear to be more concerned with finding the best

Table 4.3   Family Assistance Programs

Assistance Program	Percent of Companies Providing
Children's Education	87%
Employee Assistance	67%
Family Counseling	28%

Data Source: Global Relocation Trends, 1998 Survey Report, Windham/NFTC, p. 19.

Table 4.4 Spouse Career Assistance

Assistance Program	Percent of Companies Using
No assistance programs	41%
Networking/contacts provided	33%
Education/training assistance	26%
Career enhancement reimbursement	25%
Career planning assistance	17%
Recruitment specialist assistance	12%
Intracompany job database	6%

Note: Respondents provided multiple answers.
Data Source: Global Relocation Trends, 1998 Survey Report, Windham/
NFTC, p. 19.

technically qualified candidates at the outset, without adequate recognition of their underlying problems that could easily undermine the assignment. As evidence of this view, let's review the 1999 NFTC survey again for that data.[8] (See Table 4.5.) For you statistics buffs, please remember that this annual survey, consisting of 264 of the leading U.S. global giants and covering nearly 75,000 U.S. expatriates, is comprehensive enough to provide us a clear picture of what the managers of those competitive leaders believe to be their major expatriate assignment concerns.

Does it appear that many managers are not seeing the forest for the trees? The process of finding appropriate candidates goes to the heart of responding to the lesser-regarded categories set forth in the survey. Assuming that technical proficiency in performing the job overseas is roughly equivalent among

Table 4.5 Most Critical Corporate
Concerns in the Expatriate Process

Corporate Concern	Percent of Companies
Finding candidates	66%
Family concerns	34%
Location adjustments	29%
Spouse satisfaction	29%
Relocation resistance	21%

Note: Participants gave multiple responses.
Data Source: Global Relocation Trends, 1999 Survey Report, Windham/NFTC/IIHR, p. 24.

candidates (and notice how seldom this is ever mentioned as a key problem; apparently it is far easier to detect technical competence than all those family issues associated with each overseas candidate), then why should there not be more emphasis on all the other challenges set forth in the 1999 NFTC survey that actually determine success or failure on the assignment?

Managers and human resources people need to broaden horizons here and introduce real planning to the entire expatriate program process. Inclusion of important family issues is one of the ingredients required to make this recipe work.

If the global leaders are not devoting sufficient time to assessing family issues because they do not have sufficient in-house staff to do this overhauling competently, there are certainly enough consultants available who can supply the expertise in identifying the potential family issues, and, if need be, work with those individuals to develop their strengths in this sensitive area.

Another study, this one done by Selection Research International (SRI), and the National Foreign Trade Council in 1995, focused directly on selection processes among 52 U.S. firms that had extensive global assignments; still another cross-sample of more companies doing extensive work in the expatriate assignment field. Here's what the SRI and NFTC surveyors found as to contributing factors for faulty selections:[9]

- Eighty-one percent of the 52 global organizations participating in the study reported that faulty selection was the result of the immediate need to fill the job.

- Thirty-three percent of the respondents indicated that faulty selection was actually traced to the fact that the expatriate had been given the assignment as part of an effort to get him or her away from the home country organization.

- Twenty-nine percent of the respondent companies reported that individual departments were at fault for pressuring the assignment.

- Twenty-one percent of the companies reported that line managers who overrode important information from human resources about the candidate's suitability were at fault in the ultimate selection procedure.

- Twelve percent of respondents stated that the fault came from the failure to use the evaluation of the employee's supervisor.
- Twelve percent of the surveyed organizations reported that international assignments were used as rewards for employees.
- Ten percent of the companies in the survey indicated that faulty selection resulted from untrained company interviewers and unqualified outside vendors that had been contracted to do the assessments.

Here are other problem-generating practices that were reported by the surveyed companies, fortunately with less frequency than the corporate practices just set out:

- No true assessment tools were used in the process.
- There was a failure to identify in advance the strategic purpose of the position.
- Unforeseen problems arose with the assignee's cultural adaptation to the host location.
- No formal selection tools were available.

This laundry list could well serve as a manager's guidance manual, in reverse. Both lists of factors should provide managers with significant checkpoints for you to consider in implementing effective expatriate programs.

As a particularly heinous management process, note that no less than 33 percent of the organizations in this survey reported that some of their faulty overseas postings had derived from senior management's desire to "get rid of" the employee. Apparently the assumption is that it makes more sense to send a poor performer overseas than to deal with his or her performance issues directly in the home country. The original crime is compounded by sending the marginal performer to an overseas location where the job may be even more challenging. Taken together with the cultural challenges, that selection can only produce a failed assignment—and a human tragedy for the expatriate and family.

The SRI/NFTC study reported additional findings as to corporate practices:[10]

- Fully 61 percent of the companies participating in this survey made no connection whatsoever between training and selection.

- Only 51 percent of those organizations reported that the selection process was actually linked to cross-cultural training.

- A pitifully small percentage, only 8 percent, said that there was some connection among training, development, and selection.

What's more, not a single company reported integrating training, development, selection, and succession planning. We can find another sign of managers' failure to establish planning priorities in the responses to a question regarding how each organization was prepared to support overseas postings as part of an organization strategy. In response to this query, 63 percent of the survey respondents indicated that their organizations did little or no global organization development. The study shows that only 18 percent of the surveyed companies said that organizational objectives drove the kinds of assignment programs that the human resources people were providing. Clearly, if managers had put in place organizational objectives, and then communicated those goals to the employees, their organizations would each be going forward into the global arena as a united team.

These survey findings cause one to wonder what the *average* company is doing in terms of its integration of expatriate programs with corporate strategies. The *surveyed* companies have excellent reputations for being forward-thinking in their approaches to their domestic human resources development. Consider that these companies are regarded as multinational leaders—progressive organizations that regularly provide and review the latest survey data. One then wonders how the small, less progressive companies are treating their expatriates. But even these leaders use overseas employment practices that isolate pooling, screening, assessment, training, development, and selection programs. Managers are not only failing to link those individual process steps together, they are also failing to coordinate those steps with their the company's strategic objectives. This is particularly worrisome; those objectives ought to be driving the various developmental programs designed to produce the very profiles of expatriates who will, in turn, be most competent to tackle those objectives.

But instead, these continuing management practices are producing difficult challenges for the entire overseas postings process. This leaves one to wonder how the managers of these programs, daily witnesses to the current carnage of quits, failed assignments, and brownouts, can still honestly evaluate their effectiveness. To test that very challenge, the same survey asked those corporate management self-assessment questions. Here are some eye-opening results:[11]

SELECTION PROCESS EVALUATIONS

- Only 31 percent of the companies could report that their selection methods were producing "high" success rates.
- Almost one-half of the group, 49 percent, indicated that their selection techniques were only "somewhat helpful."
- Fully 20 percent of these organizations admitted that their selection practices were actually of "little value."

These numbers bear close scrutiny. These assessments were made by the very people responsible for constructing and managing the programs that are in place today. One might be tempted to guess that many of the respondents, having a significant proprietary interest in these programs, may be accused of looking at them with rose-colored glasses. Despite that natural tendency to look at the bright side, many of them were nevertheless candid enough to give their own processes poor grades.

STANDARDS USED IN THE SELECTION PROCESS

Over three-quarters, 76 percent, of the companies reported using "primarily anecdotal" information about their expatriate candidates. Presumably this data, obtained informally, should rise above the general quality of watercooler scuttlebutt, but why rely on any informal data exclusively when there are so many effective, more professional evaluation techniques available to the company?

Only 16 percent of the organizations sampled said that they consistently followed up with more formal research into the expatriate candidate's background.

A paltry 8 percent of the companies reported that those follow-ups had a professional structure built into the process.

None of the companies actually tested and verified by standard research techniques their organizational definitions of success and their assumptions about the effectiveness of their own selection methods.[12]

While we do not expect most midsize and small companies to go to the extreme of staffing up to the levels of a major research center, it is surprising to learn that the larger companies participating in this study have apparently not seen the need to explore professionally the issue of the quality of their own selection methods. Indeed, if companies continue to report selection as their primary expatriate assignment challenge, then the managers of the function ought to be exploring avenues to take in developing and implementing effective methods for picking the right people for overseas work.

Let's review a checklist of what procedures these companies are using in carrying through their selection process. It should provide us with indicators as to the source of the selection problems. There is an ironic feature in this listing of expatriate processes; most of these same companies tend to use each of the activities far more extensively in connection with domestic transfers and promotions. But for some reason these multinational companies are utilizing few of these useful techniques in their overseas assignment procedures. Table 4.6 shows the proportions of the companies in the survey that reported using these processes.[13]

Now pause to reflect on the fact that fully one-fifth of the companies exclude a human resources representative from participating in the expatriate interview process. Presumably, here is the company's most experienced interviewing professional, an employee specifically trained for this task as

Table 4.6 Screening Techniques Used for Overseas Assignments

Management Technique	Percent of Companies Utilizing
Line manager interview	94%
HR staff interview	78%
Supervisor evaluation	65%
Background/reference checks	41%
Medical/drug screening	33%

Data Source: 1995 Survey, SRI/NFTC, p. 10.

well as the corporate staff person who offers the most actual experience in this difficult process. The employment section within the human resources department is generally utilized as the key initial screen function in the case of domestic hires (at all levels below senior executives), so why should there be any deviation from that step in the more difficult interview evaluations of a candidate being considered for overseas work? These individuals are the firm's most experienced interviewers. Use them!

The current supervisor of any candidate clearly needs to be included in the evaluation loop. He or she has been afforded the closest opportunities to observe performances and traits that play such important roles in the potential success of that candidate in the overseas posting. If the candidate's regular performance appraisals have been fairly conducted, much of that written data will be available for the host country manager and his or her human resources representative to review and discuss together. But that data is generic to a home county position. What is needed is that supervisor's input as to how his or her employee would perform, given the circumstances of the particular overseas posting that is open to the candidate. On most performance appraisal forms, there is space provided for the rated employee's comments, not only as to the supervisor's ratings, but also for what his or her own goals and pursuits are. This section can serve as a helpful tool by which management can more accurately perceive the real intentions of the candidate. His or her comments about aspirations, goals, and so forth open a window for managers to view the candidate's thinking, unclouded by thoughts of a merit increase or an upcoming bonus.

Another facet of this survey concerns the result that less than one-half of the responding companies employed any background or reference checks on the expatriate candidate as a part of the screening and selection process. Presumably those companies see no real need for these activities on the ground that they already know enough about the candidate to bypass those procedures. But is that really true? Virtually all companies have used background checks and references at the time of original home country hire, but the passage of time often can substantially alter the findings of those two checks made years before. Managers now need to focus on the candidate's entire family unit. Human resources people understand that unlike domestic hires, where the family is generally not screened, there is an important element in the decision-making process for expatriates that involves the lives, the careers, and the school situations of every family member. Yet few major companies have utilized any screening procedures regarding the applicant's family at the onset of employment in the home country.

Unfortunately, companies need to be a bit nosy about major patterns of family conduct that could affect the posting, without, of course, violating the employee's legal rights. But appropriate testing, and perhaps development through cultural training where appropriate, can often address human relationships or other social skills that can really help the employee, the family, and management in better appraising the likelihood of success overseas.

For the same reasons, managers should consider medical and drug screenings, now done by only a third of the organizations in the study. Those tests could reveal serious issues that, if addressed early enough in the process, the candidate may have enough time to treat them sufficiently. As to positive drug results, there is an entire body of law concerning employee rights in such cases. Suffice it to say that positive results in any of these tests require sensitive management handling, best done with legal counsel's guidance.

The survey administrators listed other screening/selection techniques and their sparse use by the participating global organizations. These results are consistent with the major techniques listed earlier, which are themselves little used. Therefore it is not surprising that the more progressive techniques are used even more rarely.[14] (See Table 4.7.)

Each of these management tools has proven itself to be a worthwhile investment. A truly best practices champion ought to be using as many of

Table 4.7   Progressive Screening/Selection Techniques

Management Technique	Percent of Companies Utilizing This Technique
Structured interviews	16%
Candidate/spouse self-assessments	12%
Outside evaluations, candidate and family	12%
360-degree feedback	12%
Psychologist interview	6%
Psychological and cognitive testing	6%
Outside evaluation of candidate	4%
Assessment center	2%

Data Source: 1995 Survey, SRI/NFTC, p. 10.

these devices as the controller will allow. But their relatively infrequent use by the surveyed companies indicates that they are still not given enough serious consideration by managers and human resources people as valuable tools to be deployed in the expatriate process. Is it any wonder, then, in light of what is not being done in the selection practices, that only 31 percent of those same surveyed companies rated their screening/selection process as "effective"? That survey, conducted in 1995, was reinforced by another study done two years later, this one sponsored by Aon Associates, of more than 1,700 U.S. organizations.[15]

Table 4.8 shows the percentages of those 1,777 companies using certain selection processes as part of their overall international assignment programs.

Taken together, the two surveys would appear to indicate a trend toward increasing awareness by the global player managers of the potential value of the programs set forth earlier and their frankness in admitting that their current procedures are not working properly. But this glimmer of awareness and potential willingness to consider broader screening/selection processes represents the "glass half full." The fact remains that current multinational practices need significant improvement now. What also merits your consideration, managers, current expats and expatriate candidates alike, is that actual use of these programs is still so rare that you need to determine what the current state of usage actually is at your own company, and not assume that the array of sound, time-tested programs are utilized by your company.

Managers and expats, it is for your mutual benefit, in the long run, that these programs are available; they can save both of you much time in avoiding going through all the assignment process steps for a job that is clearly not going to be a match for this candidate.

Table 4.8 Selection Processes

Process	Percent Using in 1997	Percent Considering Use after 1997
Technical skills assessment	26%	18%
Family readiness evaluation	16%	21%
Psychological profile	11%	15%
Cultural assessment	10%	22%

Data Source: Aon Associates; reprinted in *Global WorkForce*, July 1998.

Costs of Expatriate Programs

At each of the organizations where I've had expatriate program responsibilities, in both U.S. and non-U.S. owned companies, managers were vocal in pointing out how extraordinarily expensive these programs had grown. The senior management teams, regardless of nationalities, demanded more effective cost containment. There was and always will be, a headquarters suspicion that expatriates are being excessively coddled. Senior home country managers who routinely visited expats and invariably returned with colorful tales regarding the high lifestyles they appeared to be leading, evidenced by visits to their residences located in the poshest parts of their host country communities. Further, there would be suspicions from the comptroller's corner that many expatriates were banking almost all of their base salaries and living off the allowances and premiums. Obviously their domestic counterparts could not afford that financial luxury.

The cost controversy would then be joined when the expatriate program managers would be periodically required to explain (always an issue at budget submission review) that the rationale for the allowances was to bring the expatriate even with his or her domestic equivalents, using the widely popular balance sheet approach, administered by well-regarded consulting firms. And, they would state, so many other companies use the same system that it must be the best available on the market. So the managers of the process saw the expatriate package as a leveling mechanism, intended only to keep the expatriate financially even with, not ahead of, the domestic counterpart.

Balanced against these two perspectives is the long-held expatriate view that management does not fully appreciate all the sacrifices involved in the assignment. Further, the expat will insist that the current package is not always reflective of the real discomforts of living overseas. The expats point to local cost-of-living pressures, currency exchange fluctuations, and the fattening of the expatriate packages by other global companies doing business at the same host location. They cite the need to compensate for the relocation from their home environments, and all the difficulties that are posed to the family unit in that process. I've talked with expatriates from many nations in over 40 host countries, and the consistency of their perspectives sounds almost as though they had established their own informal networks in constructing their arguments for more. Expatriates also are in positions to see how their contributions can produce enormous gains for their global employers, and consequently there is something of a profit-sharing mentality in their vocal desire to share in the product of their own contributions.

There are endless bits of evidence and logic to support the positions. All three views acknowledge that overseas expenditures are extremely high, particularly when one contrasts the size of the expat package with what it would cost to fill the overseas position with a local staff employee. While we don't expect the three sides of the traditional package dispute to agree fully with any of the others' positions, we can dissect the cost issue to determine exactly the specific sources of all these costs.

The cost challenge comes into play at the earliest stage of the process. As management sets overseas assignment strategies, there is the element of time as an expense; senior management time is incredibly important—and expensive, at today's senior compensation rates—to devote to planning how the overseas posts will be staffed and what kinds of employees will be needed to staff them. But this is all part of what management is paid to do in the first place; the only real issue is how much time should the seniors devote to these issues and whether some of them can be more properly delegated to staff. This all comes down to the realization that reasonable planning will ultimately reduce the huge out-of-pocket expenditures that inevitably follow poor assignments.

The next cost steps also stem from time—the time required of managers in properly seeding the expatriate pool—and then real expenditures for assessment and training. Consulting services in these areas do not come cheaply. On the other hand, their use and input can well serve to save the sizable costs when overseas assignments encounter problems. We have seen the wide spectrum of management training alternatives available to companies today, and there is little doubt that the costs incurred by many of these services, whether provided by outside consultants or in-house staffs, represent significant expenditures.

The next stage of the assignment involves the costs associated with the relocation itself. In the book *Globalizing People through International Assignments*,[16] Dr. J. Stewart Black et al. set up a scenario of a typical assignment of a U.S. national to Tokyo that fails (i.e., ends early). The authors break out $220,000 of purely direct relocation costs in the following manner for the expatriate and spouse:

Relocation allowance	$ 8,333
Temporary living expenses	$19,000
Broker's commission	$14,000
One-way travel to Tokyo	$11,000
Moving costs	$20,000
Property management	$ 3,000
Expenses to bring expat and spouse back	$60,000 to $70,000
Cost of sending a replacement	$75,000

These out-of-corporate-pocket expenditures represent just the tip of the cost iceberg above the waterline. Below that surface are the more intangible, but equally meaningful expenditures of downtime that preceded the expatriate's move; the loss in quality while the replacement catches up to the job standards, the time put in by peers and managers to help that replacement catch on, the possible difficulties with suppliers, customers, or clients during that orientation period, and other factors. Then we must apply those same losses to the orientation stages of the new expat trying to settle in at the host location.

Then there is the matter of morale loss at both the host and the home locations when an assignment fails completely or browns out. Local staff will view that as evidence that the opportunity could have been better assigned to a local staff employee. There is also the matter of the expatriate and family unit loss of self-esteem, again another intangible loss, but another significant one. How will his or her peers back at the home country location view expatriate work when they see how such assignments can end? What are their perceptions of management's ability to select the right person for the job? How will this turn of events affect the willingness of global assignment candidates to proceed down an apparently risky path?

Every one of these factors adds to management's concerns. Then add all the time that human resources and senior management must now put into finding the next replacement, including still more screening, selection, and training programs. Just how expensive can these assignments become when adding those training, coaching, and related expenditures? Dr. Black and Professor Hal Gregersen, writing in the *Harvard Business Review*,[17] conducted a study of these costs in 1999. Here are some of their conclusions drawn from more than 750 multinational companies, with interviews of

130 management executives representing 50 firms in Europe, North America, and Asia:

"International assignments cost on average $2 million each. . . . In 100 assignments, 25 employees will go to work for the competition within one year of returning home, which is the equivalent of letting $50 million walk right out the door. This turnover rate is double that of managers who stay at home."

Here the authors include the repatriation problems that are wrapped so closely with the employee's departure for greener corporate pastures as another damaging element to the assignment process. Now not only has the company lost the knowledge of the expatriate, but, even worse, that knowledge is now aiding the competition. Can you managers put a price tag on that kind of loss?

In light of these expense burdens, how do managers and human resources people rate the cost factor? The 1998 Windham/National Foreign Trade Council survey, cited earlier,[18] reflects the following management opinions of the 177 U.S.-based global organizations (with expatriate population exceeding 51,000) that participated in that study: Over one-half (52 percent) thought that expatriate costs were too high, 34 percent thought that costs were about right, and 4 percent felt that costs were too low. (Another 10 percent of the respondents were not sure.)

Assignment costs vary enormously by host country. Table 4.9 shows a slightly aging picture of expat costs broken down by continent, courtesy of the 1995 Selection Research International/NFTC study.[19]

Although the dollar amounts will have swelled considerably over the past five years, you can certainly get a feeling for the relative expensive-

Table 4.9   Costs of Expatriate Assignments by Region (1994)

Region	Average Incremental Cost of Expatriate Assignment
Africa	$514,000
Asia	$428,000
Europe	$293,000
Pacific	$255,000
Middle East	$218,000

Data Source: 1995 Survey, SRI/NFTC, p. 21.

ness of one continent compared to another with respect to overseas assignments there.

As to a further dimension of expatriate program costs, the same survey asked those 50 multinational firms what the corporate expenses were for a failed assignment. (See Table 4.10.)[20]

Note that these 1994 costs included estimates of corporate time in identifying, training, and preparing the expat for the assignment. Interestingly, even in those "old" days, 13 percent of the responding companies reported that the cost was over $750,000 per assignment.

Lack of Management Planning in the Expatriate Process

As we repeat, the pattern of failed assignments and repatriation quits serves as ample evidence that management has not been taking the time to plan out the strategies that would then be transferred to structuring the overseas assignments, and the kinds of people who should be selected for those tasks.

It is difficult to survey a managerial process that is currently split into mutually exclusive domains, with little real teamwork as yet used by the major global organizations. It remains a continuing challenge for managers today.

Managers, why don't cross-functional teams sit down and work the process through? Senior management has little difficulty in forming such teams when the matter at hand is an acquisition or a merger. In these instances, companies do a first-rate job of assembling teams of representatives from all the involved departments and coordinating their efforts so all aspects of the project are properly organized. What is so different about the continuing need to manage the overseas effort? And this puzzle continues to the active management of the expatriate while on assignment. Repeat-

Table 4.10   Corporate Expenses for Failed Overseas Assignments

Estimated Cost of a Failed Assignment	Percent of Companies
Under $250,000	42%
$250,000 to $500,000	37%
Over $500,000	24%

Data Source: 1995 Survey, SRI/NFTC, p. 21.

edly one hears the complaint from these overseas assignees that they feel they've been all but forgotten about by headquarters people once they have departed home country shores. That's a communication process breakdown.

We can offer some general survey data as to programs that companies are using in their global expansion efforts. The 1999 NFTC survey[21] asked the 264 U.S.-based companies to report what measures they were taking to manage their global assignments. The results are both heartening and disappointing, as shown in Table 4.11.

I submit to you that all of these measures go the heart of sound planning. The programs listed should all be used by a company truly set upon effective global expansion. The encouraging data within these statistics is that some (all too few) of the participating companies managing nearly 75,000 U.S. expatriates are in fact utilizing all these approaches. Indeed, it is gratifying to see that almost all start out on the solid foundation of making the threshold determinations of which business objectives and needs are specifically to be identified for global expansion. But then bad news emerges, as the next five categories of essential programs receive significantly decreasing participation levels. This trend continues all the way down to only 33 percent of the respondents who have taken the time to work out the criteria for assignment success. Once again, this omission by the majority of companies has to reflect a lack of recognition/planning within management's more senior ranks.

Perhaps the most compelling piece of evidence that sound planning is still a major obstacle for most global companies today is found in repatriation practices. In Table 4.12 the 1999 NFTC survey,[22] paints a bleak portrait of failure to properly plan for these moves.

At this point you've probably had enough statistics showing the need for better planning in the assignment process; but on the subject of repatria-

Table 4.11   Measures Companies Take to Manage Global Assignments

Measure	Percent of Companies Utilizing
Determine business objectives and needs	90%
Evaluate programs to ensure those needs are met	72%
Identify pool of potential candidates	53%
Plan long-term career paths	44%
Conduct cultural awareness programs	41%
Establish criteria for assignment success	33%

Data Source: Global Relocation Trends, 1999 Survey Report, Windham/NFTC/IIHR, p. 21.

Table 4.12   Repatriation Planning

When Repatriation Is Addressed	Percent of Companies Reporting
Before departure	17%
Six months or more prior to return	27%
Under six months prior to return	46%
Not discussed	10%

Data Source: Global Relocation Trends, 1999 Survey Report, Windham/ NFTC/IIHR, p. 39.

tion, let's do just one more study. For all the individuals who have been on overseas assignments, what percentage of those repatriates actually discussed repatriation issues with management prior to their departures from their home countries?

Perhaps the 17 percent figure reflects very recent management sensitivity to this traditional problem, but my own experience of dealing with expatriate issues for a long, long time would only indicate that hundreds of expatriates never received that much-needed communications opportunity.

In summary, all of these issues—assignment rejections, selection/screening procedures, cost problems, and the lack of a coordinated management planning process—have combined to deeply undermine the effectiveness of today's expatriate programs. But these issues are not insurmountable (as evidenced by the survey data showing that some leading corporate players in the global market are doing virtually all of these best practices).

The remainder of this book aims to guide you, the manager, and you, the current or expatriate candidate, along some best-practice paths designed to have you reach and thrive in the Land of Oz's Emerald City: the successful overseas posting, and return to good old Kansas.

Notes

1. "Strangers in a Strange Place," Elizabeth Olson, *New York Times*, Nov. 30, 2000, p. W1.
2. *Global Relocation Trends Survey, 1994*, Windham International and National Foreign Trade Council, p. 6.
3. "Today's Expatriate Family: Dual Careers and Other Obstacles," Reyer Swaak, *Compensation and Benefits Review*, April 1995, p. 22.
4. "The Parent Trap," Karen Taylor, *HR World*, Jan.–Feb. 2000, p. 35.

5. "Around the World," Valerie Frazee, *Global WorkForce*, July 1998, p. 6.

6. *Global Relocation Trends, 1998 Survey Report*, Windham International and National Foreign Trade Council, p. 17.

7. Ibid., p. 19.

8. *Global Relocation Trends, 1999 Survey Report*, Windham International, National Foreign Trade Council, and Institute for International Human Resources, May 9, 1999, p. 24.

9. *1995 Survey*, Selection Research International/National Foreign Trade Council, p. 15.

10. Ibid., p. 16.

11. Ibid., p. 18.

12. Ibid., p. 18.

13. Ibid., p. 10.

14. Ibid., p. 10.

15. Aon Associates. Reprinted in *Global WorkForce*, July 1998, p. 9.

16. *Globalizing People through International Assignments*, J. Stewart Black, Hal B. Gregersen, Mark E. Mendenhall, and Linda K. Stroh, Reading, MA: Addison-Wesley, 1999, p. 12.

17. "The Right Way to Manage Expats," J. Stewart Black and Hal B. Gregersen, *Harvard Business Review*, March-April 1999, p. 53.

18. *Global Relocation Trends, 1998 Survey Report*, p. 27.

19. *1995 Survey*, Selection Research International/National Foreign Trade Council, p. 21.

20. Ibid.

21. *Global Relocation Trends, 1999 Survey Report*, p. 21.

22. Ibid., p. 39.

Illustration by Liz Lomax

How Can Managers Identify the Best Expatriate Candidates?

How Can Managers Identify the Best Expatriate Candidates? What Can Individuals Do to Enroll?

"O wad some Power the giftie gie us
To see oursels as ithers see us!"
Bobby Burns, 1786,
"To a Louse"

Best Practices for Managers

Managers are charged with the responsibility for assembling the best possible candidates to represent the company overseas. Often they cede that responsibility to the human resources department and let the responsibility fall to the good old HR people to search out the potential talent for global experience. But that responsibility ought to be shared. The initial recommendations for possible assignments should begin with line management; then both line management and human resources people should review that list.

Why is there a need for both functions to get involved?

Line supervision can input the performance evaluations into the formula for selection, while the HR people can offer knowledge about the particular job requirements likely to become available at the host locations. The two functions need each other to complete the picture of candidate skills and new job requirements. HR should also be able to find other potential candidates from the remainder of the firm who should have been included in the initial list. These two functions as a team can take the initial steps to find potentially feasible candidates on a regular basis. The team can use the list of expected assignment departures to construct lists of potential replacements now.

Actual corporate practice usually omits this commonsense step. The surveys reveal a pattern of head-in-the-sand behavior by the program managers. Apparently they are content, or too busy to be proactive in this process. But if they wait for the moment when an expatriate in Paris notifies the company of her intention to quit the company, that news triggers alarms through the headquarters halls. Then urgency takes over as both line managers and HR launch a time-pressured search for a living body to fill the Paris void. The same routine occurs on regular assignment expiration dates. Managers generally behave as though the "sudden" ending of the overseas posting surprises them, even though they were well aware of those dates years ago. Why do they wait?

Had there been a planned process in place, HR would have pulled up a short list of prescreened candidates who had volunteered to be considered for overseas assignments. Now all HR needs to do is match the profile of the job vacated against those prescreened candidates. Now you'll want to know how HR would have had that ready-to-go list. Let's walk through each step from the start of the formulation of the expat candidate pool to the departure of the selected candidate.

What are the steps that you managers can take to create and continually add to or subtract from (as circumstances for candidates change) an expatriate pool?

STEP ONE: POTENTIAL CANDIDATES LIST

Senior management and human resources need to communicate on a regular, continuous basis as to what the organization's business objectives and long-term strategies are, so that the appropriate staffing plans for empowering those strategies can be undertaken far in advance of corporate time frames as possible. Changes in strategies may dictate alterations in the desirable profiles of the employees in the candidate pool. Ideally, these corporate planning meetings should be held on a monthly basis, at which time the company's senior decision makers communicate to the appropriate staff the nature of current business targets. HR needs to translate the requirements into job position descriptions with the help, if necessary, of the organization design specialist.

HR's management succession manager should then review the revised organization structure or changed job content, and begin assessing internal candidates for those eventual openings. Those lists of possible candidates would be forwarded to function management for their input as to the suitability of the people on that list for the future expatriate openings. Then line managers will want to delete or add names to the list, and should meet with HR to review the rationale for their recommendations. HR and functional management then agree on the content of the candidate list for each of those overseas postings, whether there is a short duration of assignment time remaining or not (recall that more than one-fifth of expatriate assignments are never completed). Individuals who are on the list are contacted for their interest in pursuing possible overseas postings. Those who indicate they would be interested remain on that list, while those expressing negative feelings about this career alternative ought to be removed from it.

STEP TWO: OUTREACH CAMPAIGN

HR begins an outreach campaign to encourage those employees who might be interested in overseas work and believe they are qualified. This outreach, often by corporate in-house postings, is designed to catch all potential candidates, including those that somehow fell through the netting of the line manager and HR screenings.

There is a need at this stage to create among all employees a feeling of global awareness. Some organizations conduct these briefings on a regular basis. It is a sound idea, even for those not considering overseas postings themselves. Most of those domestically inclined employees will eventually encounter cross-border projects as part of their home country jobs. They need a broad understanding of where all these host locations fit within the big picture of company operations, and good managers will supply that on a regular basis.

How should those briefings be conducted?

The starting point is to convene all-employee group meetings where the managers can outline what sorts of operations are conducted overseas, and what skills are required of the employees there, both expatriates and local staff. Managers, especially repatriates, ought to cover the basic successes and failures, pinpointing what the company's plans are for further growth. These meetings can create a feeling by employees that the company genuinely considers them as team members, and can foster overseas interest among the original "domestics." Employees who are motivated by the opportunities reviewed by the presenters should be encouraged to make known their aspirations to their managers. At this juncture, managers may want to outline specifics in host countries as to job possibilities or describe the expatriate programs more generically. Whether the employee's interest is in the general concept of overseas assignments or on a particular job or host country, that interested volunteer should be given a preliminary screening to determine eligibility for the expat pool.

STEP THREE: EVALUATIONS OF CANDIDATES

As those screening interview sessions are started, HR undertakes its own evaluation of who might be appropriate expatriate material, whether they showed the initial volunteer interest or not. The management succession specialist within HR should be able to provide some valuable input at this stage of pool development. Also, line managers should make their own generic recommendations for people who could provide greater value to the firm if they had overseas experience. HR interviews those employees on a preliminary basis; at this stage there is not a specific open assignment yet to match up with their own skills and preferences. The concept at this point is still to determine general interest and suitability for overseas work.

What are the criteria that are currently being used by HR people to identify which employees would be the most promising candidates for overseas jobs?

Prudential Relocation Services recently asked a group of international human resources managers to identify which cultural and technical factors have been the most important factors leading to successful assignments.[1] The sponsor of the study, Prudential, concluded that a potential expatriate should recognize that overseas postings are not suitable for everyone, and that some possible candidates should screen themselves out. The results of the findings included the clear recognition that lack of technical competence is most definitely *not* the major stumbling block standing in the way of expatriate assignment success. Less than one-quarter of the HR people reported that factor as the key reason for success or failure. Let's review the overall results as to what they did rate as the more significant reasons for success or failure:

Cultural Factors (58.8%)

Cultural adaptability and flexibility	34.7%
Family stability and adaptability	16.2%
Social and interpersonal skills	3.1%
Willingness to take risks	1.8%
Language skills	1.8%
Communication skills	1.2%

Technical/Benefit Factors (25.3%)

Job and technical skills	22.2%
Appropriate compensation package	3.1%

Each organization should establish its own list of guidepost factors in its search for just the right overseas posting candidate. Managers and HR must take the time to review and revise this list periodically. If they fail to do that, they risk judging the same candidate by inconsistent standards. Every company adopts its own business culture, and that culture must be reflected in the standards employed to make effective selections. (This need for consistency differs from the need to view performance from every conceivable reference point, as in 360-degree evaluations.)

STEP FOUR: NOTIFICATION OF CANDIDATES

Those who are assessed as being qualified for further overseas postings consideration are notified and informed of the procedure to be utilized when an appropriate expatriate assignment does arise. Notifications for those not considered qualified for such foreign assignments are also made, with emphasis on thanking them for their interest. In addition, managers should recommend, with the right kind of possible candidate, development or training steps that might be appropriate for them to consider if they would like to pursue such assignments in the future. The Director of Training and Development needs to step in at this point to determine whether there are patterns of apparent deficiencies that can be addressed through customized programs. If so, the content of those programs should be reviewed with the manager of expatriate programs. The development programs could well be positioned to set up a larger expat-oriented skills bank than currently exists in the company.

STEP FIVE: TRAINING OF POTENTIAL EXPATRIATES

Pool members are given generic training as to successful methods of coping with expatriate challenges. Freshly returned repatriates make very effective instructors; they have the credibility of a successful assignment behind them, and they are not reluctant to pass along valuable tips for survival that may not be in the policy book. We will focus on what kinds of formal training programs can be deployed shortly. For now, the pool members should be encouraged to make their wish lists known to HR so that when assignment opportunities do arise, there will be a minimum of time devoted to these basic generic items; the focus at assignment time will be on the particular host location and the specific job requirements there.

Guidelines for Potential Expatriates

Let's assume that you fully appreciate how valuable an expatriate assignment can be for your professional career and are willing to take that step now or in the near future. You have two processes to undertake: a self-analysis that extends to your entire family and an analysis of your company's global position. This latter bit of homework can serve you well as an indicator of whether you can rely on your employer to give fair recognition for your overseas contributions. Granted that some companies at every stage of global transition have maintained excellent track records in their treatment of their expatriates. The fact still remains that the stage of corporate overseas development strongly impacts the degree of importance senior management gives its expatriates. In other words, management may not give due recognition to an expatriate's performance in an overseas assignment where there is little corporate emphasis given that particular host country location.

You simply cannot afford to "get lost." In expatriate work, even in those companies that fully value it, it tends to be easy for those working out of sight to become out of mind. That situation worsens where senior managers are not focusing on that host country operation, perhaps because of their strategic interest in other overseas locations or in domestic operations.

If that issue is the case for your company, you are faced with a dilemma, especially so if you have come to realize that an expatriate assignment would be best for you at this stage of your career. You must decide whether it would make more sense for you to seek out a company that will give you full recognition for meaningful overseas postings or to let time take its course at your present employer, trusting that the wave of globalization will carry the company forward into cross-border expansions.

Let's view each of these two employee projects.

SELF-ANALYSIS

How truly difficult it is to conduct a fair self-examination of yourself?

We all appreciate that such a process is daunting. Have you ever done a formal self-assessment? Those processes constitute a most complex chore for many of us. It is so difficult to view ourselves as others see us that seeking others' help (friends, family, experts, etc.) can often reveal the realities within ourselves that may disclose needs for development. Mankind has indeed been searching for a way to self-evaluate for centuries. Consider the melodic tunes of Scotland's Highlands; over 200 years ago, poet Robert Burns provided readers with a wonderful lament as to our common inability to step away and realistically view ourselves as our neighbors see us.

The generic process is difficult enough as a stand-alone process. The challenge becomes even more formidable when the evaluation is undertaken to determine whether an overseas posting would be a positive or negative experience for you. Many companies have sought out consultants that specialize in these kinds of assessments, and they, if quality-driven, can provide truly professional counseling in this process.

The entire family unit represents another key factor in deciding whether an overseas posting would really make sense for you at this time. Are your family members ready at this juncture in their lives to pull up stakes and leave home for a significant period of time? Your spouse and children need to be brought into this original assessment phase to obtain their reactions to a possible relocation overseas. You need their input as to how they will perceive the lifestyle changes that foreign relocations inevitably produce. So what are some of the most essential questions to ask of yourself, and your family?

- Are you at a career stage with your present organization that would yield further advancement opportunities if you took on an expatriate assignment?

- What has been your company's track record regarding treatment of expatriates and repatriates?

- As to your relationship with your spouse, is it, in your mutual assessments, stable enough to withstand the pressures of an overseas relocation?

- If your spouse is also currently employed, how would a move overseas affect his or her career?

- If your spouse would want to continue to work overseas, is his or her avocation likely to be available outside the United States?

- As to your children, are they at critical stages of their education that would make a departure from their school impractical or socially not feasible?

- In the event that either your spouse or your children have meaningful issues regarding the overseas stay, what would be the consequences if the assignment were accepted but some or all of your family members stayed in the home country?

- What would the financial and tax implications be upon your family unit if the overseas posting was accepted? On this point, there are obvious and hidden pitfalls. If you decide to rent your residence instead of selling, that rental flow will entitle your state to its share of that income, even if you are toiling away in far distant Ushuiia. But if you do elect to sell, beware of spikes and free falls in the real estate market that may make it impossible for you to resume the homestead lifestyle with which you had become so comfortable prior to your expat assignment. Can you work out these contingencies?

- How would your family's physical and mental health status be affected by a move overseas?

- Would your departure have serious implications for any elderly or disabled relatives?

- Are there any home country network ties or religious, social, community, and academic commitments that would present serious issues when you terminate them upon departure?

- What linguistic and other cultural adaptation abilities does your family unit have that could positively influence their comfort in the host country? Conversely, what cultural adaptation challenges would they be unlikely to handle successfully?

This preliminary list of questions can be used as thought provokers for your own more self-customized assessments. You and your family can derive substantial benefit just from the process of reviewing these issues, even if an overseas assignment is never undertaken. There is relatively little internal family communication these days. Just think about modern factors such as working spouses, part-time positions for students, huge amounts of television and film watching, community-organized sports and recreational programs, and so on. I submit that a family can derive significant benefits from reviewing their capacities and willingness to relocate overseas. Family communications are being stretched by new activities, much in the same fashion as for companies trying to maintain effective ties with their overseas assignees.

These family discussions make sense also in terms of exploring whether the various mind-sets of the family members are willing and curious enough to accept all the implications of a different, and perhaps initially an uncomfortable, environment. The upside to these reviews is that they give each family member precious time to weigh all the positive and negative aspects of the assignment before a real opportunity is presented. If a family has been pressured into making a quick decision to take an overseas assignment, these factors often come into play too late into the assignment to be realistically dealt with. Mistakes will inevitably follow,

Let's assume that you have these discussions and have confidence that taking an expatriate assignment at this time or in the near future is compatible with you and your family. How do you communicate that desire to your management?

We asked that question of Michael Brookes, now a partner in the search firm Quorum Associates in New York City. Michael had been a human resources director for over 25 years, and has managed hundreds of expatriates. As a U.K. national, he became an expatriate himself, working for Nomura's regional headquarters in Hong Kong. He later came to New York to do international search. So he's seen the expatriate assignment process in action from three different perspectives. One would think from viewing Michael's conservative appearance and distinguished demeanor that he is the essence of the Oxbridge alumnus. Yet, when asked about how interested employees can make their aspirations for overseas assignments known to management, he takes a very enthusiastic, nonconservative, open, approach:

"Unfortunately too many companies assign a low priority to proactive career management, and so are generally unaware of what their staff want to do next. Therefore, my advice is not to wait to be asked if you would like some experience in an overseas office. Tell your manager and make sure HR is aware of your aspirations (not forgetting to mention how such a move might benefit the company as well as helping your career development)."[2]

Michael should know this subject. For all his years of corporate HR and executive search, both in the United States, the United Kingdom, and Hong Kong, he has dealt with hundreds of expat candidates, as employees of his company and as targets of his searches.

Each organization has its own structure and philosophy when it comes to listening to employee interests; so many of our ideas here have to be customized to your own corporate and chemistry relationships. Here are avenues that have worked successfully.

Your Manager

Starting with your own manager is the safest way to put your aspirations in corporate channels, because if you initiate your inquiry through an HR person, there could be the possibility of your manager's feeling that you have gone around him or her. Since your inquiry could be perceived as simply a desire find another boss, you ought to be careful in explaining that is not the case; you are just reviewing career pursuits overseas as a developmental process whereby you will be able to contribute even more value to the company. But if you are fortunate in having a direct, open relationship with your manager, then you don't have to engage in this fancy footwork.

You should ask for a meeting with your manager to discuss your aspirations rather than wait for the annual performance review. During performance reviews the focus is on how well you performed past tasks and what goal should be agreed upon for the future. But if you do wait for the review, there should be room allocated on the appraisal form for your reactions to the evaluations. Here is an opportunity for you also to make management aware that you would be interested in overseas work, and that you would like to take appropriate procedures to follow up on that request.

There is simply not enough time in the evaluation procedure to permit managers to fully consider the request. But in some companies, HR will pass along that desire to the expatriate program manager. You lose little in this process, and it establishes the beginning of a paper trail as evidence of your sincerity in seeking an opportunity abroad. You are confronted by the distinct possibility that the majority of HR people will be so distracted by the sheer volume of completed appraisal forms that your request will indeed go unread or not acted upon during the time of the compensation program's heavy workload.

This is why your request to discuss the expatriate possibility stands a much better chance of being seriously considered by both direct management and the HR people if you make that request known out of the formal review cycle.

Your request to be considered for an overseas posting is best made before a job vacancy is posted or common knowledge of a specific expatriate opening begins to spread around your workplace. You'll receive positive reactions from managers and HR for your general interest. Then, when a specific opening does arise, and that opportunity looks attractive to you, you have already established your foundation of interest to forward your candidacy to management. You should bear in mind that managers would assume you also want to broaden your career in the process, but it never hurts to remind them of that intent as well.

In the event there is no specific opening that looks attractive to you now, and you would still want to be considered for inclusion in an expatriate candidate pool, then your approach needs to be more generic. You can indicate a general willingness to take overseas postings, and would carefully review the particular job's appropriateness for you once it materializes. The important factor to get across is that you are ready and willing to take expatriate assignments. You could inquire about general training and cross-cultural programs that the company now is conducting or considering. Your manager should pass these sentiments along to HR, which should be your next destination, assuming that you have the go-ahead from your manager to do that.

Your HR Representative

Your next port of call is the human resources department. There may be several choices in this group that may be appropriate for you. It largely depends on the size of the company, how the HR department is structured, and how well you really know the people there.

Initially you need to determine who has the responsibility for assembling the potential expatriate assignment pool. Smaller and midsize companies often combine that responsibility with compensation or benefits, or other special functions such as organization design or succession planning. In any event, you'll need to track down the person responsible for the function to assure him or her that your interest is in fact a serious one. You'll want to describe briefly why you deem it mutually beneficial, for the company and yourself, that you be given an overseas opportunity.

The major consideration here is to demonstrate that you are sincere about taking on expatriate tasks, as opposed to finding a nice cushy haven in a pleasant host country environment. You have to make that distinction clear, since HR is bombarded by not-so-serious potential expats who are seeking only the pleasant assignments. What they do receive are requests for the London or Paris operation, preferably for a short assignment term, which actually conveys the real message "send me on an extended vacation." You must separate yourself from that suspect pack to get serious consideration. You don't need to ask for hardship tours. You simply should have a reasonable range of places and jobs that would be of real interest.

In most of the larger organizations there is a separate expatriate section that exclusively manages the assignment process. You'll need to explore that area and try to arrange an interview with the manager so that hopefully you become a face, not just a name in the batch of employee records to be reviewed when an assignment does arise. You'll want to point out the strengths in your past assignment performances as well as your perceived strengths in adapting to a host country culture. Lastly, you'll mention that you have already reviewed the concept of overseas assignments, and your entire family unit, if that is the case, has indicated an enthusiastic willingness to commit to an overseas relocation.

You should finish the discussion by asking what you can do further to move your candidacy along, including any appropriate training, cross-cultural exposure, or coaching that the company may be offering. After the responses, you should follow up on a periodic basis, perhaps every six months or so, to find out what your status is and to remind your HR representative of your continued interest.

ANALYSIS OF YOUR COMPANY OR
A TARGET EMPLOYER

The second self-help undertaking for you potential expats is to take a giant step away from your current perspective of your company as your employer, and evaluate that same organization anew as it currently is positioned with regard to its stage of growth in achieving complete globalization. The stage of international development will greatly impact the kinds of expatriate jobs that the company posts overseas, and the relative importance that managers will give to overseas operations and to the people who work in those locations. Consequently, it is to your benefit to make this expedition into corporate development to decide whether your own company will be best for your own career. Let's examine each of the four general stages of corporate cross-border growth.

Stage One: Domestic Companies Using Overseas Locations for Sales
Historically this level of corporate involvement is the first stage that companies pass through to grow into true multinational players. Essentially, the only real use of the host country is as a marketplace for products that are manufactured in the home country. There is no interplay between the various host nations to which the home country is exporting its sales items. As a result, there is no need for communication between the various host countries, and a narrowing of expatriate positions is a result. Overseas postings for these kinds of companies almost always end in repatriation back to the home county. If you are working for a firm in this stage of growth, the expatriate positions may not be highly regarded at the home headquarters because of this restriction to sales activities as well as the fact that there are no responsibilities for any activities that cross national borders. As a result, what can be learned from these jobs is generally limited to exposure to one country's sales market. The overseas experience will be fenced in by the national border.

Another element common to these companies is that the expatriate process itself does not receive the attention or planning processes that progressive overseas posting plans deserve. Perhaps this is due to the fact that most of these firms do not derive significantly large proportions of their revenues from overseas; hence senior management is more concerned with domestic activities than with what is happening far across the sea from home country headquarters.

This means that for current and potential expatriates, you need to conquer all the wide spectrum of relocation challenges while maintaining extra vigilance to what is happening back at the domestic headquarters. It is back home where the broad spectrum of promotions exists. Consequently, expatriates with these companies have a special need to remind those decision makers back at headquarters that they are performing important work, albeit for a thinly sliced function of the overall corporation. As an employee being offered the chance to obtain an overseas assignment with such a company, you should, by all means, make a special effort to determine what has become of your company's repatriates.

Incidentally, for you managers also conducting this corporate analysis, this domestically centered kind of organization represents a real challenge in trying to keep senior management focused on the need to professionally manage the careers of the expatriates. The finance people in many of these companies tend to view expatriates solely as cost centers, rather than contributors. Often they take the tack that expats are being compensated far more than they are worth. The hard value of contributions is far less tangible than the expenses required to place and maintain the expats.

Stage Two: Companies Operating Complete Businesses in Each Country
For this category of companies, the export role that we just described for stage one has bloomed into the full flower of company functions, including manufacturing. The job functions for expatriates now mirror all the functions of the headquarters unit, but there is no responsibility for any coordination across borders; that is left to the people back at home country headquarters. These companies offer an expatriate the opportunity to work with the full staff of company functions, not just primarily sales activities as in stage one, they are nevertheless constrained by the lack of cross-border responsibilities. The jobs are still fenced in at the borders.

For the patient expat, such a company does offer all the challenges of expatriate life overseas, but all outside the office. The cross-cultural challenges are all there. What is missing is the bigger operating picture. Relatively junior assignees make a good fit for this type of organization, but as they mature the only real promotion rungs that make sense are limited to headquarters positions.

Headquarters people have more of an appreciation for these jobs than their stage one counterparts, although they fully realize that the key coordination roles have been retained within the home country headquarters building. Consequently the developmental facets of these overseas postings are also viewed as somewhat limited. In addition, there appears to be a tendency for headquarters senior management to staff many of the overseas posts not with expatriates, but opt instead for local staff people who are more thoroughly grounded in what is actually the host nation's business structure. For these jobs, that delicate balance between local knowledge and corporate experience is weighted toward the local staff. This also accounts for the fact that these companies are more likely to promote local staff further up the host location ladder than their more globalized counterparts. Headquarters coordination knowledge is not required here as much as host country experience.

Stage Three: Companies Encouraging Full Coordination between Overseas Locations

These companies take the next step toward true globalization. Headquarters encourages each of the host locations to coordinate actively with other national organizations to conduct the full scope of business. The organizations in this category offer the full gamut of expatriate positions, as enhanced by their broader responsibility to work with other host unit locations in coordinating projects. Further, these companies give far greater emphasis to the training and development of their expatriates. At this stage, expatriate opportunities for advancement no longer hinge solely upon home headquarters opportunities. This is because they have broader responsibilities, including cross-border projects that can springboard to other overseas postings. Indeed, repatriation is no longer the only path to career success; other overseas postings can also serve as career growth platforms.

Headquarters people give expatriates in these organizations a lot of respect. Much of the planning that could only go on a centralized basis at stage two companies now takes place at overseas locations, giving those positions real authority.

The expatriate policies of these firms tend to be more sophisticated and detailed than those of the prior two stages, since the number and complexity of assignments, repatriations, cross-overseas-post transfers, promotions for local staff, and other personnel actions that accompany developmental assignments now come into play. A by-product of all this activity is management's greater insistence that overseas assignment policies be followed more strictly than was the case for companies in the prior two stages. Consequently the temptation to negotiate one-off arrangements is dampened by management's awareness that such precedent rises to far greater importance for these kinds of global players. There are simply too many expatriates out there who could use the proverbial whipsaw, the me-too arguments that could translate into huge expenditures for these companies.

This stage of organization development provides an ideal home for expatriate positions, as to both their increased authority and the respect that the incumbents are given back at the corporate headquarters. But even in these more progressive organizations, you should carefully follow up on how well their long-term planning has played out. Survey statistics have shown that there are so few organizations doing the basics correctly that it is likely that many of these advanced companies still have not seen the light on professionalizing the entire expatriate process. This is particularly true in their treatment of repatriates.

Stage Four: Companies Operating Businesses on a Purely Global Basis
Companies in the most advanced group are structured without regard for national borders. Both the business and the employees who conduct it are viewed as truly nationless. The regard for these "Flying Dutchmen" (from the Wagner opera about the ship that sails endlessly) of the international staff is higher than for occupants of any single domestic nation function. How one of these global players, Schlumberger, structures its expatriate operations is a case in point.

SCHLUMBERGER: A CASE STUDY IN STRUCTURING A GLOBAL STAFF

This giant oil service company started out in 1927 with a national identity question at its very inception. Two brothers, engineers by profession, came from Alsace-Lorraine, a region straddling the French-German border. As wars shifted government control over the area it belonged to each country at various times, so the company had to learn to coexist with the two distinctly contrasting cultures successfully. As the technological advances of the two brothers grew, the company rapidly became the leader in helping the major oil firms detect deposits of petroleum in the strata of the earth. The company's clients came from all over the globe, and the locations where the Schlumberger engineers had to work exceeded 80 nations, many of them in relatively difficult climate or government environments.

The nature of this business structure required the formation of an international staff separate from any domestic operation. The engineers composing this highly technical group were recruited from all over the globe, and were offered a set of expatriate compensation and benefits provisions that were not tied to any country. The programs were generous enough to attract and retain bright engineers even in the most difficult physical or cost-of-living environments. The corporate philosophy was to recognize that there could be considerable burnout of many of the new engineers at around the six-year level, so assignments were constructed on a three-year basis without regard to the nation of assignment.

Perhaps because of its peculiar nonnational identity, even the headquarters location was treated as a dual-nature concept, with a skeleton corporate staff in New York City and a slightly larger control center in Paris. In fact, the late chairman of the organization, Jean Riboud, once lamented that the issue of where central authority would best be located, New York or Paris, would best be settled by putting the corporate headquarters site on the moon.

The assignment and promotion policies had no attachment to any nation. The only exception was that if an engineer were ever reassigned to his or her (there were a few women) own country of origin, their status would be "local staff" status. That would call for significantly reduced levels of reward. Hence, the workforce consisted of many employees who had not worked in their countries of origin and were motivated by the unique international staff provisions, which treated every engineer in the same fashion.

Think of the ease of administration. There were nearly 6,000 international staff employees (out of about 100,000 Schlumberger people worldwide) who were all on the same matrix, with no need to track differences between their host and home country economic conditions. Can you imagine setting up a balance sheet comparison of thousands of engineers from almost 50 countries, doing their work in more than 75 nations?

Lastly, the prospects for career advancement in a company such as Schlumberger were enhanced, not reduced, by the overseas assignment process experience. In fact, any headquarters staff person who had not been assigned overseas was regarded as missing that critical ingredient if the individual wanted to advance in his or her own function, even if it were a staff function such as human resources or finance.

These kinds of organizations represent ideal targets for those sincerely focused on expatriate assignments, and who have the technical background. These companies value international experience and reward their people accordingly in terms of both compensation and career opportunities.

INDEPENDENT SEARCH FOR THE RIGHT OVERSEAS ASSIGNMENT

Let's assume that you've done your homework. You've analyzed your present organization, or in the case of those of you not currently employed, you are exploring the job market. How should you start out in pursuit of that one splendid opportunity overseas that is just right for you and your family? Fortunately, you are within a computer's reach, or, at most, near your favorite bookstore, in obtaining hard data and expert advice. Let's start with the literature that has proven to be helpful to others in that same quest.

Helpful Books

What Color Is Your Parachute?, by Richard Nelson Bolles, (2001 Ed., Ten Speed Press, 2000, $17) is literally the bible of all advice guides, originally written in 1970 and now in its 29th edition. For eight years I've used this text in helping support groups in New York and have always had truly remarkable results with it. Mr. Bolles puts the job seeker in charge, and not as the pleading applicant that so often used to mark the difficulties for job seekers to overcome. His upbeat approach in how to cope with rejection transcends the normal advisory texts. His positive delivery plus his effective "flower exercise" for self-assessment are worth the read by manager and expatriate alike, even if you are not considering a job change.

The author takes us through every phase of the job-hunting process. This is a comprehensive guide, its many editions an indicator of its effectiveness. Each edition is strengthened by updates from the latest wave of readers, who keep the book's advice current.

Bolles has supplemented his original book with a short but highly useful paperback, *Job-Hunting on the Internet*.[3] He gives tips on posting your resume effectively. The second key element, computer-based research of overseas job openings, is also described. For example, just going onto the Monster Board, there are 50 countries listed. Bolles describes 24 international job sites. So if you're an unhappy expat living in some remote location like Ushuiia, and feel that you are at a severe disadvantage in conducting an effective job search, take heart. With your computer you can:

- Access employer job listings.
- Post your resume.
- Obtain career counseling.
- Research geographic areas for companies and cultures.
- Make personal network contacts that may help to establish links to companies and/or countries.

The Internet can become your closest ally in getting dynamic help for your search. Here are some specific sites and information centers that are focused on expatriate issues:

- *Monster International.* Sets forth global U.S. companies by world region. Provides job posting and resume posting facilities (http://international.monster.com).
- *Career Mosaic.* This site offers search by region. It affords views of work locations, along with forums, chat rooms, tax information, and so on (www.career.mosaic.com).
- *Expatriate Moms, Escape Artist, Expat Exchange*. These are all valuable sites whose URLs are all listed in Mr. Bolles' book. Expatriate Moms, as per title, provides data on the unique challenges of raising children in a variety of host nations.
- *Network for Living Abroad.* Here is a site that provides living costs, international travel data, and residency requirements for several host countries. It also has a message board, classified ads, and various articles written by expats or local nationals advising on how best to find work opportunities at that location.
- *Federation of American Women's Clubs Overseas.* While this is not a web site, it is a central information center, located in Washington, DC, that can provide information about the 65 chapters in 30 countries devoted to the needs of the "trailing spouse." These clubs can provide helpful introductions to other spouses in your host country.
- *School sites.* There are several ways to obtain information about the schools in your host nation. One of the better ones is the Message site, which can furnish detailed data.

- *Tax sites.* All the major accounting firms have tax sites. In addition, you can opt for a site such as Yahoo!'s Tax Center.

- *Government sites.* You will have to explore what kinds of rules your host nation has concerning your ability to work there. Each nation has the details of its requirements spelled out in its site, along with the addresses and contact points for its embassies or consulates. For example, the site www.library.nwu.edu/govpub/resource/internet/foreign.htm/ is maintained by Northwestern University's library.

- *Postings for jobs/resumes by country.* Note, each country will have its own identifier; here we're showing France (http://fr.yahoo.com).

In summary, you will find help in every single aspect of the expatriate assignment or independently run job search from the wide variety of information sources available through the Web. Let's return to the world of books to review your options there.

The remainder of the books are offered in the order that I would recommend that you approach the search process; they dig into each of Bolles' subjects more deeply, and offer the advantage of being specialist works, rather than the general big picture that is outlined by Bolles.

- *25 Revealing Self-Tests to Help You Find and Succeed at the Perfect Career,* by Louis Janda, Ph.D., Adams Media Corp., 1999, $13.

- *How to Choose the Right Career,* by Louise W. Schrank, VGM Camer Horizons, 1992, $12.

- *Who's Running Your Career,* by Celia Farrell, Bard Press, 1997, $24.

- *The Good News about Careers: How You'll Be Working in the Next Decade,* by Barbara Moses, Ph.D., Jossey-Bass, 2000, $25.

- *Vacation Work's Directory of Jobs and Careers Abroad,* by Elizabeth Roberts, Oxford Pub., 2000, $17. This book is especially useful if you want to approach the overseas market directly, rather than through an expatriate assignment.

- *WEFA Industrial Monitor,* John Wiley & Sons, 1999, $24. In this book WEFA (a consulting firm), analyzes 130 major U.S. industries and provides economic forecasts for each. The book also presents helpful profiles of the major players in those industries.

- *Jobs Rated Almanac 2001: The Best and Worst Jobs,* 5th ed., by Les Krantz, St. Martin's, 2000, $17. This work focuses on issues such as which jobs call for the longest or shortest workweeks, income prospects, outlook for the future, physical demands, job security, stress, travel, and perks.

- *The 100 Best Companies to Work For in America*, by Robert Levering and Milton Moskowitz, Plume, 1999, $16. This book highlights the selected companies' attitudes toward their employees, and provides helpful corporate dimensions, such as how many facilities each of the companies operates, and how many of them are overseas.

- *International Jobs*, 5th ed., by Eric Kocher and Nina Segal, Perseus Books, $17.

- *Interim Managers*, by Diane L. Thrailkill, Randolph House, 1999, $15. This book offers the alternative to permanent employment: the short-term assignment that permits the contracted employee to view a variety of opportunities from inside the corporate structure. In fact, interim assignments have swelled in popularity. For example, in New York City, Jerry Hackett pioneered this concept by founding The Executive Source, an organization that matched company short-term needs with available profesisonals and executives. Started in 1988, this firm was only the seventh in the United States to perform this matching service. Now there are over 175 such organizations nationwide doing essentially the same work.

- *Cover Letters*, Adams Media Corp., 1996, $20. This compilation of 600 sample cover letters emphasizes that they need to be customized to the target company, clear on the career objective, and totally consistent with the enclosed resume.

- *Electronic Resumes and Online Networking*, 2nd ed., by Rebecca Smith, Career Press, 1999, $14. This book takes you through the adaptations you'll need to make to your mailing resume to bring out your best points when it is transmitted over the Internet. It also provides guidance on how to apply for jobs online.

- *The Perfect Interview: How to Get the Job You Really Want*, 2nd ed., by John Drake, AMACOM, 1996, $17.95. This book probes in depth into the techniques for successful interviewing.

- *Personality Testing—Ace the Corporate Personality Test*, by Edward Hoffman, Ph.D., McGraw-Hill, 2000, $16.

- *Dynamite Salary Negotiations: Know What You're Worth and Get It*, by Ronald L. Krannitch, Ph.D., and Caryl Rae Krannitch, Ph.D., Impact Publications, 1998, $16.

- *The International Career Employment Weekly*, Carlyn Corp., $4.95 per issue. Can be ordered via 800-291-4618 or cc@internationaljobs.org. The same organization publishes a monthly newsletter, "The International Employment Hotline," that can be ordered from its regular mail address, 1088 Middle River Road, Stanardsville, VA 22973.

These paper resources can provide general support and specific guidance for your search.

Let's turn to several other job-hunting avenues that you need to consider.

Networking

This tried-and-tested method still accounts for the largest proportion of all direct job interviews, notwithstanding the arrival of Monster.com and similar vehicles for job postings and resume postings on the Internet. Why should the person-to-person job search approach still be so effective in light of all these fine books and web sites?

You probably know that many of the most important job openings never make it to the Internet boards or the newspaper listings. Companies hiring people often give openings to search firms with the intent of avoiding the time that would be wasted if they had to wade through all the response mail and messages regarding a really juicy job opportunity. It is worth paying the search firm to make its own discrete inquiries, often hunting out candidates from competitors or other successful firms who may need real enticing to come in and talk about the opportunity. And how do these search people locate the appropriate candidate targets? Through friends, former associates, and the search firms' research departments. The first two categories are basic networks that the headhunter continues to nurture throughout the year.

For this reason it will be truly helpful for you to nourish contacts with the search people, even if you are not sitting on the edge of your chair hoping for a better job today. If you don't happen to have any current search contacts at present, you may want to refer to Christopher Hunt and Scott Hanlon's book, *Job Seekers' Guide to Executive Recruiters*,[4] which outlines virtually all of the major U.S. search people and what are their areas of expertise. It will do you no harm to try to contact the search people in your geographic and functional areas through a resume and cover letter (after your preliminary introductory phone call). This will generally be retained by the firm's director of research for approximately six months. Today more firms are entering resumes into a computer database and they are retained indefinitely. You will need to emphasize your strategy of trying for an expatriate assignment in both the cover letter and the resume (they frequently become separated).

Networking with friends and peers can also prove highly productive. Frequently they will know of an employee's departure from a firm at about the same time the HR people begin to figure out whether they should do the search themselves or send it out to a search firm. During this window of opportunity, it will be highly beneficial for you if you send a resume that matches the job requirements. HR people want to avoid the search firms' charges of up to a third of the successful candidate's first year's compensation. Because many of their domestic-oriented candidates may want to decline an overseas posting, you may have a better chance of getting in the front interview door than if the opening occurred in the United States.

You will need to circulate regularly around your network of friends so that you can update them to your current job status and what kinds of overseas opportunities you are seeking. The career support groups we had in Westchester County provide unique opportunities for the attending members, many of whom are targeting the same companies at which others are still working or which they have just left. We were fortunate in having four major international firms—IBM, Reader's Digest, Texaco, and PepsiCo—with headquarters and operating units within a few miles of our meeting place in Mount Kisco. Consequently the group always seemed to have some members who could answer the inquiries of other group members about their companies.

As to guidance for effective networking, we were delighted to listen to words of wisdom from an experienced outplacement counselor, Jack Driscoll, who described the sensitive nature of maintaining a meaningful network. Jack's presentations would always feature a description of a juggler with a dozen tall, thin bamboo reeds, trying to simultaneously spin china plates precariously perched on each bending reed. Jack likened each plate to a network contact, emphasizing that you continually had to be aware of the dishes that had been spun early on in the process and were beginning to wobble. Jack would dash about the conference room, saving the imaginary plate just before it fell to the floor. We understood the principle: Don't let the network contacts grow stale! Keep coming back to them with your status reports no less than six months after the last contact.

TARGETING COMPANIES

Still another avenue for you potential expatriate candidates to explore is to research companies of potential interest to a point where you narrow the field to as few as are appropriate targets for you. Today all the major organizations have constructed helpful web sites available to you at your computer desk. Many offer the opportunity to view their current job openings (granted this will not be their complete list, considering internal candidates and those jobs already contracted out to search people). You will do well to try out the system, finding out who the interview players are, how they operate and what they are looking for. Then, when an attractive job opening does arise you will already have the knowledge of the ground rules of how that firm conducts its screening process.

TARGETING COUNTRIES

In addition to *Directory of Jobs and Careers Abroad*, listed previously, there is another practical guide, *The Global Resume and CV Guide*,[5] which features a chapter on each of 40 countries, written by veteran search experts from each nation. Each of the chapters sets out a country overview, resume specifics, cover letters, job information sources, interview advice, and cultural advice.

Let's suppose you have a desire to work in France:

- *Cover letters.* In France they are traditionally handwritten because many companies there use handwriting analyses.
- *Employment ads.* The six national dailies are set forth along with the weekday when the job section is published. Their Internet sites are also available; indeed there are more than 450 Internet job sites in France.
- *Work permits/visas.* There are two different authorizations required by the government, one to work and the other to stay, including the requirement for a long-term visa (over three months) with your con-

sular authority prior to departure. France also requires a promise to hire or a copy of the employment agreement. Once in France there is still another requirement, an authorization to stay within the prefecture of residence, and there you need to obtain a residency card, which must be renewed annually. Incidentally, France requires your employer to obtain a work authorization from the national employment agency—a certificate that justifies why a French national is not being hired for your job opportunity.

- *Cultural advice.* The French consider hierarchy important; "they like titles and status. This hierarchy is often reflected in the layout of offices; the higher the floor, the closer one is to God. . . . The influence of the Catholic culture means that discussing money and business are taboo. The French do not like to talk directly about business and money; conversations about these subjects always take an indirect route."[6]

Having worked in Paris, I would add to the culture section a strong recommendation that the expatriate have some knowledge of the language. Parisians especially appreciate that you have recognized their unique cultural heritage if you have taken the time to master their language.

The editor of this valuable book, Mary Anne Thompson, accurately sums up the critical nature of international careers for a person's career development:

> Interest among college graduates and young professionals in pursuing international careers has skyrocketed in recent years. Such interest has been enhanced by chronic personnel shortages in home markets that are causing companies to actively search beyond their borders for talent.
>
> The new generation of employees is not waiting to be hired at whim by just any employer. Young professionals around the world are targeting specific destinations *first* and then choosing career partners who can take them there. A recent survey of the chief executive officers of many of the world's largest companies lists working abroad as the most important employment experience for young professionals who are interested in becoming the CEOs of tomorrow.[7]

You potential expatriates can also see Ms. Thompson's summary as further incentive to take that overseas posting sooner, rather than later, because the other half of that worldwide trend is that there may be someone at present residing outside the United States who may well be a prime candidate as an "inpatriate" for your own position. Similar to borderless products, the world's workforce is becoming increasingly mobile; your corporate opportunities competition is no longer limited to the U.S. domestic labor market.

TARGETING EXPATRIATE ASSIGNMENTS BY FUNCTION

Suppose you are a human resources person and need to broaden your knowledge of your occupational field by practicing it somewhere, anywhere, outside the United States.

In addition to the various search alternatives already listed, there remains the professional association as a worthwhile resource. Virtually every function has a variety of these groups, and many specialize in international subgroups. The field of human resources, for example, has several major associations, the largest being the Society for Human Resource Management (SHRM) and its international group, the Institute for International Human Resources (IIHR). These groups, like other function-based associations, conduct meetings for updating technical knowledge, but also are magnificent vehicles for counterpart networking for searches. Additionally, these associations publish their own open jobs listings, all of which are available through the Internet at the price of the annual dues. Professional associations also are common when broken out by industry. So as a human resources individual working for a financial securities firm, there would be three different associations available to join, the Wall Street Human Resources Directors Association, the Wall Street Compensation and Benefits Association, and the Wall Street Employment Association. They all hold monthly meetings that feature speakers on the technical developments occurring in each of those fields and also serve to be networking sessions.

Professional associations represent a continuous practical development program for you in addition to the overseas postings updates that you can obtain from actively participating in these meetings. So, as the old U.S. Navy ads once proclaimed: "Join now and see the world!" (. . . with diligent research and active lead follow-ups).

Notes

1. *Global Human Resources Management: Developing a Pool of Qualified Candidates*, Valhalla, NY: Prudential Relocation Services, 1999, p. 1.
2. Message of Michael T. Brookes, Oct. 3, 2000, New York, NY.
3. *Job Hunting on the Internet* (2nd ed.), Richard Nelson Bolles, Berkeley CA: Ten Speed Press, 1999.
4. *Job Seekers' Guide to Executive Recruiters*, Christopher W. Hunt and Scott A. Hanlon, New York: John Wiley & Sons, 1997.
5. *The Global Resume and CV Guide*, Mary Anne Thompson, New York: John Wiley & Sons, 2001, p. 1.
6. Ibid., p. 80.
7. Ibid., p. 1.

Illustration by Liz Lomax

How Should Managers Assess and Train the Candidates?

CHAPTER
6

How Should Managers Assess
and Train the Candidates?

"Training is everything. The peach was once a bitter almond;
cauliflower is nothing but cabbage with an education."
Mark Twain, *Pudd'nhead Wilson's*
Calendar (1894), ch. 1

A ssessment and training work effectively only if they are closely linked into one process. Otherwise the costs of these two programs will not bring appropriate value to the company and will not serve to properly develop the potential expatriate.

Some writers place the training process as an afterthought to help the selected candidate get ready for the overseas assignment. But common sense dictates that once management has invested time and effort in screening potential candidates for expatriate work, a follow-up process should start before a specific opportunity arises for which the pool member should be considered. That process is a continuing assessment and training program designed to ferret out areas for further employee development and to train the individual to overcome the identified needs. The entire focus is on turning weaknesses into strengths for a generic overseas exposure, not for a specific assignment requiring a lickety-split replacement. This is by way of saying that you managers must view training as a truly continuous process.

Sound training planning starts on the date of hire. Professional training

133

people ought to be able to identify those employees with the required strengths to develop into first-rate expatriate general managers or function heads or advanced technology people. The training manager must continually scrutinize the employee population to determine who will be identified and included in the next generation of expatriates. Training and development people use a variety of sources to produce candidate lists for the various programs designed to improve their skills. The direct managers, HR, the performance appraisals (including that small, but significant space devoted to the rated employee's own comments), and a variety of other sources are blended together for the decisions as to which employees should receive what kinds of formal training. Then management will have the responsibility of ensuring that the training occurs and that the results are properly monitored.

Conversely, if managers permit the assessment and training tandem to be postponed until a job vacancy materializes, there will be too much pressure exerted by host country management to squeeze the home country management for an expedited replacement. That pressure always takes precedence over the training, assessment, and customized preparation courses that all should have been administered as building blocks for the new expat's growth.

Current assessment practices of the major global leaders are relatively difficult to isolate and study. Many of the companies deploy an assessment process (lasting as little as a few hours in some cases) as a last step prior to boarding the aircraft, along with some brief preparation courses, generally lumped together as a so-called training program.

But a significant number of failed assignments are traceable to cultural and family strains. Those issues can be ferreted out in professionally administered assessment/selection programs. So clearly it is in management's best interest to include assessments as a keystone in constructing a sound expatriate program. If managers forgo using this critical measurement tool, they risk exposing the assignment process to unnecessary risk. Then the procedure takes on all the aspects of a guessing game, with the ultimate question being: Who *is* this person?

The stakes are far too high, in human and monetary terms, to take that gamble. Whether management has the degree of professionalism within corporate staff or elects to outsource the assessment/training functions is a matter for senior management to judge. That judgment needs to be realistic, free from internal pressures. You managers should take a hard look at the capability levels within the company to perform these functions. If those skill sets are not there, you should explore the consultant market to find a firm that possesses those proven capabilities.

Assessment

Let's begin our review of assessment by identifying the traits and skills that are being assessed. While it is well understood that managers are asked to probe the minds and hearts of their employees as potential expatriates, the initial difficulties for them are that they are not positioned at the host location, they don't generally know the candidate's family, and they are not themselves trained in assessment. So their knowledge upon being asked by HR as to their assessment of how well one of their subordinates will do in an overseas environment is limited to an evaluation of how well that candidate has performed in the job he or she has done in the home country. Is it any wonder, then, that this narrow reference leads to major errors when the selection decision is largely based on that supervisor's limited evaluation? A bit of historical perspective will be helpful in viewing what assessment practices are today.

CORPORATE ASSESSMENT PRACTICES

The traditional selection process for expatriate assignments excluded genuine assessments because the process was managed by individuals who either didn't know or didn't care about assessment programs. Historically, the manager would arbitrarily pick a friend to go to Paris and an unlikable chap to a less attractive location, often motivated by a smoldering desire to dispatch that unfortunate employee off the home premises. So off to Devil's Island the out-of-favor employee was sent, regardless of his or her relative technical skills and characteristics. Who is to say that today's managers don't continue to follow those old, much-maligned, arbitrary assignment patterns of decades ago? Certainly the failure rate statistics suggest that those traditional decision-making processes survive.

In the 1980s the wave of globalization appeared on the horizon, sending some managers to experiment with assessment programs, usually as a last-minute step just prior to the already selected employee stepping onto the departing jet.

Then, by the 1990s, the globalization wave escalated, with increasing pressures to send more and better expatriates to guide overseas locations into the difficult waters of expansion. Now there was begrudging awareness that something in the selection process was seriously flawed. Voluntary and involuntary terminations continued at unacceptably high rates, plus there was an extraordinary volume of quits shortly after repatriation. We've reviewed the surveys identifying the causes generating the difficulties: partner dissatisfaction, family concerns, and inability to adapt. Those are all conditions that can be identified during proper assessments. The second step of the process, training/preparation, would then come into play in a mutual attempt by the company and the employee to properly address those issues.

Professor Edgar Barrett, who founded and directed the international consortium programs at Thunderbird, the American Graduate School of International Management, has many years of teaching and consulting in the global context, and at his retirement in June 2000, he observed:[1]

"We've often heard that an ounce of prevention is worth a pound of cure. In international assignments, a modest amount of well-reasoned assessment (before the fact) is likely to provide a major competitive advantage to your offshore locations."

Despite this recognition by both corporate management and academia of the need for assessment and training programs, the surveys already cited appear to tell us that the companies, even the major ones, make sparing use of them. We are left with a paradox; companies know why assignments fail, but strangely continue to retain dubious selection practices such as sending away poor performers or selecting on the basis of giving a reward to the employee for a prior project. Genuine assessment programs appear to have been only sparingly used as a part of the procedure.

RECOMMENDED MANAGEMENT PRACTICES

For you managers, the planning for a thorough assessment/training program should start with the gathering of the evidence of costs being wasted by the failed assignments. Senior management will always listen when there is an opportunity to stop financial hemorrhaging. Assessment/training devices can effectively stop the bleeding, whether using in-house staff or hiring an outside consulting firm to do the assessments. Obtain that budget approval and go to work!

Managers need to analyze the volume and flow of overseas employment turnover to accurately gauge the size of the expatriate problem in their own companies. If there are really a substantial numbers of openings and they surface at more or less a predictable rate, then in-house staffing of an assessment/training section might be the optimal choice for your organization. Consider that the advantages of in-house staffing include their knowledge of corporate background, policies, and familiarity with corporate culture, and rapid access to management. Consultants become familiar with the particular corporate basics over time, but there can be an expensive start-up phase when the outside professionals are still getting a feel for their corporate client. Another management approach is to bring consultants in to train in-house assessors, who would first observe how the program really works and then gradually take over some of the more basic parts of the process.

If there are relatively few overseas openings, or they rise and fall in turbulent surf fashion, it is not generally cost-effective to hire an in-house staff for this work, and consideration must be given to exploring the consulting marketplace, where expertise is available but must be carefully probed for, since there are regrettably some less than quality suppliers in this business.

ASSESSMENT TOOLS AVAILABLE FOR MANAGERS

Let's once again start with a typical assessment scenario. The initial screening for the expatriate candidate pool has resulted in the management decision to select employee John Jones. He had indicated a strong interest in taking on an overseas assignment, and in particular the Paris operation. You are the manager of the overseas assignments program and need to obtain all the pertinent information available about John's qualifications to work overseas and whether there might be any family issues involving spouse Jane and children Jay and Kay. We will follow this family through the various stages of expatriation and repatriation.

The first step is to retrieve the HR file on Jones, whether from your new computerized files or paper files. The most important documents for you are the performance appraisals and the employment application.

The application furnishes the outline of prior employers, prior overseas assignments, and family status. Wife Jane is also employed, and the ages of their children are not anywhere near the critical high school near-graduation years, so there appears to be little in the way of threshold inquiries. The application reveals that both John and Jane studied French, and he asserts the he speaks it "fluently" (but Parisians might have something to say about that). The Jones family owns a house rather than rents (raising potentially difficult resale issues) and participates in many community activities (how deeply are they rooted into their community?). There are several other assessment clues set forth in the application, but the basics show no major stumbling blocks to overseas assignments.

The second major reference items in the file are the performance appraisals. What do these ratings really say about how well an individual does the job? Well, the ratings themselves don't tell us much, because of management's tendency to rate virtually everyone a 4 on a 1 to 5 scale. This evaluation inflation has been a management malpractice since the rating scale itself was constructed. Managers, being quite human, have proven to be susceptible to human frailties such as avoidance of unpleasantries. Their behavior reflects the need to consider all subordinates a little better than average but not outstanding performers. By manipulating the final rating numbers, supervisors can avoid nasty confrontations over a subsatisfactory rating such as a 2 or even a satisfactory rating of 3. Who wants to be appraised as only a satisfactory performer today? Managers have thereby created a Frankenstein's monster, adorned with a glowing halo—now virtually all employees are better than average. What does that do to the term "average"? Managers cheerfully accept the fact that the bell-shaped curved has shifted its peak to 4. As for 5, most companies have placed safeguards preventing the halo from advancing that far by requiring specific rationales from the managers who give that rating.

Let's return to our example. No managers would be surprised if candidate John has a 4 performance rating through his entire career with the company. But the appraisal forms do offer some real guidance as to how John performs his work, and that is of significance. The manager's comments include notations that John works well with others, is flexible in terms of adjusting rapidly to changes, and does not need close supervision. The openness of the appraisal form required constructive evaluation thoughts rather than check marks; they can be of real value.

Likewise, the form also calls for employee comments on the rating and offers an opportunity to set goals with the manager, which will serve to fashion business objectives over the next year. The comments as to the fairness of the ratings are invariably devoid of real meaning. But managers can take a longer examination of the goals section. Here they can explore to see how aggressive the rated employee has been in formulating new objectives. Managers should be especially watchful for employees who appear to be satisfied performing at the same level of effort each year. Appraisals ought to produce mutual agreement about specific objectives that need to be finished by specified target dates. Those goals then are reevaluated on a quarterly basis through the remainder of the performance year. Evaluations should have a continuous existence and not be confined to the file drawer until the next annual compensation/performance appraisal review.

The candidate's personnel file may also disclose letters of commendation for projects completed successfully, certificates for attending various training classes, and, hopefully, evidence of John's seeking more formal education, whether it is by part-time courses or time off to pursue a degree. These documents evidence a person who completes his work and a feeling on his part he can develop further with more general education—another indicator especially applicable to overseas attitudes.

You as the manager then need to verify and amplify the written data by talking with the supervisors who completed those appraisals and obtain their input as to how they would perceive the candidate in an overseas assignment. Because the focus of most of the appraisals is reviewing work already performed, the supervisors can give valuable opinions as to future prospects, even in generic overseas postings. Since we are still at the generic stage of expatriate assessment, we need not be too concerned about whether the point ratings are a bit higher or lower than average (such as 4.1 versus 3.9 averages) since we don't know as yet what kind of expatriate job, requiring what new skill sets, will be in the offing for John. It may turn out that when an overseas opportunity does arise, its skill requirements may be compatible with those already demonstrated by the candidate.

Managers may also want to consider direct assessment interviews at this point, either with the on-staff people or with consultants. The earlier in the process that a clear portrait can be drawn of the candidate, the better. Issues that may arise can be converted to training and development programs so that the risk of removing a truly good potential candidate for overseas consideration is minimized. The same "do it now" philosophy ought to govern any testing with which the organization feels comfortable. Well-constructed interviews and testing techniques can only serve to help both the manager and the candidate decide what the best course of career planning ought to be, regardless of whether that includes expatriate assignments.

SELF-ASSESSMENT TOOLS AVAILABLE FOR THE CANDIDATE

Once again, these devices must have stood the test of verification, whether applied by in-house assessment people or consultants. In fact, the very process of inviting competitive bids for your assessment/training work should produce value for your company's staff people. They will gain exposure to the thinking and programs of professionals who have worked through the same kinds of programs with other clients. That experience is extremely valuable, since it should remove much of the risk in developing a new assessment approach for your own candidates.

Similar to some other consulting firms in this field, Prudential Relocation Services has come up with an evaluation tool for employee self-assessments. Their instrument, called Overseas Assignment Inventory, has the objective of helping the candidate to increase his or her understanding of the cultural factors inherent in overseas assignments, and asks the candidates to complete their own assessments of how they believe they measure up to each of the identified traits. Here is Prudential's list of the 14 essential attributes:[2]

1. Your expectations.
2. Your open-mindedness.
3. Your respect for other beliefs.
4. Your trust in people.
5. Your tolerance of others.
6. Your personal control.
7. Your flexibility.
8. Your patience.
9. Your social adaptability.
10. Your initiative.
11. Your ability to take risks.

12. Your sense of humor.

13. Your interpersonal interest.

14. Your communication level with your spouse.

To this list let me add another significant factor, a genuine *desire* to work with host country nationals, unhampered by impatience. This feeling is either there or it is not. It apparently is an inherent trait that some of us have and others are not so fortunate to possess. It would be difficult to learn to have such a desire. It is perhaps similar to teaching a person to learn to love apple pie after years of not really relishing that dish. Perhaps Professor Edgar Barrett, whom we quoted earlier in this chapter, put it most succinctly:[3]

"Sometimes we get too sophisticated. In truth, if you have a burning desire—in your gut—to understand and work with people from other cultures, you're a long way down the path already."

But if an individual, through the process of assessment, is made aware of how his or her outward behavior comes across to people from other cultures, there is an opportunity to change that outward behavior, through proper guidance, to establish the kind of thorough awareness that is fundamental to cross-cultural relationships. An effective facilitator, such as in our Zorba example, can stimulate the awareness and sensitivities facilities that we possess. But assessors or trainers can't stoke a fire inside that isn't there.

One of the major attributes of the self-assessment process is to trigger the self-screening mechanisms that we all possess. If the potential candidate and family unit can carefully evaluate their own suitability for the stress of an overseas relocation, they will be far better positioned than if they blindly take the risk of going overseas only to discover some fundamental roadblocks to completing the stay—a process in which everyone loses—expatriate, family unit, and host and home country management.

The key to identifying appropriate candidates, according to Rita Bennett, cofounder of Bennett Associates, a consulting firm based in Chicago, now a division of Cendant, "is to use an assessment program based on research indicators and interviews to determine the individuals who can adapt and perform well. Bennett Associates provides daylong assessments that actually get the candidate to determine for himself or herself whether he or she is appropriate for the assignment. By using behavioral interviews, the assessment examines the candidate's interest and curiosity. During the interview process, the candidate demonstrates those characteristics."[4]

Ms. Bennett adds:

"In these days, where an international assignment is becoming a prerequisite to career advancement, a person can open himself or herself to trouble. When we're doing the assessment, we're giving the person the tools to make the assessment himself or herself."

For both of you, the potential expat and the manager, that process will be mutually beneficial. Management makes a positive effort to help the employee decide whether an overseas opening would be appropriate. At the same time, the expatriate candidate comes to be aware that the assessment feedback, if rendered early enough in the assignment process, can open the door to counseling or developmental training.

STRUCTURED INTERVIEWS

Another valuable tool for you managers is the structured interview. Similar to assessments, they can be a potent indicator of likely success or failure on an overseas assignment, but they also can inflict a great deal of harm if they are not done professionally. These interviews contrast with the free-form employment screenings that all of us have conducted every time there is a job opening in our area. Instead of concentrating on technical qualifications, these interviews focus on those character traits deemed essential by the company. Such interview questions have been worked out with experts, usually consultants in the field, with a preset pattern of gauging the candidate's responses.

Whether formally structured or not, the candidate can expect that the same standard issues will be raised during the screening that are basically universal in their applications. Consider the following advice from Geneva-based Bill Twinn, currently director of human resources for the International Air Transport Association, and Patrick Burns. They have been expatriates in more than a half dozen countries for more than 25 years. They advise candidates for expatriate opportunities as follows:[5]

Assuming you, the prospective candidate, can provide the academic and professional qualifications and skill . . . you should be able to show evidence of some of the following if you are going to beat the probable "competition":

Experiences and exposures accumulated throughout your life which suggest that you will enjoy the challenge of adapting to an environment which is different from the one in which you currently live and work . . .

A clear explanation of your motives for wanting to live overseas . . .

Your research into the country that you hope to be expatriated should extend to a review of possible negatives that may be raised by the interviewer as to why somebody with your profile would not be able to adapt . . .

This advice may give the impression that, with little careful thought, you can talk your way into an expatriate posting. Up to a point, this is true, but it is critical that, in building your arguments, you look honestly at whether you would be a good expatriate.

PERSONAL CIRCUMSTANCES REVIEW

This interview is usually held well along the screening process, and generally signals that the managers are looking at your candidacy for overseas postings in a very serious manner. The reason for this is that the session probes into personal and family matters that are not considered in domestic transfers. The interviewer, whether corporate staff or from a consultant firm specializing in expatriate screenings, will home in on family matters such as the spouse's work situation, the children's school timetables for graduations, health issues, financial problems, and a variety of other issues that might affect the performance overseas. Statistics indicate, as was seen earlier, that not many organizations currently avail themselves of these background-finding expeditions. But the major reasons for assignment failures are the very targets of the questions in this form of interview.

TESTING

Tests need to be thoroughly validated before they can be taken seriously as an effective screening/assessment device. There is no shortage of consultants in the testing field. The major judgment factor for management is to investigate the background of the test. Who used it? What were the results? Did the results accurately predict the success of the candidates? Let's examine one of these standardized tests to see what they ask the candidate.

Dr. Stewart Black and coauthors describe in *Globalizing People through International Assignments*,[6] a test called the Global Assignment Preparedness Survey, (G-A-P-S), which appraises candidates for six criteria:

1. Cultural flexibility.
2. Willingness to communicate.

3. Ability to develop social relationships.
4. Perceptual abilities.
5. Conflict resolution style.
6. Leadership style.

According to the authors, "Our research has found that G-A-P-S results are related to a variety of incomes, including expatriates' work and nonwork adjustment, job performance, satisfaction, and level of commitment and loyalty."

The book goes on to describe how each individual's report is sent to the candidate, who frequently self-selects out of the candidate pool, having discovered elements of personality or traits that would be troublesome in an overseas environment. Other candidates can look to the report as a guideline for self-improvement. Good managers ought to step in at this point and work with the candidate to plan how the detected shortcomings can be resolved. Perhaps further training or individual counseling can be arranged so that future eligibility for selection can be restored.

BACKGROUND CHECKS

Here is another management device that is rarely utilized in the expatriate assessment programs, apparently because managers do not feel the need to review the same history that was presented to them when the individual first applied to them for employment. But that reasoning is flawed because it assumes there have been no major changes in the employee's circumstances, which, as time rolls on, is hardly realistic. Debts may pile up, or problems with drugs or alcohol may develop, among a host of conditions that will give the company pause to reflect as to whether an overseas assignment makes sense for this employee at this time.

The candidate ought to be alerted regarding the procedure and asked if he or she has any objections to it. In the event there are objections raised by the candidate, you managers should be concerned, and should follow up as to precisely why the candidate does not feel comfortable with what is in essence a reasonable request. After all, the company is placing significant responsibilities on expatriates, not to mention the considerable costs that will be incurred in the overseas assignment process. Managers are conducting due diligence efforts in the pursuit of this information. This may need to be spelled out for the reluctant candidate.

Drug screens and health examinations fall into the same category. Most companies do not include these screening devices as part of the overall assessment procedure, yet they could produce valuable information, either at this preselection stage or when the overseas opportunity has materialized and selection has begun.

Training

As assessment progresses, managers will become aware of developmental needs of the candidates for the expatriate program. Those needs may be specific to individuals, or they can be required of groups of employees. Both forms of development are essential for healthy corporate growth and should flow from a needs analysis that corporate training people should conduct on a continuing basis.

EXECUTIVE TRAINING

All training programs represent serious investments by the company in the participants. As with financial investments, the investor is seeking a substantial enough return to justify the company's commitments in time and expense. Executive education lays a foundation from which an expatriate can make good on that investment.

These general programs are focused on employees who will be enabled to use the expanded globalized approach whether they remain at the home country operation or are fortunate enough to obtain an expatriate assignment. Such courses range from a few days up to six months, and either are offered as regularly scheduled courses by prominent universities or consultants, or are customized to the specific needs of a single company. In the case of the former, consortiums of companies send candidates to the campus of the host university, where the value added to learning about the best of global practices is a valuable by-product of exchanging practical approaches with participants from other organizations.

Let's examine the main categories of executive education available today—the consortia, the customized programs, and distance learning alternatives.

CONSORTIA

In a consortium, a university hosts several companies on campus, usually requiring a half dozen or so participants from the 6 to 10 participating companies. The faculty members are drawn from the business school, and are usually also part-time consultants, which brings much-needed practicality to their academic approaches.

The consortium members work with the school's administration and faculty to fashion a combination of case studies and lectures, featuring the best-case and worst-case scenarios, as learning tools for the individuals to carry back to their respective companies. Some of the participants have been expatriates, but many are sent to these courses as general preparation for future assignments.

There is a distinct advantage for this kind of executive education over the other two alternatives, customized courses and distance learning programs. That advantage is the ability to mix with the other company participants, academically and socially, an interchange in which participants gain the broadening awareness that their own companies' practices could bear reexamination in light of other companies' successes (or failures) in the same kinds of undertakings.

In a recent *Wall Street Journal* article entitled "Executives Head Back to Polish Skills and Rub Elbows," reporter Carol Hymowitz had this to say about the increasing popularity of this form of executive training:[7]

> At Harvard Business School, enrollment in executive education jumped 80 percent in the past five years and now accounts for 25 percent of the school's total revenue. Last year, about 5,000 executives and managers attended one of Harvard's executive programs, which vary in length from 3 days to 10 weeks at costs ranging from $4,000 to nearly $50,000. Several hundred more participated in programs for particular companies.

How do these host institutions keep current with changing global practices and issues? This certainly has to require more than furnishing a classroom with international faces in it. It is a continuing challenge to track current practices from around the globe and incorporate the lessons learned in the curriculum. An analysis of this challenge to the schools was recently discussed in the *International Herald Tribune*:[8]

Schools go global in several ways. The most typical is through their course materials. Schools know they just can't add the word "international" to an accounting course. International subject matter means case studies that cross borders. Business cultures vary, and cases should illustrate these differences. MBA directors are constantly on the lookout for them.

"We scan the world for the best case studies," says James Teboul, professor of operations management at INSEAD. "We use them from all over, France, America, Asia, and Europe. Sometimes we have to adapt them for Europe."

In addition to the lessons to be drawn from the case studies, the consortiums deliver that precious interchange of participant experiences, which writer Hymowitz noted:[9]

For many, the biggest benefit of executive programs is the chance to meet and mingle with other managers, particularly those sharing similar experiences. They prefer getting practical help with problems they face on their jobs, rather than more theoretical learning.

"You can study lessons from a book, but lessons from life are more valuable," says Claude Boruchowitz, manager of major accounts and government for Minolta in Brussels, who attended the IMD program. "I could talk about problems and solutions to problems with people who work in very different industries than mine, but like me, must work globally."

CASE STUDY: THUNDERBIRD'S INTERNATIONAL CONSORTIA

Let's explore a typical executive program consortium, to see precisely how it operates and what is being taught to the corporate participants.

The American Graduate School of Management, "Thunderbird," administers several executive training programs throughout the year—both general programs for consortia of companies, and curriculums customized to one corporation's needs. Currently, three different consortia are in action, holding three two-week sessions each year on the Phoenix campus. We'll focus on Consortium II, a group of nine global players: AT&T, Dow Chemical, EDS, Fluor, GM Powertrain, Goodyear, Honeywell (now GE), Lucent Technologies, and the SK Group (the fourth largest Korean-based company). This group of companies, with some membership switches from other consortia, has been meeting three times each year for almost 10 years in Glendale, Arizona, the campus of the school.

Each session lasts two weeks, and companies usually send anywhere from 5 to 10 participants to each of the three sessions. Faculty is lent from the school's regular degree program and is evaluated by the participating company board members, after meeting with their participants at the conclusion of the two weeks. The Consortium Advisory Board (consisting for the most part of corporate training and development officers) meets with the academic directors to review the effectiveness of the teaching and the current relevance of the general subject matter and case studies. As an example, here are some session subjects and the cases discussed in exploring those subjects:

Subject	Case
1. Industry Globalization	Singapore Airlines
2. Global Leadership Development	Konigsbrau Hellas, A.E.
3. Value-Based Management	Dell Computer
4. Global Finance & Valuation	(lecture)
5. Analyzing Competitive Strategy	Barnes & Noble, Amazon.com
6. Sustaining Competitive Advantage Cross-Culturally	Euro Disneyland
7. Assessing the China Market	(lecture)
8. Merger & Acquisition Strategy	(lecture)
9. Global Licensing & Partners	Benecol: Raiso's
10. Leading & Teaming: Finding the Balance	EcoChallenge Morocco
11. IT Integration Strategy	Cisco Systems, Inc.
12. Knowledge-Based Technical Change	Chaparral Steel
13. Developing World-Class Affiliates	Motorola–Penang
14. Performance & Control	Multiquimica do Brasil 1999
15. Global Diversification	Asahi Glass Co.
16. International Market Entry	Enron Development Corp.
17. Global Competitors, Central & Eastern Europe	Gerber Products Co.
18. Building Competitiveness with Customer Service	Southwest Airlines 1999
19. Acquisitions & Privatizations in Emerging Markets	P.T. Semen, Gresik
20. Global Strategy Implementation	Phillips–Matsushita
21. Managing Change	Ogilvy & Mather
22. Global Brand Management	Procter & Gamble in Japan

In addition to using these case studies, the course also challenges the participants in negotiation simulations, in which the class is split into various teams and asked to come up with strategies to be deployed against the other side. And to complement this team-building exercise, there are individual personal action plans to be drawn and discussed as a follow-through from class to application back on the job.

The SK Group
This course has proved to be an outstanding vehicle for the development of SK Group managers. For almost a decade these participants, drawn from Seoul headquarters as well as from SK expatriates from all over the world, spend a concentrated week prepping up on business English. They then participate in the two-week course of lectures and small group discussions. While they do not generally actively participate in the give-and-take of the larger lecture sessions (with some notable exceptions), they weigh in with great enthusiasm in the smaller group formats. They are eager to learn of Western company approaches to mutual issues. They are willing to exchange their own experiences with procedures that worked or didn't work in country X with the eight other companies' participants who are similarly enthusiastic about probing for what sorts of strategies can prove to be effective in various parts of the world.

These practical exchanges are encouraged as a complement to the use of business school case studies. The faculty is on loan from the school's degree program, or consists of visiting professors from other universities. They review the cases in the same manner as do most business schools, using questions to elicit learning points rather than employing direct lectures.

The corporate participants can be exposed to as many as eight different methods of solving problems (derived from the participating companies actual experiences) in addition to the more academic-driven alternatives. The SK Group attendees, like the others, leave Arizona not only armed with increased global awareness; they have established networks with the other participants that have proved most valuable in terms of seeking informal guidance in difficult situations. This experience has clearly prepared them generically for a specific expatriate task or, in the alternative, to better understand the nature of the company's cross-border operations from their desks in Seoul.

The other eight companies report similar usage of the course, often mixing the participating group with a few expatriates to add an extra dimension of perception.

CUSTOMIZED PROGRAMS

Unlike the consortium approach, the customized programs start with
the premise that a particular global player has some unique objectives
that management seeks to achieve through academic or consulting channels. Again, no specific overseas assignment is in sight. The goal is to
provide a sound foundation of global thinking for the employee's future
development.

The company's first step is to identify whether the kind of learning involved is more suited to an academic approach through a university or institution possessing a first-rate faculty equipped to deliver the customized
message, such as Harvard, Thunderbird, Babson, Cornell, and the University of Washington, among others that have established international
reputations for globalized instruction. These professors can offer a wealth
of solid research on who has done what in the international arena, and
those who have been active in the consulting field also bring the wealth
of their practical experience to the classroom.

The SK Group mentioned earlier in connection with the Thunderbird
consortium was one of Asia's pioneers in establishing a customized course
with U.S. universities, including general developmental courses of four
months at the University of Washington and Thunderbird, finance courses
at the University of North Carolina, human resources courses at Cornell
and the University of Illinois, and technology courses at the University of
Colorado and Denver University. All these courses called for specific learning targets for those managers deemed prospective global people. The costs
as to tuition, transportation, housing, and so on were considered by SK's senior management to be well worth this commitment in helping that company stay ahead of the globalization wave. After a decade of sending these
selected employees to American universities, SK has now developed a
whole cadre of senior and middle managers who are well grounded in Western approaches to effectively developing businesses and is using the best
practices for treatment of its expatriates in the process.

Some consulting firms have made great efforts to create a niche for
themselves in the cross-cultural market, for both general use and in connection with specific assignments. As an alternative to the campus approach, most of these consultant-led sessions can be held on company
premises and scheduled to suit corporate work requirements.

CASE HISTORY: THE NOMURA RESEARCH INSTITUTE (NRI)

This organization, NRI, has been called the world's largest think tank. It is Tokyo-based, and has operations sprinkled throughout the globe, including New York City. It primarily deals with providing financial service research and technology to its parent, the Nomura Securities Company. Similar to Nomura operations elsewhere, the workforce in New York consists of both Japanese expatriate managers and local U.S. staff nationals. The expatriates were generally assigned on a three-year basis. The expats were familiar with the parent's Tokyo-based research methodology and technology but needed U.S. expertise in properly applying that knowledge here. They would also have to learn how to modify practices that had proved successful in Tokyo, in order to fully meet the special needs of the American financial marketplace.

The U.S. local staff, by contrast, included no one who spoke any Japanese or was really familiar with Japanese culture. Some of their Japanese expatriate counterparts had developed fair English language skills, but many of these overseas assignees had never been out of Japan prior to this assignment. So the expatriates and local staff needed each other's support in achieving their respective goals; but they really weren't comfortable in seeking it or working together through projects.

Communication problems developed as the business began to expand. This produced the inevitable frustrations that communication gaps engender, and each group began to feel that the other was not being as straightforward in their dealings as they could have been. The director of human resources, an experienced U.S. national, Jordan Thompson, another veteran internationalist, searched for good consulting firms that could home in on the cultural differences that he had isolated as the main issue generating the failure to communicate.

Twelve managers—six Japanese expatriates and six local U.S. staff—were asked to attend a four-session program created by the selected consultant to stimulate both groups to better understand the cross-cultural barriers that were underlying their communications difficulties. The second target, of course, was to position each group to come up with ways to overcome those cultural barriers.

At the outset of the program, both groups were cautious and even suspicious about how any real improvement in the working relationships could be developed out of a consultant's training program. This was reflected in the way both sides initially seated themselves at the first session; each taking their own side of the table, facing their counterparts, who were also staking out their exclusive turf.

Readers of the Robert Ardrey trilogy, *The African Genesis*, *The Territo-*

rial Imperative, and *The Social Contract*, would have immediately recognized the mutual staking out of protective space that Ardrey so well described in his portrait of the origins of this behavior in mankind.

So we took stock of the divided classroom and worked through the consultant programs designed to foster closer understanding between the two nationalities. Would the course produce a totally divisive confrontation or produce a mutual recognition of what cultural factors were at work? Considering the sharp contrast between these two cultures, the odds were not at all favorable. The extreme cultural dissimilarities are aptly summarized by Professor Samuel Hayes of the Harvard Business School:[10]

"The cultures of Wall Street and Japan's stereotype firms could not be more different. Wall Street is practically a caricature of American frontier values, strangely transported through time and space to the canyons of Manhattan. Its youthful gunslinger traders and investment bankers brashly confront each other across the deal table . . . talent is for hire. This ambiance is a far cry from the culture of Japan's security industry, which, like that of the nation's corporate mentality in general, honors the virtue of teamwork, subordination of individual agenda to those of the group, a get-rich-slowly attitude, and the 'good soldier.' "

The consulting firm utilized the research of cultural pioneer Geert Hofstede in setting forth four dimensions of cultural contrasts for the group to study as their first step in uncovering what were the underlying stumbling blocks to their understandings. Along with contributions by other pioneers such as Nancy Adler, Robert Moran, and Fons Trompenaars, Hofstede's work has led the way in research that is still being conducted by academic institutions and consulting firms today. He explored the cultures of 40 nationalities, including the U.S. and Japanese societies, focusing on what criteria could be statistically valid in contrasting how each of those cultures operated. After six years of evaluations, he came up with four main aspects of cultural behavior, which he termed "dimensions."

1. Power-distance.
2. Uncertainty avoidance.
3. Individualism-collectivism.
4. Masculinity-femininity.

His project team examined over 116,000 completed questionnaires by employees of MNC, who were nationals of 40 different countries. The scores for each nationality were averaged together for each of the four categories, and the results showed some significant contrasts among the participants in the survey. Hofstede constructed a matrix setting forth these disparities.

Hofstede's research placed the Japanese and U.S. national traits, as measured by the dimensions standards, on opposite ends of the dimensions index. At Nomura, the consultants began to spell out each dimension, and participants were regularly asked to comment as to whether they would agree with the Hofstede findings based on their own upbringings and then their working relationship difficulties in the New York office. As members from each group offered validations of the Hofstede ratings, both nationalities slowly began to appreciate that the reasons for the difficulties in understanding were not solely due to the other individuals' desire not to help the situation, as both nationalities had suspected, but rather that there were deeper factors that needed to be appreciated on both sides.

The consultants then divided the group into six pairs, and asked that each pair (Japanese expatriate and U.S. local staff) walk through the dimensions together, using brief case studies that set up the two different cultural approaches. They were asked to come back to the overall group with a recommendation as to how best to work out solutions to the case problems in a way that would be comfortable for both cultures.

It was invigorating to see how this process played out. Staff members who had not been very understanding toward each other were being asked to consider how the other culture really felt about solving the case problems. This understanding grew noticeably through the last session, at which, it should be noted, each national group seated themselves in a totally commingled fashion. Indeed, the longer-term results proved highly beneficial to the firm, at least until the next expatriate rotations and the normal U.S. staff turnover.

DISTANCE LEARNING PROGRAMS

A considerable drawback to global training on the university campus is the time spent away from the desk by the participant, not to mention the costs of transportation, room and board. The countervailing thought is, however, that the participant will not be as likely to be distracted by ongoing job issues if he or she is away in Arizona, available only by cell phone during restricted times. It comes down to the analysis of each candidate's ability to defer job distractions. What is abundantly clear is that the advance of technology has brought the campus classroom to the company premises via the computer and the distance learning studio technology that all leading universities can now offer to the global corporate community.

Now it is possible to learn from the academic gurus via simulcasts that are beamed throughout all company overseas locations simultaneously. The distinct advantage is to call upon the university's very best faculty, reaping the benefits of their wisdom on a broad-based scale. Huge savings to companies such as the SK Group, with the majority of their executives based in Seoul, are thereby created—albeit offset by the restricted classmate-to-classmate interchanges, which, of necessity, are narrow in terms of time and effectiveness.

In the field of global human resources, and in particular compensation, there is an illuminating example of how companies can effectively construct customized programs with the elite of university faculty. Cornell's School of Industrial and Labor Relations houses one of the nation's more advanced distance learning facilities, which receives a full workload from corporate clients. Professor George Milkovitch, a prolific author on books about global compensation, is able, through the Cornell studio, to reach out to corporate employees around the globe from remote Ithaca, New York. Professor Milkovitch can lecture about the finer points of overseas pay to clients sitting in their company offices on three continents simultaneously. He can see all three locations and can zero in on a questioner from Bogotá, while other employees in Asia, Europe, and the United States can observe the exchange, and also contribute and even directly converse with each other.

Professor Milkovitch remarked to me in 1999 that "distance learning is the most exciting thing I've done"—a remarkable statement coming from a teacher who has spent so many years, in so many places, passing along expertise on compensation matters. We'll revisit Professor Milkovitch in our discussion about future compensation trends.

DISTANCE LEARNING COMBINED WITH CLASSROOM SESSIONS

It was only a matter of time before universities would roll out programs combining the distance learning technology with the campus classroom. Fordham's Graduate School of Business is a case in point. This school, located in Manhattan, has produced a course called a Transnational MBA program. It enables attendees to keep their full-time jobs while earning an MBA in a little over two years.

Business Week called it a "good blend of face-to-face schooling and net learning, a model of the future."[11]

The distance learning portions are transmitted from the school's studios in New York. Then the class is assembled in various locations around the world for on-the-spot instruction by school faculty.

VIRTUAL CLASSROOMS

Here is another new concept, somewhat similar to distance learning programs, but it opens up the exchange of ideas among the learners themselves, and is not driven by the faculty. Preselection of the work that the participant will do is not made up front; rather the students themselves largely determine it. As described by Francis Beckett in *HR World*:

> The flexibility of this approach is demonstrated by Henley's in-house MBA run for IBM. 250 IBM managers in Europe are taught by distance learning based on the company's own software. . . . Students only meet physically in the same room for about 18 days, either at Henley or in IBM workshops with Henley tutors. They learn at work, at home, or even in airport lounges using electronic notepads. The attraction, from the company's viewpoint, is that they can ensure their managers learn the things they actually need to know, while on the job.[12]

UNIVERSITY PROGRAMS GEARED TO INTERNATIONAL CAREERS

For potential expatriates there are several university programs that have been structured to prepare them for careers as internationalists, whether specifically designed for eventual expatriate assignments or for jobs closely tied into cross-border businesses. We've already visited the American Graduate School of International Management (Thunderbird) for our inspection of an international consortium in action. But Thunderbird stands out as one of the first institutions to concentrate exclusively on international careers.

Founded just after World War II, using a hangar left behind by the Air Force, Thunderbird has grown into a highly regarded school through the years since. It offers a one-year master's program in international business (MIM), and has attracted a first-rate faculty from around the world. A typical student profile would be that of a college graduate about three years out of school, with direct business experience in the interval before starting with Thunderbird.

The University of South Carolina offers two graduate school approaches with two-year programs. There, in the Darla Moore Graduate School of Business, is a unique program for human resources people with undergraduate degrees and intervening business experience. This program requires the first-year students to take globally related HR courses. At the summer break, the students are then assigned (and fully paid) internships with one of a number of participating global organizations. They then return for their second year of study, graduating with a Master of Human Resources (MHR) degree. Graduates from the school (all 100 percent) each year go on to work for the likes of Sony, Exxon Mobil, Citigroup, General Electric, General Motors, IBM, PepsiCo, and TRW. What I found especially interesting at this school was its emphasis on bringing into the classroom the veterans of the corporate wars to relate HR experiences away from the textbooks, a splendid element of practicality to go with the more academic focus of the program. A second program, for business majors, requires the candidate to spend the internship overseas. This degree is masters of international business studies (MIBS).

Cornell's School of Industrial and Labor Relations also offers an advanced program, master of industrial and labor relations, (MILR), in addition to its undergraduate program, producing a BS degree. Both programs are outstanding.

Incidentally, I've just joined the USC faculty, but this evaluation was written prior to my start there.

Both managers and potential or current expatriates, this spectrum of new learning programs presents opportunities. Does your company or your target company have ongoing programs in these categories? The booming popularity of the distance learning programs is beginning to cause some global leaders to rethink their traditional classroom setting arrangements with universities and consultant organizations. But the trade-off, time on the job versus the contacts with other participants, remains a thorny dilemma for most organizations today. Managers appreciate the intangible benefits from having their participants mix with representatives from other global leaders, both in and out of the class setting. Many participants with whom I've talked have stated that they actually brought away more from those discussions than from the lectures and case reviews guided by the university professors.

In summary, there are significant benefits in all of these methods of instruction, and each individual and company needs to weigh carefully the benefits and drawbacks of each method to best suit their own corporate needs.

Notes

1. Statement of Professor Edgar Barrett, American International Graduate School of Business, Phoenix, AZ, June 12, 2000.
2. *Global Human Resource Management: Developing a Pool of Qualified Candidates*, Valhalla, NY: Prudential Relocation Services, 1999, p. 4.
3. Statement of Professor Edgar Barrett, June 12, 2000.
4. "Looking Out for Mr./Mrs. Right: How the Experts Weed Out Inappropriate Expats," *Immigration Advisor*, LRP Productions, 1996, p. 6.
5. *The Expatriate's Handbook*, Bill Twinn and Patrick Burns, London: Kogan Page Ltd., 1998, p. 23.
6. *Globalizing People through International Assignments*, J. Stewart Black et al., Reading, MA: Addison-Wesley, 1999, p. 66.
7. "Executives Head Back to School to Polish Skills and Rub Elbows," Carol Hymowitz, *Wall Street Journal*, Sept. 12, 2000, p. B1.
8. "New Strategies for Going Global," J.J., *International Herald Tribune*, May 18, 1998, p. 1.
9. "Executives Head Back to School," p. B1.
10. *Investment Banking, A Tale of Three Cities*, Samuel B. Hayes III and Philip M. Hubbard, Boston: Harvard Business School Press, 1989, p. 291.
11. *Business Week*, Oct. 4, 1999.
12. "Virtual Classrooms," Francis Beckett, *HR World*, Jan.–Feb. 2000, p. 48.

Illustration by Liz Lomax

How Should Managers Select the Best Candidate
for Each Overseas Assignment?

CHAPTER

7

How Should Managers Select the Best Candidate for Each Overseas Assignment?

"Many are called, but few are chosen."
Matthew 22:14

Judging from the high rates of failed assignments, successful selection practices remain an elusive goal for many global competitors. For most of them there are three fundamental issues that have not been resolved. Depending upon your company's own history, it may be one, two, or all three of them that continue to plague the process. They are:

1. Selection is not positioned as part of an overall screening, training, and development process.
2. Many of the critical indicators of possible success or failure are omitted from the selection procedure.
3. The decision-making process itself is seriously flawed.

We will take a brief look at each of these current practices and then focus on how they could be reshaped to produce higher rates of successful overseas assignments.

159

Selection as a Stand-alone Process

We've seen that less than a third of multinationals link their selection process with cultural training, and that only 8 percent link selection with training and development programs. These company practices are a living testament that managers have not yet made the connection between choosing a candidate and preparing that individual for the basic requirements of the job. You managers are doing no favors for the company or the expat candidate when you permit that disconnect to happen. Managers can assure that the candidates possess the very skills and/or traits that overseas assignments demand when they build those factors into the preselection training and development programs. If managers believe that there may be a quality issue regarding in-house training staff, there are numerous consulting alternatives that, if properly researched, can provide the much-needed expertise that training and selection processes require.

When selection has no tie to training, managers are left with a gamut of questionable candidate factors that may be so inappropriate that the final choice might as well have been accomplished through a lottery. Company knowledge of employee profiles can be sketchy (through performance appraisals) or stale (from the original employment application). Why not reduce the gambling risk by assuring that the candidates know what you want them to know?

All three types of programs are set forth in the SRI study—general training, cross-cultural training, and development sessions—and should be included in the preselection process. Since these programs are so sparsely deployed, what other factors are driving the actual selections?

Selections actually appear to be driven by the departure of the incumbent expatriate as opposed to being the result of a screening and training process that had already identified appropriate candidates well before the overseas opening emerged. Managers and HR often manage the selection process like any time-pressured project, so hurriedly that the factors they ultimately use as selection criteria are dubious at best. HR frequently winds up picking whatever parts of a full program appear to be available to squeeze in the newly nominated expat's brief time frame before departing.

Prime Indicators of Candidate Success

What do companies look for in identifying who would be the best fit for an expatriate opening?

Once again, let's refer to the SRI/NFTC survey of 77 leading corporations to view what indicators managers are using to make their selections.[1] (See Table 7.1.)

These same companies were asked to set forth the main reasons for their faulty selection experiences; the results are shown in Table 7.2.[2]

Taken together, these two survey results portray current selection practices that defy logic. The basic reasons for the mistakes can be fused down to the lack of time to make a proper decision (which really goes to the heart of the process not being properly linked to screening and training, as just discussed) and the questionable skills of those entrusted with making the selection decisions. That factor is directly tied into the priorities of skills and traits that are being used as the essential guideposts in the selection process.

Table 7.1   Selection Criteria Used by Managers

Selection Criterion	Percent of Companies Using
Technical requirements of job	96%
Business needs	94%
Candidate availability/willingness	88%
Reputation within organization	71%
Personal traits/ability to adjust	60%
Language knowledge/fluency	54%
Prior international experience	48%
Stable work history	44%
Academic degree	25%
Career of spouse	21%
Children issues	21%
Formal assessment results	13%
Marital stability/status	10%
Care of elder parent	2%
Other factors: cost, experience, performance ratings, flexibility, etc.	6%

Data Source: International Sourcing and Selection Practices, SRI/NFTC, p. 10.

Table 7.2   Reasons for Faulty Selection Experiences

Reason for Faulty Selections	Percent of Companies Reporting This Reason
Driven by need to fill job	81%
Used to rid people from the organization	33%
Driven by departments	29%
Line managers override HR	21%
No line management buy-in	13%
Supervisor's evaluation not used	12%
Assignment used as reward	12%
Untrained company interviewers	10%
Unqualified vendors	10%
Not controlled by HR department professionals	2%
Other: failure to identify strategic purpose, no true assessment tools used, no formal selection tools, cultural adaptation issues	13%

Data Source: International Sourcing and Selection Practices, SRI/NFTC, p. 13.

Let's start by examining the overly emphasized influence of technical skill proficiencies. While technical knowledge of the work is the easiest element of a position to test for and evaluate, the actual percentage of failed overseas assignments due to that factor is minimal contrasted with cultural adjustment, spousal, and family problems. How can managers effectively test for those assignment elements? Each of those factors could well form the basis of an entire treatise, but let's just take a quick snapshot of the growing importance of spousal issues.

SPOUSAL ISSUES

To get a feel for the multiple pressures that set upon the expatriate spouse, try to imagine how our model expat John's wife, Jane, would be positioned with regard to his posting to Paris. Her likelihood of successfully coping with these issues becomes a factor in the selection process.

She must be concerned about where their two children will receive the best education in the city. How will they be safely transported there?

Where can she locate the most appropriate housing for her family? How secure are the neighborhoods? What are the ins and outs of Paris shopping—food, clothing, and so on?

How can she squeeze a job search into all these other immediate priorities? Having been an administrative assistant in the United States, what are the chances, given her poor French, of locating a job within reasonable commuting distance from the Jones family's new apartment home?

This means that she must either be able to negotiate the Métro or take a chance on competing for driving space to navigate Paris' diabolical roundabouts.

Are there enough hours in her day to give household pet Fang assurance that he has not been forgotten in the turmoil of relocation?

Yes, wife Jane, like all expat spouses, faces a multitude of difficult challenges and should receive meaningful support from family, new friends, and John's company in coping with those issues.

The survey set forth in Table 7.1 showed that only 21 percent of the participating companies considered the spouse's career as a factor in the selection process and a paltry 10 percent reviewed marital stability/status as an evaluation factor. But the demographics and social implications over the past 20 years call for rapid and effective management responses to the two-career marriage. Indeed recent statistics bear out the trailing spouse's difficulties. The 1998 NFTC study,[3] reports that 49 percent of spouses were employed before the overseas assignment, but only 11 percent were actually able to secure employment at the host location. Further, the 177 participating companies there cited that spousal resistance was one of the three most critical expatriate challenges (54 percent), along with family adjustment (68 percent) and children's education (67 percent).

The net effect of the growing spousal concerns by many companies was also made crystal clear in the 1999 NFTC survey,[4] in which those 264 responding organizations reported an enormous increase in spousal assistance programs. (See Table 7.3.) That survey reported that 70 percent of those companies now provide formal spousal assistance programs, compared to only 59 percent in 1998, a significant 11 percent increase of surveyed companies. This positive trend, although late in coming, reflects managers' realizations that the spousal dilemma has grown to enormous proportions. So what are you managers doing to address that issue?

These percentages should increase significantly over the next decade. Managers are learning by increased assignment rejection rates the reality of how difficult it will become to successfully attract and retain dual wage-earning couples for overseas assignments. You managers should more fully

Table 7.3   Spousal Assistance Programs

Form of Spousal Assistance Program	Percent of 264 Companies Utilizing
Education/training	37%
Establish/find networks	36%
Reimburse career enhancement	21%
Identify volunteer activity	20%
Assist career planning	20%
Financial allowance	16% (average $4,740)
Compensation for lost income	7% (average $8,500)

Data Source: Global Relocation Trends, 1999 Survey Report, Windham/NFTC/IIHR, p. 30.

understand that the trailing spouse is being asked to give up a way of life as well as the income that had been coming into the household. Then you can add to that boiling pot all the cross-cultural challenges and other traumas that tag along with every uprooting for an overseas location. In light of those critical issues, it is truly baffling that managers in fully 30 percent of the organizations reported that they furnish no spousal assistance programs whatsoever. How many more refusals will they be forced to accept regretfully before that 30 percent is finally reduced to zero?

The best practice for you managers is to include the spouse and the entire family unit in the selection process.

Selection Decision Makers

The final third of the selection process predicament concerns who, within the corporate structure, has been delegated the power to render the final yea or nay as to picking the candidate to be offered the overseas job. As we view current practices, we'll again encounter unsatisfactory procedures, void of the teamwork that is so relevant to other major projects that a company undertakes as a standard business operating procedure. Table 7.4 shows the pertinent parts of the Selection Research International/NFTC survey.[5]

These results should cause you managers to raise a large red flag over a process that demands the immediate attention of your senior management. The numbers show that the majority of these companies place the exclusive responsibility for selection on the shoulders of just one individual, the line manager. Is that individual always the best-qualified person to make that

Table 7.4 Responsibility for Selection of Expats

Final Selection Decision Responsibility	Percent of Companies Reporting This Position
Line managers	58%
Cross-functional teams	44%
Corporate staffing	6%
Human resources	6%
Combination of above	10%

Data Source: International Sourcing and Selection Practices, SRI/NFTC, p. 10.

decision? Consider that most line managers have little more experience in effective interviewing than the juniormost employment representative in the HR department. While we have nothing against line managers, they do not usually receive the kind of intensive training that employment representatives receive in order to professionally interview. Clearly, the line manager will know about the technical requirements of the job under consideration, but there are other facets of the position on which other members of the corporate or line staffs can offer different insights.

This need for broader perceptions is at the heart of the rationale for giving the final selection responsibilities to cross-functional teams. They ought to be empowered to contribute their own expertise and/or experience to the collective wisdom of the company. Rather than setting up still another power struggle for corporate guerrillas to wage, why not position the decision as a shared responsibility, with the line manager charged only with the extra tie-breaking vote?

One of the valuable by-products of the traditional concensus-building technique is that it distributes ownership to more than one function; hence there is mutual effort to ensure that the selected candidate *does* succeed—a far cry from what we've all observed when a single decision maker rejects others' advice and a failed assignment ensues. At that juncture, the usual reaction of the left-out corporate staffers is: "I told you so."

Now let's turn around the three selection issues just identified and construct a selection process that can be used as a model. For this purpose, we will use our hypothetical example expatriate family, John, Jane, and the Jones children, as John is being considered for a selection to an expatriate position—that of manager of marketing for the Paris operation of his U.S.-

based employer, Dot.com. Set forth next are the recommended selection steps for Dot.com's management.

Selection Process Model

UPDATE JOB DESCRIPTION

This step is fundamental to the selection process in that it draws an accurate portrayal of what technical skills and human traits this expat job requires. This description must be comprehensive, whether written by HR or the incumbent. Ideally, both should collaborate on it. Without a comprehensive position description there is the distinct probability that some of the key managers in the selection process will have entirely different perspectives as to what any specific job opening is all about. Most of these managers, in both the host and home countries, are not likely to be close to the entire breadth of the position's responsibilities. Nevertheless, each will be able to offer views about portions of that job that the other managers are not positioned to view.

In our example assignment, manager of marketing, Paris, the Paris HR manager would be charged with taking the current job description to the departing incumbent to review what substantial changes have occurred since the last update. They need to discuss any changes in technical skill requirements and traits that are necessary to succeed at that marketing position in Paris. This is often a difficult first step, since many expatriates depart the host location without a significant amount of planning time being afforded to management to capitalize on the departing employee's first-hand knowledge of the job. As mentioned earlier, this lack of adequate time is almost always traceable to a falling-dominoes series of last-minute assignment opportunities and departures within the company. If the vacancy stems from a quit or involuntary termination, the incumbent will be long gone before any replacement arrives at the host county. In either event, the company loses the benefit of the individual who had the most intimate knowledge of the job, and hence would have been the primary source for the job description update.

For many years managers viewed job descriptions as limited to a breakout of the position's technical skill requirements. The completed descriptions were done either by the incumbent from a structured job questionnaire or by an HR representative, who would interview the incumbent and occasionally observe the incumbent perform it—a "desk audit." Either format would lead to its subsequent use as a basis for job evaluations. Managers use those evaluations with the help of compensation people in HR to attach salary grades and ranges to the job.

Consequently job descriptions are often formatted to furnish the kinds of data that a job evaluator or committee could go to for the basic information to use for an evaluation. Such was the case when I conducted job evaluation sessions for clients of the Hay Group. That job evaluation system, then the bible for many industries, pinpointed necessary know-how, problem solving, and accountability as each job's key dimensions.

But today that technical skill focus has been broadened by several new approaches. The newer evaluation systems, such as competency models, describe the particular combination of knowledge, skills, and characteristics required to perform a particular job. What is most relevant to expatriate work is the portion given over to personal characteristics, which are defined as a pattern of traits or ways of reacting to the external environment. Examples would be self-confidence, energy level, self-sufficiency, and emotional stability. These traits are at the heart of expatriate success. On a case-by-case basis, they need to be accurately identified by the company so that candidates can be more precisely compared to the complete job profile, not just the technical skill requirements components.

In our marketing manager case, the current incumbent should review all the technical skills and personal traits with HR as they compose the description. In addition, Paris HR would need to obtain the perspectives of superiors, peers, and subordinates to round out the job description.

The list of required characteristics should be reviewed by Paris HR and the Paris director of sales and marketing (the job to which this open position reports) and then finalized, furnishing copies to the U.S. marketing and HR people as the primary sources of triggering the screening for final selection. All these managers should sign off on the final version of the position description.

Generic Traits Requirements for an Expatriate Position

Let's consider eight general skills that should be required of an expatriate assigned to any location. There will be additional, more specific needs depending on the particular host country. The basic eight, as set forth by Dr.

Ernest Grundling, a Ph.D. from the University of Chicago.[6] They should serve as the basic starting points as you managers begin to fashion complete job descriptions with your HR people.

TRUST.
The ability to build trust across cultural barriers is vital, especially when some of the behaviors that we regard as evidence of trustworthiness may be interpreted as signs of unreliability in another environment.

With regard to the first of Dr. Grundling's points, experience at several host country locations has given me the distinct impression that there is a general tendency for newly arrived expatriates to overdelegate matters to local staff. Expats often assume that local staff members have already proven themselves to be worthy of that trust on the assumption that the "survival of the fittest" corporate jungle principle prevails globally. That is a mistaken perception in many host locations. A wise expat will thoroughly research each of his or her new associates. Office and national politics have a way of combining in some areas to perpetuate the continued employment of some individuals who, in Darwin's terms, would have otherwise become extinct. A local staff person may still be there for a variety of sheerly political or poor management reasons.

There is a fine line to walk here. A new expatriate needs the local expertise from these staff members. Expats soon understand that their delegation of authority is eagerly received; yet not all of those local staff people are going to turn out to be skilled enough to execute all that authority. Expats need to listen carefully to their host country mentor, their manager, and other expats to research which members of the local staff can be given what levels of authority.

RESPECT.
The member of a multicultural group must develop behaviorally encoded forms of respect that are practiced by each participant. (Examples: asking for input from each participant; waiting for others to finish their thoughts.)

Let's view some examples of Dr. Grundling's principle at work:
The Japanese culture immediately surfaces as an illustration of the need for respect. At Nomura Securities in New York, we viewed the usually fast-

paced Wall Street types trying to modify their behavior when dealing with their Japanese expatriate managers. Deliberate consensus building is a complex process for most business cultures to master. Indeed, most of the local U.S. staff found this initiation into the world of patience to be an extraordinary transitional challenge.

For both Japanese expatriates and U.S. local staff, there were distinct trust issues. The expatriates were highly competent in the areas of Japanese equities and how Tokyo management wanted the various U.S. operations to fit within the company's overall strategy. Their U.S. counterparts were in great need of understanding the latter. But the expatriate managers of the various departments understood little about the U.S. products, such as fixed income and investment banking. They had to learn from their subordinates, and that meant they had to rely on straightforward and comprehensive explanations from their U.S. local staffs.

The U.S. local staff had to rely completely on the Japanese expatriates to explain the firm's corporate workings, particularly in terms of where in the Tokyo corporate hierarchy the decision-making authority rested. The U.S. employees also had to count on their Japanese managers for guidelines as to proper coordination with the other Nomura overseas branches.

Both Japanese and U.S. nationals had to work on the assumption that their counterparts were going to be forthright as to the continuing issues of separate lines of knowledge and authority. They came to respect the other once the trust had been verified by successful results. This was a very gradual process indeed. What hampered complete assimilation was the rotation system that always seemed to call for the return of an expat at about the time he had finally mastered the basic knowledge required to fit smoothly within the coordinated setup.

LISTENING.
The challenge for managers in a multicultural environment is to listen for what they do not expect to hear. Can you deal with new information that is beyond your normal common sense assumptions?

Good listening is a rare skill. There are books and training courses that describe the problems and techniques available for overcoming those obstacles. In the U.S. business world we are witnessing a curious trend. As we progressively resort to more nonspoken communications such as e-mail and fax, we begin to lose the clues for greater understanding that accompanied the sound of a speaker's voice. Speakers can communicate different authentic meanings by the tone, volume, and pace of their speech. As we move to more convenient and less costly channels of communication, we begin to lose some of the sharpness with which we had originally honed our listening skills. Effective listening is a rare skill that is getting rarer because we have fewer opportunities in today's hectic business process to exercise and improve it.

Now let's add the cross-cultural challenge to the universal requirements for effective listening skills, and then confront a more complex obstacle, a daunting one indeed. We'll return to Geert Hofstede's two extremes, the U.S. and Japanese national cultures.

Recently we have read that the Japanese are rapidly adopting more individualistic Western ways, such as forgoing group-oriented behavior for individual approaches to everything from self-help programs to filing malpractice lawsuits.

Many of us who continue to work with Japanese nationals in both Japan and the United States will attest to the fact that there are many Japanese, particularly at the more senior levels, who are still uncomfortable giving a direct "no" to a proposal. Instead they offer a variety of options that may or may not be tenable; the real underlying intention is for you to understand that you'll need to move on to consider another proposal.

Listening carefully to Japanese speech patterns takes on extra importance because of the various meanings some words carry, all dependent on the precise nature of the conversational context. For example, the word "hai" in Japanese, which is so often used in everyday conversation, can be translated as "yes." But it doesn't always mean "yes." Frequently it really means "I understand," or, with a solemn face, "No, but I'm not going to tell you that directly."

Conversing with Japanese nationals also requires the gaijin (the foreigner) to be watchful in terms of the physical clues that accompany the speech. There can be signs of meaning in a sigh, the intake of breath, or the closing of eyes that accompany spoken words that often give those words special meaning. They often use long pauses to consider their next statement or to evaluate what you've just said. Americans must learn to conquer their temptation to interrupt. Another cardinal rule for U.S. listeners is to give ample silence after the apparent end of your Japanese friend's statement. There could be another one to follow, and your comment will throw the conversation direction off by interjecting a new thought.

We can look to the Middle East for another set of special listening challenges. There, depending on which nationality is involved, you will encounter speech patterns that border on a volume level equal to a Nine Inch Nails concert in Madison Square Garden, a decibel challenge for any listener over the age of 21. Recently arrived expatriates often mistake these high-decibel exchanges for heated disputes. They're just exchanging pleasantires.

At the outset of one's experience with these barely controlled outbursts, you become a bit taken aback by the number of interruptions, often accompanied by highly animated gestures. But the cultural mores in many of the Middle East countries where I have worked with expatriates really mean that both parties to the conversation are signaling their own knowledge of the subject matter, not necessarily in total disagreement with the other party to the discussion. Once they have established their assertions of knowledge or business contacts, they reach out for your acknowledgment of respect. As soon as you provide that, you can move on to the subject matter of your talk.

OBSERVATION.
In certain cultural contexts what is not said is more important than the literal content of the discussion.

In the Arabian Gulf region, the manner of dress, whether traditional or Western, is often a clue as to the extent a person has taken steps to signal his adopted mode of thinking. At the Dowell-Schlumberger headquarters in Dubai, there were two third-country nationals on the human resources staff, both with the same name, Hassan. But there the resemblance ended.

The Hassan from Iraq always wore the *dish-dasha*, the traditional white robe of the Gulf. He was in every sense trying to become an accepted Dubai national. Consistent with many local customs there, his entire demeanor was reflected in his clothing preferences. Despite a particularly annoying habit of positioning himself just inches away and yelling "through" the listener, often accompanied by strenuous gestures, he made literally no effort to modify any of his behavior patterns to the customs of the listener. He didn't care for most of the international staff and wore that disdain on his sleeve.

By contrast, the other Hassan, an Egyptian national from Cairo, would always be nattily attired in the latest and smartest of Western casual garb. True to his clothing preference, he made every effort to be associated with the international staff expatriates from around the world. His mastery of English, as well as his highly polished demeanor, were awesome: both severe contrasts to his Iraqi counterpart. Both Hassans had adapted their outward behavior to their sharply contrasting ways of thinking.

EMPATHY.
Being able to sense and respond to the feeling of your foreign counterparts, while vitally important, can also be difficult because the clues are unfamiliar. (Examples: the smile that could signal discomfort, or exaggerated emotional displays that are calculated to probe for concessions.)

Let's take an example from the world of baseball, as culturally adapted by the Japanese. As all baseball fans know, the Japanese have taken to the American national pastime with a high level of unrestrained enthusiasm that seems totally out of the culture's mainstream habits of reservedness. Games in Tokyo are punctuated by enthused brass bands that play rousing fight songs that remind an American spectator of U.S. college football music. Another unique cultural adaptation is the organized cheering, monitored closely by colorfully attired cheerleaders. A non-Japanese visitor has a truly difficult question to answer: Are these fans genuinely enthusiastic, or is this organized spirit another group role that is followed to the hilt, including the mandated enthusiasm?

Still another unique Japanese bit of baseball behavior is a practice of smiling after making an error or striking out, a gesture that would bring down on the player all kinds of scorn if practiced by an American playing ball in the United States. This tendency to smile in the face of adversity extends to the business office, where many Japanese nationals often conceal their real feelings with smiles that are difficult for gaijin to read as clues to their inner feelings.

FLEXIBILITY.
Can you adapt to what you heard with new ears, seen with new eyes, and felt with a new emotional register, transforming your management style in a way that makes it more locally effective? (Example: learn to solve a problem by offering indirect feedback instead of tackling it directly.)

This trait was emphasized in the Geert Hofstede cultural dimensions matrix that we described in Chapter 6, on training. The Japanese participants had been put off by their American colleagues' forwardness in virtually all aspects of their conversations, while the Americans saw little need for the time and effort required to attack issues indirectly.

Another eyewitness experience for me came at the Schlumberger headquarters in Paris. There my assumptions about Parisian character traits, including the reputed stereotyped arrogance, had to be quickly reworked. While the French staff on rare occasions did evidence some excessive pride in terms of their superior oilfield technology, I encountered none of the anticipated social loftiness related to their cultural acceptance standards. The French nationals turned out to be far more concerned about whether you had sufficient field experience to understand the work conditions on the rigs or platforms.

INFORMED JUDGMENT.
The finely honed skill of quickly reading and assessing business counterparts may go terribly awry when we are outside of our cultural familiarity zone. Clues that we normally rely upon as windows into another's soul may turn out to be also leads or dead ends; meanwhile we miss what is locally obvious. Judgments are best made when one is fully informed by guides who know the local business territory.

The need to seek out help in judging new peer and subordinate capabilities is never more important than at the onset of the overseas assignment, when most expatriates are susceptible to associating technical competence with a person's command of English. We've already reviewed the local staff evaluation issue, and Dr. Grundling's perspective here offers the commonsense advice that all expatriates, regardless of what home and host cultures are involved, must be highly selective in the process of obtaining sound advice concerning activities relating to the host country culture.

PERSISTENCE.
People who give up the first time that something goes wrong will not last long overseas. Individuals and groups who face adversity by coming back and trying again and again to create solutions—that doesn't mean repeating the same mistake—are the ones who will prevail.

Dr. Grundling points out here a universal trait, the concept that each of us has the desire to do a job perfectly. Mistakes at the onset of an overseas posting are inevitable. The important thing is to remember that those errors should be perceived and remembered as learning points. Some of us have the tendency to view those missteps negatively; they are then seen only as steps in a downward slide, regardless of the importance of the error. But we should have the patience to wait out the learning process, and learn from the missteps, not be demotivated by them.

There are many, many other traits that are common to overseas assignments generically, and still more that would apply to particular nations, cities, or work sites. Those traits need to be identified as specifically as possible so that candidates will be accurately measured against those standards. Let's return to the expatriate assignment process as we move on to the second step.

REVIEW LOCAL STAFF CANDIDATES

Once the job description has been completed, the host country HR function (Paris HR people, in our sample case) should perform a comprehensive screening of local staff employees who might be feasible candidates for the marketing manager position. This search should include other expatriates working in the European region as well as other local staff individuals. Since our company, Dot.com, has a European regional headquarters, the HR function there should also be actively involved in that search. Managers cannot afford to ignore considering candidates from local staffs. Yet most managers automatically assume that if an expat leaves a position, another expat should replace that person. Most local staff individuals have serious career aspirations of their own, and it would be unfair not to offer them opportunities to develop and be promoted provided they are qualified now or could be developed for future jobs.

The company will reap advantages in several ways.

First, if managers can effectively promote a local staff national into a position formerly held by an expatriate, they have just sent a positive message to the remainder of the local staff: There are genuine opportunities for advancement for you here.

Second, when managers promote local staff nationals, the host nation's business and social communities will warmly welcome that policy decision. In some countries, in fact, the local promotion will sometimes be required as part of a legally mandated quota system.

Third, local nationals have a deeper knowledge of the local community than expats can learn in three years, but the drawback is that they generally lack the corporate headquarters perspective that expats bring to the host location.

Fourth, the selection of a local staff person will generally translate into significant cost savings of one-quarter to one-half of what the company would have had to pay for an expatriate to fill the post.

For all these reasons, management will be well advised to give serious consideration to all feasible candidates in the host nation and region staffs before moving to the expatriate pool.

REVIEW EXPATRIATE CANDIDATE POOL

In the event there are no suitable candidates from the local staffs or other expatriates already assigned to the European region, Paris HR transmits the job description to the corporate HR function to begin the screening process of the expatriate pool candidates. In the event there are no serious contenders, the alternative for HR is to post the job for interested employees or open the search to the public, either by search firm or by electronic postings.

If there are viable candidates found in the pool, such as John in our example, HR contacts each of them to verify that they still have an interest in expatriate work and would be willing to pursue the marketing manager job in Paris. At this juncture, HR may want to conduct some testing, structured interviews, background checks, and so on that will be utilized in the final selection process.

HIRING MANAGER REVIEWS SHORT-LIST CANDIDATE PROFILES

The profiles of the screened candidates are then transmitted to Paris for review by the manager of the open position—in our case, the director of sales and marketing—together with Paris HR. They will review test results, assessment findings, and any recommendations that the corporate marketing function and corporate HR would have regarding their reactions to each of the candidates. The Paris director of sales and marketing and Paris HR set up a priority list of candidates, contact corporate HR in the U.S. headquarters of Dot.com to obtain that function's views, and then proceed to coordinate notifications and interviews.

What materials should be included in the profile to be considered by the hiring manager?

- A copy of the completed application form.

- All reference checks.

- All performance appraisals.

- Compensation history, to include any bonuses and copies of the recommendations that supported those bonuses.

- Any correspondence in file that describes projects, special assignments, letters of appreciation, and so on.

- Any managers' notes reflecting objectives, plans, and so on.

- Family background profiles. This data must include whether the spouse is still employed, which grades the children have reached at school, and any special health or family concerns that could bear upon their comfort in accepting an overseas assignment.

- Formal education, special training, language proficiencies.

- Assessment and special test results.

- Informal evaluation by current manager as to how candidate would likely perform in the overseas job and culture.

HIRING MANAGER AND HR CONDUCT ON-SITE INTERVIEWS

The Paris director of sales and marketing along with Paris HR conduct interviews with each of the short-list candidates at the Paris location, or by closed circuit. The spouses of the final candidates are also included in the interviewing cycle. If appropriate, Paris HR requests that the succession planning function review the short list and make recommendations as to how the expatriate assignment would play out for the longer-term benefit of the employees and Dot.com. Let's presume that candidate John has survived the short-list cut, and he is selected to visit the Paris operation for a final round of interviews.

HR SETS COMPENSATION AND FULL EXPATRIATE PACKAGE

While the interviews are being completed, the corporate compensation people begin to construct the general boundaries of what the expatriate package will be for this job. In this process, they study the packages and local rates of direct superiors, peers, and subordinates at the Paris location. This package will be subsequently refined to fit the successful candidate's own compensation history. That final package would be reviewed and approved by the corporate marketing director and the Paris director of marketing and sales, as well as Paris HR.

SELECTION PRIORITY IS FINALIZED

The Paris management reviews its final selection priorities with corporate management and begins the process of setting up the offer interview(s). The corporate HR function notifies the first candidate on that list, John, that he has been selected and will be shortly presented with an employment agreement.

Corporate HR drafts that employment agreement, with corporate legal review.

OFFER IS EXTENDED

Corporate HR invites the successful candidate, John, and makes him the formal offer, giving him a reasonable time frame to accept, modify, or reject it. HR warmly congratulates John, reminding him of all the potential opportunities that can be opened through a successful overseas assignment. HR invites John to sit down later with the manager of succession planning to discuss the various paths that might be open to John following completion of the overseas assignment. John understands a good expat practice when he sees one and will follow up on that offer. If HR doesn't offer this meeting to John, he should state that the postassignment career alternatives are of such concern that he would pursue that avenue with or without HR's direct involvement.

Corporate HR reviews the major provisions of the agreement with John, asking for any questions that John may have. Then HR asks John to return with his final answer in a few days, after he has had the opportunity to carefully review the contract (best with his own attorney and tax adviser) and to discuss the assignment with his spouse, Jane, and family.

NEGOTIATIONS

Companies strenuously avoid making alterations to the standard boilerplate expat agreement. As we've noted earlier, the expat community is extremely sensitive to one-off arrangements, so that when that group learns about a new goody that has been granted by the company (and they *will* learn) the expats will queue up the next business day at the HR office. "Me, too!"

Consequently, the contract that John takes home is pretty much non-negotiable unless there are substantial, unique, issues that could be agreed upon without the danger of setting a corporate precedent. The other factor that could mitigate the company's hard-line resistance to modifying the agreement is the special degree of importance given to the particular job or the candidate. In these cases, corporate HR may agree to some contract revisions, but only after obtaining expat agreement that the changes will not be shared with others. That seldom works out, but it slows down the process of dissemination.

Let us suppose that John's spouse, Jane, holds a full-time job and has no intentions of giving up her career. When John returns home with the agreement, they notice nothing in it regarding the company's intentions on helping her job search in Paris. This could be, and often is, the deal breaker. Everything else in the agreement is acceptable, but John needs to find out what the company intends to do for his spouse prior to making a formal acceptance of the offer.

John has been given a copy of the corporation's overseas manual, and as a good expat candidate, he carefully reviews those general rules to round out the picture of all the policies that govern the assignment. The manual contains no corporate policy on spousal job aid, either.

John has no choice but to ask corporate HR what the company's practice is in helping expat spouses find jobs at the host locations, and in particular Paris. HR will generally explain the company's standard practice, generally not written anywhere, for providing training guidance, setting up informal networks with other expat spouses, and so on. If the company offers a lump-sum payout, that, as an exception, could be in the manual. However, John needs a formal commitment. How can he insert that into the contract?

Whatever oral commitments HR makes at this meeting are generally not enforceable by the expat. Only a signed memorandum will generally bind the company. Suppose HR states that Paris HR has an effective network of other HR directors in Paris and promises to contact those people energetically on Jane's behalf. This kind of commitment may or may not be satisfactory, but if it is, John needs that promise to be reduced to writing as part of the contract.

Other contractual provisions John should consider are a guarantee of minimum job level on repatriation, the selection of a home country mentor, and a commitment to assign a host country mentor as well.

Still other special provisions could be a special schools reimbursement or special medical treatments that the Jones family will want during the overseas assignment. In fact, the best approach that the Jones family can take to this proposed agreement is to draw up their own wish list and see what the HR's reaction will be to the proposals.

Let's assume that the contract has been fully negotiated and that John signs it. What are the next steps in the assignment process?

SELECTION OF EXPATRIATES'S TWO MENTORS

Now that the ink is barely dry on the contract, several steps must be taken by corporate HR to set the assignment process in motion. They should all be undertaken simultaneously, but we've identified them as separate steps in order that none gets lost in the shuffle of the chaos that invariably accompanies the overseas assignment process.

The home country mentor should be a home-based officer not likely to be reassigned in the near future. He or she should be in a position ideally senior to the expatriate, who can relay appropriate news to the expat and obtain feedback as to how the job overseas is coming along. John must be asked for his input as to who would be a comfortable person in that role. John's complete trust in the selected coach is critical to his mentor program's success. If the expatriate is not genuinely happy with the choice, there will be little direct communication between them, and the fragile link of information exchange between expat and the home country headquarters is likely to be severed.

The host country mentor, to be selected by mutual agreement, will be finalized once John arrives in Paris, at a meeting with Paris HR.

How can HR managers best build effective mentor programs?

Coaching is not for everyone. Some individuals truly enjoy imparting guidance, and others feel uncomfortable doing that. Let's borrow an illustration of this from baseball.

Ted Williams, the Boston Red Sox hitter, was empowered with such natural abilities that he could actually see the seams on a pitched baseball. In addition, his hand-eye coordination was extraordinarily fast. He combined this awesome natural talent with a smooth, powerful swing that produced long line drives. He is baseball's last .400 hitter and a member of baseball's Hall of Fame.

Equipped with all this natural talent, Ted was named manager of the Washington Senators, in those days a very weak team with very poor hitting. It seemed like a natural mentoring choice; Ted was revered for his batting success, and the Washington ball club desperately needed to upgrade the talents of their hitters. What could go wrong with a pairing like that?

Patience. Because all facets of hitting had come so naturally to Ted, he was faced with coaching less naturally skilled hitters into a practice that came to him like an art form. When the Senators' hitters could not immediately follow through on Ted's basic instructions, Ted became frustrated. You can almost hear him now:

"Are you guys really trying? It's so easy, just hit the way I'm showing you."

Of course they couldn't come up to his standard, and because of that Ted quit his brief career as a manager and mentor.

That lesson applies directly to the business world, home of the Peter Principle—promoting individuals on the basis of past performance rather than their likelihood of success on the new job. Some of the greatest doers are poor teachers. Teaching requires patience and understanding of others' mental and physical skills. In fact, we found through mentoring programs that the best mentors were those individuals who originally had found mastering the job somewhat difficult, and had to learn to overcome those initial issues. Mentors need the patience and understanding of how to cope with the basic items, and then be good communicators in getting that information across to the learner in a positive way.

So HR will need to establish and then recognize the traits of employees wanting to be mentors, and then will need to set up a mentor roster from which individual mentoring assignments can be selected.

Let's walk through each step:

1. The position description of a mentor is drawn up by HR and submitted for senior management approval.

2. Those descriptions are circulated among management to elicit nominations.

3. HR screens the nominees; those found to be meeting the standards of the profile are notified that they will go on a continuous roster of mentors.

4. The selected mentors are given appropriate training, which is conducted on a regular basis.

5. As new senior managers move into positions at the firm, their managers are asked to review their candidacy for mentor positions going forward.

6. No less than 12 months from the end of the assignment, host country mentors are to meet with the management succession people to identify feasible jobs in the home country organization.

7. Once the overseas assignment is concluded, the two mentors and the expatriate are asked to provide corporate HR with feedback analysis as to what the strong and weak points of the program were and what recommendations each would make as to strengthening it.

ORIENTATION TRIP IS SCHEDULED

Corporate HR finds alternative visit dates for John and Jane, transmitting dates to Paris HR for coordination with other expat family units, relocation coordinators, school staff (children Jay and Kay will need to be registered as quickly as possible), real estate agents, and, of course, the key members of the local staff. Interview opportunities for spouse Jane are coordinated through the various human resources people who indicated to Paris HR they would have opportunities for her to consider.

Orientation trips represent superb openings to gauge the true nature of host location conditions. Local HR ought to schedule an informal welcome for the newcomers with other expat families. The Jones family can discover the really helpful, proven techniques for dealing with the new culture's challenges. Expats tend to be highly helpful to each other, regardless of whether they are working for the same company.

Expat housing and schooling form the backbone of establishing a comfort zone within which the expat can then begin to concentrate on the work that he or she was sent there to perform. But if either of those raw ingredients is not satisfactory to the expat family unit, the expat will not be able to progress to the point of making the expected contributions to the company's efforts there. The current expatriate community at the host location will traditionally gladly share their experiences in finding accommodations and selecting appropriate schools for their children.

The Jones family would be well advised to seek out recommendations as to effective real estate agents. Really good ones can save lots of time and often money in showing only the kinds of housing that the newcomers are interested in.

Likewise, the Joneses would do well to find other expat families with children at the same grade levels as their own. They need to solicit opinions about the quality of teaching and course content at each of the schools they are exploring.

POSTSELECTION ASSESSMENTS REVIEW

Paris being Paris, French language skills are incredibly valuable for community acceptance, whether you are asking for directions or trying to attract a waiter's attention at your local bistro. If there is some precious time between selection and departure, French language training should be arranged for both John and Jane.

Dot.com, John's progressive, global employer, has seen the wisdom of working through the following five procedures for each of its selected expatriates-to-be:

1. Technical skills assessment.
2. Cultural proficiency assessment (spouse included).
3. Psychological profile (spouse included).
4. Family readiness evaluation (spouse and children included).
5. Health, drug, and alcohol screening.

REPATRIATION ALTERNATIVES REVIEW

The manager of succession planning reviews the various career alternatives that should become available once John has completed the Paris assignment. The newly appointed mentor for John ought to attend this meeting so that he or she can be updated as to any changes that may affect the various paths that are outlined and agreed upon. Since this assignment is for a three-year term, it is unlikely that any positions will be specifically reserved for John this far in the future, but the essential learning point is that there is mutual agreement on what kinds of jobs and locations would make sense for the company and John to consider as the assignment nears completion. A schedule of review dates with the succession people should be set up no less than 12 months prior to the term completion date.

This aspect of assignment planning *must* be closely linked to the continuous assessment and training processes that should continue through the overseas stay. Monsanto's Carol Jones had this to say about the overall process:[7]

"Developing selection criteria and selecting the right person for the overseas assignment is key to success. Too often management fears that too much distress will alienate prospective expatriates, resulting in a refused assignment. Clarifying repatriation plans at the time of expatriation, however, eliminates employee confusion and uncertainty about their future with the company."

Indeed, Monsanto's expatriate planning process stands out as proof that a company's senior management team can allot the time and effort to make an expatriate assignment program work effectively.

CROSS-CULTURAL PROGRAMS

Now that the Jones family is scheduled for the Paris assignment and there is still time prior to departure, management can avail themselves of the window of opportunity to customize a cultural awareness program for John and family.

What are global competitors doing today in terms of providing this form of customized preparation? Once again, we can look to the 1999 NFTC survey. The results are surprising and disappointing:[8] Only 37 percent of those companies even offered this kind of training for the entire family, 23 percent for the expatriate and spouse, and 3 percent for the expat only; an astounding 37 percent offered no such preparation whatsoever. But the blame for unawareness cannot be placed solely upon management's shoulders; the same survey found that of those selected expat candidates being offered these invaluable programs, 30 percent of those selected opted to reject the training that had been made available to them.

Taken together, that means that almost one-third of the 63 percent being offered these training opportunities rejected those programs. The low levels of companies offering such programs, combined with the surprisingly high levels of employee refusals to participate in such preparation, mean that more than one-half of all expatriates currently on assignment have never experienced any cross-cultural preparation.

But does that really matter?

The managers of expatriate programs were asked that question in the same study. Their replies have significant value for us because these managers are in positions to evaluate the effectiveness of this preparation. Table 7.5 shows what the 268 respondents to the survey concluded:[9]

This highly favorable rating suggests that more companies should be offering such preparation. Those organizations that do offer this training will need to reduce the significant proportion of candidates' rejections. This would include adjusting their design and content to provide a more attractive program as well as marketing their importance to the new expatriate family unit in a more effective fashion.

Let's examine a recent expat cultural challenge story that found its way from Saudi Arabia to the pages of *The New York Times*.[10]

John McNamara, 54, the national director of international assignments for Deloitte & Touche, also worried about how his family would adapt to his position overseas. But for him, the issue was cultural. Not only was his wife, Agate, not allowed to work while his family was in Saudi Arabia, from 1998 to 1999, she was rarely able to leave the small community where the couple and their two sons lived. "It was very difficult for her to get used to the societal restrictions on women," Mr. McNamara said.

Table 7.5   Value of Cross-Cultural Preparation

Estimated Value of Cross-Cultural Preparation	Percent of Companies Reporting This Level
Great value	42%
High value	39%
Medium value	17%
Little value	2%

Data Source: Global Relocation Trends, 1999 Survey Report, Windham/NFTC/IIHR, p. 27.

How extensively are global organizations generally using preparation procedures? Aon Associates conducted a survey of 1,700 U.S.-based organizations to see which programs were being utilized. Table 7.6 shows the results.[11]

Managers continue to evaluate these very devices as invaluable corporate tools, yet their 1997 actual usage of those tools remains so low that they've created a credibility gap between what managers say and what they actually do about utilizing these processes. We do see some glimmer of enlightenment in the column setting forth whether the participating organizations were actually "considering" implementing each of the eight predeparture programs set out in the study's questionnaire. Perhaps there will be a trend toward more implementations of these practices in the near future.

For you managers charged with responsibility for running the expatriate programs, there is still another hurdle to clear after deciding that cross-cultural training is really worth the time and costs: Who should best provide it? Anne Riordan of Bennett and Associates, Inc., now a division of Cendant, has offered some illuminating thoughts as to the dimensions of what to seek in looking for the right kind of consulting services for this niche of training:[12]

"Predeparture cross-cultural training is a key component in the cycle of assistance offered to corporate families moving abroad. The ability to identify cross-cultural values, norms, and behaviors and, subsequently, to assess the manner in which these issues affect communication and business activities are fundamental skills for all expatriates."

Table 7.6   Utilization of Preparation Procedures

Preparation Programs	Percent of Companies Using in 1997	Percent of Companies Considering Use
Preassignment visit	50%	13%
Language training	37%	20%
Health, drug screening	34%	8%
Realistic job previews	33%	17%
Technical skills assessment	26%	18%
Family readiness evaluation	16%	21%
Psychological profile	11%	15%
Cultural proficiency assessment	10%	22%

Data Source: Aon Associates; reprinted in *Global WorkForce,* July 1998.

And as to the requirements for identifying what you managers need to assess in terms of the quality of the consultant, she continues, "An effective cross-cultural training program should go beyond acquisition of basic knowledge. Information alone does not provide adequate tools to promote effective employee performance or useful transition management for the spouse. Cross-cultural training consultants must be exceptionally adept in change management consulting and counseling. Long-term expatriate success involves attitudinal shafts, breaking of stereotypes, and changes in perceptions. An introduction to these changes begins in a predeparture cross-cultural training program."

Cross-cultural programs should continue throughout the assignment. Many experts in the field believe that the entire expatriate family unit should take such a course somewhere after the second or third month into the assignment. At that stage they have learned enough about the host country culture to be able to ask better-focused questions than if they were just starting out.

As the needs of the expatriate family unit develop, a sound management practice would be to revisit the continuing needs for further training in this uniquely important area. When the family begins to settle into the host location, they will invariably encounter cultural issues for which they need to obtain explanations. Consultant experts can explain what really was at work in those mysteries. Assignees must be furnished the knowledge and given the opportunities to develop skills to adapt, expand their skill sets, and thereby be able to perform at their highest levels for the duration of the overseas assignment.

Now that you are convinced that your company needs to work on establishing such a cross-cultural program, what should be the standard components of such a program?

We asked Cass Mercer Bing of ITAP, one of the major experienced consultants in this area, for a brief description of a typical cross-cultural program. This particular program, a two-day seminar, was required for every new employee of one of Mexico's major corporations. ITAP used a questionnaire called the "Culture in the Workplace Questionnaire" to introduce the new expatriates to the cultural differences to be encountered in each of the countries in which the company was doing business. Let's review the training agenda.

Day One

This day's program is delivered by the consultant along with an in-country cofacilitator, a native-born resident of the host country. Topics covered include:

- The cycle of culture shock.
- Social differences between the United States and the host country.
- The logistics of functioning in the host country, such as accessing health care, transport, postal services, and addressing the specific issues presented by the expatriate family unit.
- Use of a culture-profiling instrument based on the work of Hofstede, which, according to their understanding of their own cultural preferences might have an effect on their own appreciation and enjoyment of the new culture.
- Review of purpose-designed critical incidents illustrating how local people deal with situations in which the expatriate family might find themselves.

Day Two

The second session includes a review of this expat's working issues and his or her role in managing a "foreign" team, and further use is made of the Hofstede-based culture profile questionnaire, using the host country norms to show the expatriate the approaches and attitudes that are likely to be faced in the new job. The focus is on exploring the adaptations the expat is happy to make once he or she understands the reactions behind what he or she is seeing.[13]

This customized program offers guidelines for the many other varieties of preparation programs. It includes specific, practical data about surviving in the new environment and proceeds to explain basic behavioral differences between that host county culture and the expatriate family's home country culture.

You managers ought to review the gamut of the consultant services in this area. The costs and time allotted are so insignificant compared to the costs of failed assignments that these training programs will be well worth your investment. You potential expatriates ought to be pleased if it turns out that your own company or your target company offers these kinds of programs, either in-house or on an outside provider basis. It's a clear indication that the managers have recognized the scope of the expatriate challenge and have acted to support the expat's entire family in coping with expatriate challenges in the host country.

RELOCATION SUPPORT SERVICES

HR works with the new expatriate in locating and contracting with movers of household goods, contacting the appropriate visa and work permit people (for spouse Jane), coordinating moving dates, and setting up temporary living arrangements for the Jones family while they wait for their permanent residence to become available. The Paris HR function makes the appropriate contacts on the Paris side. HR Paris coordinates visits to the various international schools there for appointments to meet with the administrators to examine the teaching staff, record of successful graduates, the facilities, and so on.

Today most major companies have arrangements with their own law departments or outside law firms to assist with the visa and work permits. These services are particularly helpful because many nations still insist that these processes be slow-moving and exasperating for corporate expats and their families.

ORIENTATION TRIP CHECKLIST

What are the components of an ideal orientation visit? Let's consider the following musts.

Meetings with Host Location Staff

The initial meeting is with the new expat's new manager. In our case, the Paris director of sales and marketing. Goals, objectives, and timetables should be generally spelled out so that the new expatriate is aware of what timetables will govern the assignment, at least at the beginning stage. The next visit is with that manager's manager, generally a courtesy call. Here is the person who can relate the bigger story of the host county operation.

The next visit is with the Paris HR function to work out the pieces of the relocation process that can be facilitated by that function, including the arrangement to meet with a well-screened real estate broker who can direct the Jones family to the kinds of properties that would be of real interest to them. The HR function should also arrange for the Joneses to visit socially with the other expatriate family units in Paris, so that the really sound shortcuts in adapting to the Paris scene can be utilized, and they can acquire knowledge of what techniques do and do not work there.

HR or John's line manager will conduct a walkabout with John, introducing him to all members of the staff. Brief chats with subordinates ought to be scheduled as soon as possible during this trip so that any feelings of chemistry discomfort may be put to rest.

John's next visit is with the training director to investigate what further training, including language, of course, will be required to bring the Jones family up to French cultural acceptance. For Paris, and in the world of marketing and advertising, there is no substitute for a sound basis in French; the more concentrated the preparation, the better. Consider the following expat war story, this one from Paris:[14]

> UK-based Keziah Cunningham, international development manager of resources solutions consultancy Bernard Hodes, recalls one campaign that nearly went live in France. "In English the ad talked about the need to embrace corporate values," she recalls. "The perfectly accurate translation in French, we found out in time, used the same word as street slang for 'breast' . . . In Germany and Spain it's fine to use English if you're an international company, but in France it's not. They assume people are not interested in them if they can't be bothered to translate." Indeed, there is an old adage, "Buy in your language, and sell in your customer's language."

Our marketing expat John, and other expats starting out, ought to be sensitive to the subtle cultural pitfalls. If you are in doubt, seek the help of local staffers. They will be pleased that you came to them for advice rather than assuming that your own approach would automatically succeed in their nation.

Meeting with Incumbent

The employee with the most direct knowledge of the expat vacancy is the departing incumbent. Because this individual will inevitably be preoccupied with moving away and revving up for his or her new employment step, this meeting will present a challenge for the newcomer, John, to attract and retain the attention of the incumbent. In fact, the manager can provide real help in this regard by scheduling a reasonable amount of overlap time so that neither department nor the arriving expat feels rushed in this vital exchange of information. It will behoove the new expat to elicit as much formal and informal information about the job as possible while the incumbent is packing his or her bags.

Here are main issues to ask about:

- What are the central challenges of your job?
- Who have you relied on for valuable support in meeting those challenges?
- What are the office formal and informal methods of communication?
- How much detail *and* how often does the boss need to be updated?
- To what degree is authority really delegated?
- What are the factors that arose in performance reviews that were deemed most important by the boss?
- As to local staff, what are your estimates of each of the major contributors?
- If you could have changed your approach to the job, what would you have done differently?
- What is your next assignment like and when were you advised of that opportunity?
- Were you contacted on a regular basis by your mentor back in the home country, and did you find that relationship valuable?
- Who would you recommend as a mentor here and why?

Also elicit any other comments about the company, the host country operation, the regional operation, competitor marketing people and practices, or anything else that will be relevant and helpful.

Meeting with School Staffs

Expats need to keep in mind that schools overseas can operate under some rigid time lines for interviews, applications, and so on, so the earlier expats can start this exploration the more likely it will be successful.

Often HR will maintain a central file on the international schools. If so, the expat should locate the families whose children are attending them for a firsthand evaluation of their quality. The central issue is how good is the teaching staff. That question can be answered in a variety of ways, depending on individual student needs. Therefore, a possible approach for the Jones family is to find similar profiles of other expatriate families' students, to see how those children fared in each of the school environments that are being investigated. For this exercise, you may want to bring along the grade transcripts of each child to compare what are his or her strengths and weaknesses.

Meeting Other Expatriate Families

This orientation visit is a golden opportunity to get a feel for the real cultural environmental issues governing the host location. Where are the better places to shop for groceries, what is the best means of transportation, how safe is the neighborhood, what kinds of clothing should be worn? Of special interest to the Jones family is their beloved pooch, Fang. As in many American families, the family dog is considered an essential part of the family group. But how to safely transport him and what are the issues involving dogs in Paris? Again, all these way-of-life issues are best asked of the families who are residing in Paris at the time the Jones family moves to that city. Spouse Jane, in particular, will be spending lots of time with other spouses discovering the do's and don'ts of expatriate survival in Paris. In her case these efforts must be comfortably prioritized with the steps need to conduct her job search.

Meeting with Real Estate Broker

The location for the residence will most often be tied to the convenience of transportation to the school selected for the children. Since this is so frequently the case, the Jones family will be well advised to make their school selection before the choice of which Paris neighborhood in which to settle. Most of the larger companies use relocation consultants who can be generally relied on in steering the expatriate families to quality housing. But be alert to the possibility that there are indeed pirates among these brokers who look upon newly arrived expatriates with great relish. They can sense naive clients, and unless there is a long-standing contract with a particular broker, be very cautious in your selection. Again, the advice of other expatriate families becomes invaluable in making this selection.

First-time expatriates should keep in mind that the company's housing allowance will be reimbursing them only up to a point measured by base salary, family size, and, for some companies, position status in the company. This practical consideration is spelled out in the expatriate policy manual that you will be furnished by the host location HR function.

Meeting with Host Country Mentor

Because John's company is a progressive, global organization, its senior managers recognize the wisdom of structuring a host country mentorship into the expatriate support program. This individual should be senior in the organization to John and should not be in a directly related function. That way, straight performance issues can be avoided. As with the home country mentor, there needs to be a comfortable coaching relationship that can serve to answer the many questions that will arise in the new expatriate's mind as he acclimates into the Paris operation.

The recommended procedure here is for Paris HR to make a preliminary list of mentor candidates for John, and to discuss the possibility of being selected with each of them to determine their willingness and ability to lend constructive aid to the newcomer expatriate. This short list is taken by Paris HR and reviewed with John to see if brief interviews can be arranged to determine where the greatest comfort lies for the appointment. If there is some doubt, this selection can be postponed until the expat arrives for work, but should be completed with a mutually agreeable choice as early in the assignment term as possible.

It is time for John and Jane to return to home country headquarters and begin to wrap up all the relocation issues before they move to Paris for the start of the assignment.

Notes

1. *International Sourcing and Selection Practices*, National Foreign Trade Council and Selection Research Institute, 1995, p. 10.
2. Ibid., p. 13.
3. *Global Relocation Trends, 1998 Survey Report*, Windham International and National Foreign Trade Council, June 1998, p. 6.
4. *Global Relocation Trends, 1999 Survey Report*, Windham International, National Foreign Trade Council, and Institute for International Human Resources, May 9, 1999, p. 30.

5. International Sourcing and Selection Practices, p. 10.
6. "The Future of Global Management," Dr. Ernest Grundling, *International Focus*, Summer 2000, p. 3.
7. "Vowing to Go Abroad," Ruth E. Thaler-Carter, *HR Magazine*, Nov. 1999, p. 94.
8. *Global Relocation Trends, 1999 Survey Report*, p. 26.
9. Ibid., p. 27
10. "The Foreign Assignment: An Incubator or Exile?," Melinda Ligos, *New York Times*, Oct. 22, 2000, p. B1.
11. Aon Associates, as reported in *Global WorkForce*, July 1998, p. 9.
12. "Training for International Assignments: Fables, Fiction and Facts," *Runzheimer Reports on Relocation*, Aug. 1995, Vol. 14, No. 6.
13. Letter from Stephen I.P. Martin, managing director, KCL, and president, ITAP, Europe, Sept. 28, 2000.
14. "I'd Search the World Over," Kate Dale, *HR World*, Jan.–Feb. 2000, p. 25.

Illustration by Liz Lomax

How Can Managers Design a Sound Expatriate Rewards Package?

How Can Managers Design a Sound Expatriate Rewards Package?

*"This is a world of compensation;
and he who would be no slave must consent to have no slave."*
Abraham Lincoln,
Letter to H. L. Pierce, April 6, 1859

There is no perfect expatriate compensation model; if there were, all of today's multinationals would have eagerly adopted it. Instead, each of the multinationals continues to try out its own kaleidoscope of reward systems. These organizations are torn between creating programs that will effectively attract and retain the best possible quality of expatriates and increasing pressures to hold down the expensive cost spirals that have lately received so much publicity. This struggle has been waged for decades, and every few years a bold company or consultant emerges touting a new reward approach as being the long-sought panacea for the expatriate package ills.

Some multinationals are experimenting with lump-sum payments, others are trying destination pricing, and still others are exploring customized programs for different locations. The majority of firms continue using the balance sheet approach, often inserting their own modifications. These various expatriate reward packages do have a very tangible element in common: All of them continue to draw criticism from cost-conscious managers.

Expatriates respond that management does not adequately appreciate the costs (in both monetary and human terms) of the relocation and cultural adaptation processes. They point to currency fluctuations and local inflation spirals that are seldom remedied promptly enough. They read and talk about the violence that affected so many expats in Indonesia, and the January 2001 closing of the U.S. embassy in Rome for fear of bombings. They wonder what is really going on back at home headquarters—with rumors about job and people changes, organization restructuring, layoffs, mergers, acquisitions, and so on. In light of all these factors, overseas assignees believe they should be entitled to a reward package commensurate with all of their needs.

Financial people take issue with none of those specific concerns. It is the totality of the package that seriously concerns them. They labor over all those premiums and extra bonuses that do not apply in domestic transfers, where families are also uprooted. They can point to surveys such as the 1999 NFTC study that showed that the majority of HR people running the programs felt they are in fact too costly.

Authors William Sheridan and Paul Hansen picture this corporate tug-of-war in the following terms:

"In response to growing cost pressures, expatriate program managers are looking for ways to reduce expenses across the board, including expatriate expenses. At the same time, these managers are prepared to do whatever is necessary to encourage staff to take overseas assignments quickly and to keep expatriates relatively happy."[1]

You who are charged with managing expat programs, or who are managing expatriates, are left with a Herculean dilemma: how can you fashion reward packages that will attract and retain the best employees for your overseas locations while holding down the truly significant costs that these programs have spawned over the past four decades?

We'll try to guide managers and expats as you respond to the challenge. We'll study current practices and examine how they developed. Their history is particularly relevant because the conditions that governed their original construction and subsequent growth have changed dramatically, leaving us with the question as to whether the traditional plans still make sense today. In this process, we'll retrace some of the same history outlined previously in describing the transition of assignments. But these topics are so inextricably intertwined, that will be unavoidable.

Background of Expatriate Reward Systems

Historically, the development of the allowance systems that are common to most of today's expatriate packages, similar to the kinds of overseas assignments described earlier, were fashioned and developed by the petroleum industry. In the early days following World War II, the majority of U.S. expatriates were employed in just two countries: Saudi Arabia (31 percent) and Venezuela (24 percent). Consider that only 8 percent of all U.S. expatriates in those days were on assignments in Europe.

The compensation programs provided by these essentially petroleum industry organizations reflected the highly capital intensive nature of those companies. They could afford rich packages for their employees, particularly in the context of relatively short-term assignments in difficult work environments. Those companies addressed the hardship issues by paying high compensation rates. The oil company programs produced a system devoid of longer-term connections to corporate strategies or career pursuits. In the process, these programs set an extremely expensive cost bar.

To motivate the mercenaries to work in remote and difficult places, the oil companies resorted to a host of special premium payments for mobility, foreign service, hardship, completion, and so on to complement the short-term rotations. This produced policies that were extravagant, but nevertheless acceptable given the economic structure of the petroleum industry at that time.

When nonpetroleum organizations representing a broad spectrum of manufacturing multinationals began their global expansion campaigns in the 1950s and 1960s, those managing the expat programs, not blessed with the fat profit margins of the oil companies, had to find more economical approaches to sending their people on overseas assignments. At the outset of this new U.S.-based corporate invasion, the companies adopted relatively generous packages (particularly in relation to their own bottom lines) because there were as yet no reasonable alternatives.

The 1960s and 1970s were decades when many companies used overseas assignments as rewards for close friends of senior management. There was little thought about linking the rewards of the programs to the company's strategy in the host country or, for that matter, any long-term career planning for the expatriate. Most of the newly arrived companies adopted many

petroleum premiums although the underlying conditions for them contrasted with the difficulties confronting oilfield employees. Now they were
dealing with bankers, traders, salespeople, manufacturing people, and others who were required to live within the host communities and to remain
there for around three years. This was a far cry from working on remote
desert rig sites or platforms, housing furnished in company-owned compounds, and assignments measured in months, not years.

The newly arrived companies found themselves searching around for reliable data on host county costs. They uncovered either meager information or data that was not directly applicable to their own situations. Some
multinationals tried to do the research themselves. In 1955, for example, a
Conference Board study of 117 organizations employing 12,725 U.S. expats
showed the following data-gathering techniques.[2] (Note: Some companies
used multiple data sources.)

U.S. State Department	37%
Other providers	26%
Individual company research	24%
General information regarding cost of living	19%
Individual treatment	9%
United Nations	3%

After 40 years of development the expatriate compensation field saw the
emergence of a system that began to link the expat's base pay to his or her
home country and attempted to equalize the expat's purchasing power between the home and host locations. This approach came to be known as
the balance sheet system. It was often supplemented by the company's offering additional carrots to get the candidate to take the overseas job. The
extras included the premiums of the petroleum era plus a group of new allowances that would vary by country of assignment. To some extent, then,
companies were putting in motion programs that looked like the oil company's original approach of front-loading pay packages while sacrificing
strategic links to longer-term compensation, corporate strategies, or career-
path planning.

Companies continued to wrestle with the extravagance issue over the
next two decades, but no organization could break through with a new sys-

tem that would constitute a balanced way of satisfying expat basic needs at reasonable costs. Today, that search continues.

In Chapter 2 we considered the variety of expatriate assignments from the point of view of job content. Now we need to review those kinds of assignments from the perspective of how the expatriates are rewarded for each of those types of overseas postings. The form of assignment should greatly influence the manager's choice of the format of the reward package.

SHORT-TERM ASSIGNMENTS

As we saw earlier, these projects include systems installations, periodic audits, and so on and are performed by individuals who are not accompanied by their families. Most of these assignments do not carry the full weight of expatriate rewards packages. There is no need to find a residence. Rentals and even hotel arrangements are often utilized.

In fact, many of the shorter assignments are really extended business stays. The time and effort, much less the costs, are simply not worth the company's putting these employees on full expat status. The only exception would be for those short-terms assignments that are a part of a pattern of multiple short-term postings. Then there would be a need to come up with a full expatriate package that we will describe for the longer-term postings. For example, GTE uses a concept called "just-in-time managers," who continually roam the globe on projects involving its new personal cellular services.

The spectrum of allowances and premiums is not applied; rather the expat is generally continued on the home country payroll, with no significant adjustment made to base pay or benefits programs. Living expenses are treated as fully reimbursable, so the assignment takes on the character of an elongated business trip.

LONGER-TERM ASSIGNMENTS

For all other overseas postings, the company will need to construct a full expatriate package.

Today's managers need to assess the corporation's strategy in the host location to lay the groundwork for determining how the position ought to be structured and its duration. Is it a position that could lend itself to becoming a transitional one, setting up a local national to take over those duties? Or does senior management see a continuing need for extensive headquarters experience in order to facilitate host and home country cooperation?

Methods for Calculating the Compensation Package

Today there is no general agreement as to how many different reward systems are being administered by U.S.-owned multinationals for the overseas assignment people. The basic programs have been so altered that they are often unrecognizable. Each company has developed its own unique provisions that invariably interlock with the more standard sections to provide distinctive financial consequences for the expatriate family unit. We will do some research here from which you can derive a sense of all the varieties of packages that are being utilized today. For an example, consider the findings of Windham International/National Foreign Trade Council's 1998 survey:[3]

Companies using home country as standard for calculation	62%
Companies using host country as standard for calculation	3%
Companies using both home and host countries as basis for calculation	35%

The survey sponsors noted that there was a 2 percent increase in companies using both home and host countries over the prior survey year, 1997. The corresponding decrease came from those companies that used the host country exclusively as the basis for their programs. Let's examine each of these systems.

Home and Host Countries as Standards

The home country as the basis for expatriate package calculations was the historical starting point for virtually all multinational organizations. This was because the assignment patterns, as in the petroleum industry, were based on the understanding that the expat would be returned to his or her home country, which was almost always the headquarters country as well, at the conclusion of the assignment. Virtually all the major corporate players then, particularly the oil companies (and almost two-thirds of them now), built in repatriation as part of the system. Hence the home country appeared as the only feasible reference point for the expatriate family unit. As a consequence of dynamic growth of the expatriate populations in the 1960s and 1970s, consultants devised systems that would lend a measure of credibility to the calculations of the cost differentials between the home and host countries—the balance sheet approach.

BALANCE SHEET

We are all familiar with a balance sheet, aren't we?

Well, frankly most of us nonaccountants review such documents only from the companies that we have invested in, via their annual reports, and in those circumstances they are difficult to understand. Although expats had some initial difficulties grasping the details of the mechanism, they generally accepted the program's procedures as being essentially equitable.

What is being balanced?

The answer is the expatriate family unit's standards of living, between their home and host locations. The basic concept targets equality, assuring the family that they will be no better or worse off in the host country than if they had stayed at home. The system relies on fact finders, usually one of the major specialist consulting firms engaged in this global field, such as the Associates for International Research (AIRINC), Buck Consultants, Organization Resources Counselors (ORC), Prudential Relocation Services, Runzheimer, and Watson-Wyatt, among others. These firms have consultants working all over the world to engage in advice giving and fact-finding.

The balance sheet is all about the family's purchasing power at two locations—the home and host countries. The consultants gather data continuously to ensure that the family will be keeping pace with the purchasing power they would have had at the home country, at the same salary level and family size. The expat's base salary is broken down into four kinds of expenditures: income taxes, housing, goods and services, and reserve (pension contributions, savings, investments, etc.). When the assignment location costs exceed those that would have been incurred at the home country, the company makes up those differences as allowances. In addition, many companies add incentive payments, such as " foreign service" or "mobility" premiums, as further inducements where host country conditions would appear to warrant them.

In our assignment case, John, Jane, and two children are heading from the United States to Paris. How will the balance sheet be worked out for the Jones family?

Base Salary

Virtually all U.S.-based organizations start out with the determination that a U.S.-based salary will be utilized for the expatriate package. The consequences for this threshold decision are important to multinationals because the allowances and premiums will be calculated off the base salary amount. Let's review the impact of that standard practice.

First, base salaries for most management and professional positions in the United States are tied to surveys, either of the same positions or comparable ones, as they are currently being paid in the United States. That means that managers are looking backward for base salary competitiveness—back to the home country, not forward to the base salaries being paid at the host location. Managers see logic in the look-back approach when the expatriate is relatively certain to return to the home country within the average period of assignment duration. They recognize that base salary rates for comparable work being paid at most host locations will be considerably less than U.S. pay practices, but this difference is justified as a means of adding incentive for expat candidates to accept the assignment.

This widespread practice can lead to significant compensation discrepancies at the host location, especially where two conditions are present: The local wage rates are substantially lower than those in the United States, and local staff nationals have climbed up the corporate ladder at the host location to assume roles that are comparable in skill requirements to those positions being filled by expatriates. This practice creates an equity issue for the country manager and a morale problem for local staff, but is reluctantly followed by managers because they realize how demotivating a salary reduction would be for the new expat.

Let's see how Dot.com's compensation people would work out the determination of John's new salary in Paris. Let's assume that John had been at a

$100,000 base as manager of marketing. The salary administrator would evaluate the same job in Paris as being either higher rated, at the same grade level, or below the U.S. job rating. If John's company, Dot.com, has a formal job evaluation program in place, the administrator looks at the two grade levels of the U.S. and Paris jobs. They will both have salary ranges that were constructed based on job worth in each of those two labor markets. If the Paris job were rated a grade higher, that would constitute a promotion for John; had that job been in the United States. This would usually carry a promotional increase of about 15 percent of his old salary as a reward for moving into a more difficult position.

So if John were moving up a grade or two, his new base could be set at the equivalent of $115,000. If the Paris job is at the same level or below the U.S. position, the corporate salary administrator would make no adjustments to John's base salary.

Had John's company adopted the host country approach, also known as "destination pricing," the Paris HR manager would have to recalculate John's new base salary there so that it would be in line with the other expats' salary levels and externally equitable in the Paris labor marketplace. In compensation talk that's the double measure: internal consistency and external competitiveness. Those are the two targets of compensation professionals everywhere.

If Dot.com had opted for destination pricing, then the actual rate would be determined by HR research on the current internal base pay rates for comparable jobs, and using the local Paris wage surveys covering people who hold comparable jobs to John with other companies in the Paris or European areas (whether or not they are expats or local staff). This would depend on the locations from which candidates are generally drawn for the level of John's marketing position in the Paris organization structure.

Housing
The first calculation is to determine the portion of John's salary that represents Paris housing costs. To determine this representative portion, the consultant selected by Dot.com calculates a "normative expense" in the United States.[4] These norms come from national statistics of average housing costs at John's new salary base and the Jones family size of four. These numbers are reviewed each year and adjusted when appropriate. If the Paris housing costs are found to be higher than the U.S. costs, the

company can either deduct the U.S. housing norm, with the employer paying the difference, or, if that norm is not deducted, the company could pay a housing differential (where the actual approved Paris housing cost has exceeded the U.S. housing norm).

Goods and Services

This is the largest expenditure for most expats in their host countries. The balance sheet operates to pay the excess of these costs in Paris over what they would have been had the Joneses stayed in the United States. The consultants calculate the portion of John's salary spent on goods and services in the United States, and the amount in French francs needed to purchase the same items in Paris. This is an important variable in John's expatriate package; it is the assignment location "spendable income." In making the calculation of this key differential, the consultant uses "data published by national government agencies."[5] Here are the items that compose both indexes, which are adjusted to John's base salary and family size of four:

Food at home	Food away from home
Clothing	Transportation
Recreation	Personal care
Furnishings and household operation	Medical care
Tobacco and alcohol	Domestic service

Goods and services differentials can be either positive (Paris costs are higher than costs in the United States) or negative (vice versa). The index for Paris and the United States is calculated through the surveys of pricing agents, which in the case of one of the consultants in this field, Organization Resources Counselors (ORC), translates into the use of more than 100 individuals collecting an average of six prices for each of about 120 representative items in retail outlets where expatriates actually shop. The pricing is done a minimum of twice each year, up to four times per year. The surveys are then weighted to represent "typical spending patterns" and are compared with a base of 100, which represents the home country costs (the United States for the Jones family). That 100 is compared with the host country location (Paris) calculated at the current exchange rate.

The excess differential (assuming Paris was higher) is reflected as a number added onto the original 100 index for the home country, so that Paris might be calculated as 125, which is then factored against John's base salary to produce a cost-of-living allowance. Housing allowances would be similarly calculated.

What recalculations are made in terms of inflationary pressures at either the home or host countries? The natural concern here is that expatriates are tracing only the cost of living at their host locations, carefully monitoring every movement up as the cost of the baguette and croissant rise ever upward. The consumer price index movements back home are not of real concern to them. So adjustments are made periodically (usually quarterly or semiannually) when the host country inflation rates have in fact moved up against the home country rates. This is not the U.S. Consumer Price Index. Consultants do not use the CPI numbers because they include costs of housing that are separately accounted for in the balance sheet methodology.

Reserve

This group of expenditures covers contributions to social security, company pension, savings, insurance programs, and so on. Consultants expect, under the balance sheet approach, that the expat will continue to make these payments in the home country.

Taxes

Managers have two options in determining how to administer the expatriate's tax obligations.

Tax Protection

When managers select this program, expatriates could come out of the tax process with a windfall. This system requires that the expatriate calculate his or her actual tax liabilities (in John's case, to the French and U.S. federal governments, as well as province, state, and city taxes) and compare the total owed to what would have been paid to the U.S. and other governments had he or she remained in the United States for the entire taxable year.

If the expat's new total is in excess of the hypothetical home country tax, then the company owes him or her the difference. When the company makes such a differential payment, that payment becomes subject to further taxation, which triggers the whole cycle of payment, additional tax, payment, additional tax, forever. Most companies "gross up" the tax differential payment so that it already includes the anticipated additional tax that the originally calculated sum would have produced.

If the expat's new tax liabilities are less than what would have been owed had he or she remained in the United States, the company gladly permits the expatriate to retain the "savings" differential. That feature of expat programs becomes especially important in low or no income tax host locations. The companies relish this aspect of enriching the attractiveness of the overall package because the monies being saved by the expat are not coming out of the corporate coffers.

Tax Equalization

This program is used by nearly 90 percent of U.S. multinationals for their expatriates. Companies deduct the tax liabilities that the expats would have incurred had they remained home from their base salaries. Then the companies pay the expats' tax liabilities in both the home and host countries. Managers who select this approach understand that the hypothetical tax deduction they are making serves to reduce their organizations' tax liabilities.

While the windfall to the employee is eliminated, managers have gained through this process a smoother repatriate transition. Had the expat been sent to Dubai or other nations with no personal income tax, there would have been a sharp tax liability blow to the repatriate upon return to the United States. The choice of tax equalization eliminates the wide disparity between low or no tax host nations and the United States.

STRENGTHS OF THE BALANCE SHEET APPROACH

Expatriates' Perceptions of Fairness

Because there is a well-entrenched, large-scale system of obtaining and then calculating the various indexes that constitute the allowances, expatriates often feel a true third party is furnishing compensation advice to their employers. This feeling is to be contrasted with the expatriate feeling that if the company had total control over its own reward system there would be a substantial opportunity for the company to implement cost-savings programs by sharply reducing the dimensions of the expat package.

In those situations where a company has relatively small numbers of expatriates, the HR departments frequently do save substantial administrative costs by selecting overseas location surveys from consultants and then making their own calculations using the third-party raw data. By using an entire methodology that has been established for many years and utilized by hundreds of other global organizations, you managers can avoid suspicion. And if you have large numbers of expatriates, another distinct advantage of using the balance sheet is that it can save large amounts of your own staff's time in obtaining data and then calculating the final allowances on their own.

Continuous Link

Where no assimilation is expected and the expat is to be repatriated, the continuous link to the home country makes sense. If your company's assignments are the traditional "out and back" three years or less terms and the expatriate population comes from one country, the rationale of maintaining a continuous comparison of economic conditions between the home and host countries is a well reasoned policy. The expat family is expecting to be repatriated, and their sense of fairness is that their overseas actual costs of living be roughly equated with what they would have spent for housing, goods, and services had they stayed put.

Japan serves as a striking example of how this expat mentality can play out for the typical expat using the balance sheet. Prices in Tokyo are extraordinarily high by any standard. But when you add the expat tendency to live in expat clusters, those neighborhoods, like Hiroo, grow into islands of outrageous expenses for housing, goods, and services. Adjoining districts can offer similar items at extremely low prices, but the general tendency for expats to continue to buy their favorite toothpaste or cereal, and pay the premiums for those items, seems to be universal. Indeed, the Japanese expat clusters in the United States are examples of precisely that same tendency. Consider the status of Scarsdale, New York, one of a dozen metropolitan expat clusters, this one appealing to Japanese expatriates. Here is an observation from *The New York Times* in May 2000:

Scarsdale, in fact, is famous in Japan, standing for quality schools and housing.

"It's a brand name, and the Japanese like brand goods and brand names," said Kuniko Katz, a Japanese expatriate who raised a family in Scarsdale after marrying an American social studies teacher years ago. Last year, Mrs. Katz, who has tried to bridge the gap between the two cultures, founded Japan America Community Outreach, a nonprofit organization which helps Japanese expatriates become acclimated to American society while introducing Westchester residents to Japanese life.

Wherever they are, expatriates tend to live in impressive homes in costly neighborhoods, the result of generous housing allowances that can hit $8,000 a month and up."[6]

The balance sheet recognizes the expat lifestyle and uses the selected expat communities in each host country to make their pricing surveys, rather than using national data. This method is viewed as reflecting the facts of expatriate life, according to the overseas assignees, but is often criticized by the corporate financial people as being too generous.

WEAKNESS OF THE BALANCE SHEET APPROACH

Costs

The cost of maintaining the balance sheet approach is the most often cited criticism of the system. We mentioned costs as one of the key challenges to the expatriate assignment process back in Chapter 2. Now we can zero in on the leading suspect for those excessive costs: the balance sheet process. Consider the following conclusions by Ernst & Young consultants Don Robins and Robert Buwalda:[7]

"A typical expatriate costs his or her employer two-and-a-half times more in total compensation than a counterpart based in the United States. More than half is often attributable to housing and tax reimbursement costs, with the balance after base salary attributable to premiums and cost equalizers. Many expatriates have come to expect such premiums and cost equalizers. The infrastructure developed and maintained by multinationals to handle the task of computing, paying, reviewing, updating, and communicating these amounts is also costly and cumbersome."

How can these costs associated with the balance sheet approach be effectively reduced? Thomas S. Tilghman, a Towers Perrin consultant, recently offered some suggestions in the *American Compensation Association Journal.*[8]

1. "Reducing or eliminating the 'foreign service premium,' especially in those locations that are culturally similar to the home country."

Premiums such as foreign service or hardship periodic payments referred to by Mr. Tilghman have engrafted themselves onto the regular allowances within the balance sheet. Yet they grew when managers needed extra monetary incentives to offer potential expats and held on, even in the face of the global trends toward more civilized environments, offering all kinds of facilities that were not present even a decade ago. The real problem here, I would suggest, is management's lack of desire to take away a traditional benefit at the same time they are desperately trying to stimulate good employees to take overseas assignments. Frequently companies would term this premium a "mobility allowance," a substantial up-front payment to the expat for being willing to relocate in the first place.

As human resources practitioners, we defy logic in awarding the same foreign service premium to a news correspondent covering Paris as to those risking their lives in Beirut or Kosovo.

2. "Reducing or eliminating cost-of-living allowances through 'efficient purchaser' cost-of-living tables, or customized tables that eliminate duplicate benefits."

In this suggestion, Mr. Tilghman takes on a formidable foe, the innate clustering and home way of life issues that are simply facts of expatriate life, and have been for scores of years. All those Americans in Hiroo and Japanese in Scarsdale are aware that they could shift their spending habits by "going native," but their patterns of behavior through all these years tell us that they are not about to venture out and make those sacrifices.

Of course there are the rare exceptions to this generalization. For all the years I worked with Japanese expatriates coming into the New York area, very few ever elected to live outside the confines of Fort Lee (termed Fort Apache by some) and Scarsdale. One such independent expat, a wonderful, jovial character, happily moved to the Upper East Side of New York City with his wife and young children, and proceeded to dive into that young, vibrant neighborhood with gusto. For several years I would trudge up First Avenue in the New York City Marathon, and as I would approach the 77th

Street intersection, there he and his family would be positioned, replete with a homemade sign urging me on and, that priceless marathon commodity—cold water. Out would come his camera, we'd pose with each family member, and after the requisite handshakes I'd be back to the running grind but with their waves and broad smiles.

There was no doubt that Takaya-san was relishing his family's foray into a New York City neighborhood that was totally devoid of other Japanese experts. Indeed, Mr. Takaya has American counterparts sprinkled around Japan who have no intention on settling into an expatriate cluster. But no expatriate system that I know of expects that to happen. The costs are constructed on highly inflated clustered living, not branching out alone in the local economy.

3. "Replacing monthly allowances with lump-sum payments at the beginning and/or the end of the assignment, especially if these payments can be made in a low-tax location."

Here again, the obstacle in the way of getting this done will be management's need to reduce the entitlement tradition that has plagued overseas assignments ever since the first oil programs of the 1950s. Steadfast traditions die slowly, and even if the management of a company recognizes the sense of changing over to lump sums paid outside the host country (should tax rates be an issue there), the main objection of the expats will be that the other multinationals are not implementing that "take-away."

4. "Timing the payment of various components (including performance incentives) in a tax advantageous manner to limit tax equalization payments."

Here you managers will not find any expatriate resistance. The entire matter of excessive management costs for tax equalization is, for them, a matter for the financial people to work out. And as long as they continue to receive the same amounts after tax Mr. Tilghman's proposal makes sense.

5. "Reducing or eliminating allowances over time."

As expatriates begin to feel comfortable with the host location, there is no doubt that they become better shoppers, more effective users of public transport, and so on. The only issue here is the length of the transition period after which the allowances would be reduced and, finally, eliminated. That topic will be revisited in our discussion of longer-term assignments.

Strategic Issues
The balance sheet approach does not link up with long-term planning, whether it be for the company's or the employee's future. Instead "it cre-

ates a pay-to-buy mentality that causes people to focus on pay more than on the career opportunity and performance. It's also inconsistent with the approach of thinking globally, acting locally. The more expatriates are paid differently from local nationals, the less likely alignment with business goals is, and the more probable are equity concerns of local nationals," write authors Patricia Zingheim and Jay Schuster in their aptly titled book: *Pay People Right! Breakthrough Reward Strategies to Create Great Companies.*[9]

In other words, the emphasis of the balance sheet is to solve a problem of today's difference between the home and host countries' economic impact on the expatriate family unit. The size of the package has nothing to do with the future. And with no link to business or compensation strategies, the balance sheet would appear really to be a Band-Aid approach, rather than serving as a fundamental part of a remedy to enable both the company and the employee to look forward to the next steps of growth.

Just consider the significant incremental compensation allowances and premiums; they overshadow the critical piece of what compensation was intended to be, a reward for performance. If the merit increase, noted universally for its stress on pay for performance, is totally overwhelmed by all the premiums, special bonuses, and allowances of the package (all of which are not within the direct control of the expatriate), then the underlying message to the expat becomes abundantly clear—"Performance is not that important anymore." Yet, now more than ever, intense global competition ought to stimulate the major players to construct reward systems that leave no doubt that good performance will be abundantly recognized and rewarded. The balance sheet simply ignores performance.

Earlier we looked at the stages of development that companies transition through on their way to becoming truly global players. In that chapter we perceived those steps as a way to figure out how important overseas jobs were to the company at each phase of the global development process. Now we can return to those same four stages, but this time to analyze how differently each of those categories of companies can link their growth strategy to rewarding the efforts of their employees on overseas assignments. As each of these companies moves from one stage to another, the expatriates become increasingly important in implementing further overseas growth strategies.

In their 1996 *American Compensation Association Journal* article entitled

"Linking International Business and Expatriate Compensation Strategies," authors William Sheridan and Paul Hansen observe:

> Each stage of globalization leads to a set of inherent assumptions about the employment conditions under which expatriates should operate. In turn, each expatriate compensation approach also is based on a set of inherent assumptions about expatriates. . . . For example, if the stage of globalization is at the export level (global strategy: representation of product/ service), the human resources required would be heavily expatriates, whereas if the company had reached the truly global stage of development (global strategy: borderless management and the leverage of internal capabilities) the use of its human resource would be a cost-effective blend of expatriates and locals.[10]

Consequently, the export organization will use "out and back" expats more than the global-bound organization that may want to stimulate growth everywhere with the help of expatriates who have built effective local staffs before and can be counted upon to live a full career in expatriate/local staff development. Those "out and back" expatriates would be far more appropriate for the balance sheet approach than the three other stages of corporate growth. Those two types of expats should have totally different reward systems and career incentives, not to mention how their performances are going to be evaluated. While the export firm is simply looking for a quick fix by the expat, the global firm needs an expat who can thoroughly understand how to work with and grow the local staff; and that could take a very brief period or an eternity.

For all the debate over the effectiveness of the balance sheet approach, it continues to be utilized by about two-thirds of the major multinationals—a large majority of the multinational firms today.

Home (Parent) Country as Standard

Instead of employing comparisons between the host country and the individual employee's country of origin, companies using the parent country plan treat the expat in the same compensation mode regardless of where he or she is assigned. Unlike the balance sheet, which tries to reach back to the country of origin (difficult when the expat is a third country national; there are separate tables of indexes for them), the parent country sets up one compensation system matrix that applies to all expatriates, regardless of their country of origin. The glorious simplicity is here—no adjustments are made to the pay levels (usually set by a combination of corporate hierarchy and years of service, generally in a matrix format by salary grade).

The benefit of simplicity must be balanced against the need to create program standards that will be generally perceived as fair to the expatriate populations—and the price the company pays for this is to select for use a relatively high-cost country such as the United States or France as its headquarters standard. Then once the base salaries are set for the expatriates, they include what would have been separate allowances. Housing is reimbursed or provided for and all benefit plans are company sponsored, with little in the way of contributions required from the expatriate. These packages are indeed rich, but there is some offset for management in the sense that it creates a highly flexible basis for transfers anywhere. There are few administrative difficulties and no need to make continuous cost-of-living comparisons between home and host countries.

Let's see how this system operates.

A CASE STUDY:
SCHLUMBERGER'S INTERNATIONAL STAFF

We've described this global player before, in connection with its successful overseas posting pattern. Now we'll focus on its compensation approach.

To attract and retain those engineers, the company decided it would construct a generous package; after all, what was being offered to the young engineer expatriates was a series of three-year assignments in some of the most difficult work sites in the world. We often heard the engineer lament, "Why is it that nature put these reservoirs in these places—the North Sea, Prudhoe Bay, the Sahara desert, northern Sumatra? Why not just outside San Francisco?" No such luck for these twenty-something engineers; they were going to endure physical and mental hardships.

Recruited from the best universities around the world, these engineers have joined an International Staff, with a completely independent set of compensation and benefits programs from their countries of origin. There is no need to track cost-of-living indexes. The base salary structure is substantial enough to protect against those economic issues. They are paid in U.S. dollars, and their base-salary calculations are drawn on the highest of Western competitive rates for engineers. They have a profit-sharing program that ties bonuses to company performance.

Should the expat ever be repatriated, he or she loses the International Staff status and is returned to the local staff employment conditions. Those reward levels are designed to be competitive in their respective marketplaces. However, these are often considerably less attractive than the International Staff schedule. The net effect is to keep the engineers on the cycle of overseas assignments until retirement or voluntary termination.

Parent country systems can also work effectively if there are relatively small amounts of expatriates being employed overseas. The size factor usually comes into play by virtue of the fact that contracting for a full balance sheet approach with a consultant is too expensive, given the few employees assigned overseas.

Parent country programs offer the distinct advantage of facilitating successive overseas assignments, which is the Schlumberger strategy. Unlike the balance sheet, which may call for a huge increase or decrease in company costs to maintain the host/home countries cost of living balance, the parent system continues to govern, in the same way it had been administered at the last host country.

Another unique factor about this system in its particular application by Schlumberger is that the actual work sites—the rigs and platforms—are often so remotely located that there is little opportunity for these engineers to spend their base salaries. At early ages these engineers would be forced to save or invest their substantial earnings. By way of example, I encountered a 28-year-old Canadian engineer in El Tigre, by the Orinoco Basin, who had already saved more in his six years with the company than his parents had earned in their lifetimes. He proudly described how he had just finished arranging a purchase of a new home for his parents in Manitoba. Here was a young man with a forced savings plan that worked. He freely admitted that had he been posted near a desirable social center he would have blown the money away, but as a young bachelor, he figured that could all wait until his departure from the company.

The parent system has at least one distinct disadvantage; it gives birth to a two-class system of employees. The economic benefits of being on the International Staff can cause local staff resentment, particularly if the work being performed is roughly comparable. But the company has to maintain a generous reward system for the demanding work in difficult work sites. Otherwise there is little about such a career that would attract and retain bright engineers. These engineers are given thorough technical training, and their responsibilities, testing for oil reservoirs under the ground, have such huge financial implications that the high level of reward still makes sense for the company.

Region of Countries as Standard

Where countries have similar economic structures and there are frequent transfers of expatriates among those countries (particularly true in banking today), another expatriate rewards program that can be used is the averaging together of those countries into one consolidated region for the purpose of making the balance sheet adjustments. The combination process allows the company to make some cost-cutting adjustments that result in substantially lower allowances than would be generated from a pure balance sheet, and is certainly far less costly than the parent country system. Generally, companies using this system do not add the foreign service premium to the rewards package, under the philosophy that there are no serious adjustments to make if one is being expatriated from and to countries with similar cultures. Consider the economic and cultural differences between Denmark and Norway. They are unquestionably important, but in degree they do not represent the same level of challenges as a United States to Tokyo expatriate assignment, or vice versa.

Western Europe, Scandinavia, and the Middle East are all prime candidates for companies desiring to consolidate and simplify their nation-by-nation balance sheet accountings, particularly if they frequently transfer expatriates between nations in the combined group. But if there are substantial amounts of transfers out of or into the region, then the old specter of perceived unfairness through differences in rewards levels raises its ugly head.

HOST NATION AS STANDARD

This program, also called "destination pricing," is also simple to administer and can be extremely cost effective, depending on the costs at the host nation. It assumes that all employees working at the host location should receive the same rewards packages. This approach has the benefit of removing the two-class system that the parent program has built in to it, and that depending on the expatriate's country of origin, the balance sheet would produce.

Several compensation professionals have recently debated the merits of moving to the host location as standard for expatriate rewards, and their points are worth consideration for you managers who are charged with responsibility for managing the expatriate program. Rick Swaak, formerly Vice President, International Human Resources Services, National Foreign Trade Council, Inc., reviewed the rationale for selecting the "destination pricing" system in an article in *Global Outlook*:[11]

> With talents being sourced from all over the world and a very competitive global economic environment to contend with, companies will emphasize the importance of keeping expatriate costs in line with local compensation practices. It does not make sense to treat expatriates as "favored" employees. They are in a foreign location to do a job—often to hire and develop another employee. U.S. companies do not give special privileges to transferees within the U.S. who perform similar tasks. Treating expatriates differently from their peers in the host country will eventually backfire.

One notable exception to the rule that all expatriates and local staff will be treated alike is in pension coverage. Most companies will see the wisdom in maintaining the home country pension eligibility while overseas, since the outcome of a series of overseas pension entitlements will be a disaster for the expatriate. Under such a scenario, an expat would have small entitlements in the various plans and would have not gained vesting rights in those accrued amounts. Another exception to pure local adaptation is found in the housing allowance, where many organizations recognize the extreme contrasts between housing levels of acceptability between cultures, and consequently these organizations often provide a special housing allowance, depending on the particular circumstances of the host country contrasted with the country of origin.

This system can create wonderful windfalls or financial tragedies for expatriates, depending on their original cost-of-living standards and whether the host nation happens to be more advanced or backward than their countries of origin.

In our example, expatriate John would be offered French compensation and benefits coverage. That package would be similar to one in the United States, so it might not be a meaningful factor in his decision to accept or reject the Paris offer. But suppose he were up for consideration for an overseas vacancy in Mexico City? Or Calcutta?

Such "downers" offset the career benefits for taking an overseas assignment, so that some enhancement is needed for these programs, usually in the form of a premium paid up front but not technically considered part of the ongoing compensation package. Without such an incentive, John's knowledge of pay in Mexican pesos at Mexican compensation rates would be a deal breaker. But just think of Juan, his coemployee working in the Mexico facility, who would be delighted to be transferred to the United States with a complete set of U.S. standard programs covering his entire spectrum of compensation and benefits.

What is the net effect of constructing these starkly contrasting reward levels? The mobility issue becomes a significant obstacle to further expatriate assignments. In the two situations just posed, it will be like pulling wisdom teeth to get Juan to leave his New York assignment. John, used to a U.S. way of living, may want to leave his Mexico City job, no matter how challenging it is, for a position that will more comfortably suit the entire Jones family. For this reason, companies that do not have work operations in developing countries do not utilize the destination system.

Even though there are logical arguments for the host-based system, few companies have actually been bold enough to try it.

Better of Home or Host-Based Systems

These programs offer the more generous option to the employee and the more costly to the employer of the two programs already described. What makes these programs unique is that no one is ever certain, depending on the country of origin and the host country, which system will be utilized, since economic conditions for the two nations are bound to change continually.

This element of uncertainty stands in the way of accepting a single program that will benefit the expatriate most fairly. Table 8.1 reviews the 1991 and 1998–1999 usage of the various plans as surveyed by the International Human Resources Guide, an e-commerce organization making its results available over the Internet, quoting in turn a PricewaterhouseCoopers (PwC) Survey of Expatriate Tax and Compensation Policies.[12]

What do these practices tell us? The balance sheet (home-based) continues to dominate although it is widely recognized for its long-term shortcomings. Perhaps this is why so many companies are making modifications to the basic process to allow career and merit considerations to play their justly critical roles. The better of home or host–based programs continue to receive low popularity because they are patently difficult to rely upon, since economic circumstances could cause a switch in systems during assignments. For all the reasons why host country–based compensation makes sense, it remains too onerous for most companies to tackle, perhaps because the perceived "takeaways" by the expatriates will amount to assignment rejections by the bushel.

"Other" in this survey set forth in Table 8.1 presumably means individually negotiated packages, which can only spell trouble in the future for any firm that is serious about global expansion. The precedence that every individual deal carries with it will seldom be limited to one expatriate. There will always be trading of compensation data as long as expatriates are assigned anywhere around the globe. It is to their best interest to compare, and any package that has a particular piece that is not included in one's own will soon be presented as a grievance for the company to consider, just to catch up.

Each company, in the end, needs well-informed managers to guide it

Table 8.1   Headquarters-, Home-, or Host-Based Systems

Method of Expatriate Compensation	1991 Results	1998–1999 Results
Headquarters-based	29.8%	28.3%
Home country–based	47.8%	50.6%
Modified home country–based	12.2%	16.4%
Better of home or host–based	2.1%	2.6%
Host country–based	4.6%	1.1%
Other	3.6%	1.1%

Data Source: PricewaterhouseCoopers, 1999 Survey of Expatriate Tax and Compensation Policies, as quoted by International Human Resources Guide.

through the process of selecting and implementing the kind of compensation program that fits snugly into its strategic growth mode. The right system will serve to attract and retain the kinds of expatriates it will need to further expand its global presence. The financial people will always present costs as a major factor in this process, and indeed they will always play a key role in deciding which compensation course to take.

Developmental Assignments

We reviewed the various reasons prompting these assignments earlier in Chapter 2.

Originally the developmental assignees were treated under the same compensation policies as those performing ongoing jobs. As companies began to appreciate that these people were not really contributing value to the host operation (at least in the initial stages of their assignments) they began to curtail some of the more expensive premiums and allowances, the rationale being that the nature of the assignment did not really represent a sacrifice for the expatriate; but rather a growth opportunity. It should be looked upon by the expat as a "glass half full." As such, these companies do not offer a foreign service or mobility premium, and do not offer a completion bonus at the end of the tour.

The other elements of the expatriate package were essentially retained. The duration of these assignments was shorter than the job replacements, often just of one or two years' duration.

Long-Term Assignments

Some positions, such as country manager already discussed, by their nature are going to require substantial periods of time to assimilate into the host country culture. As these assignments proceed, usually past the fourth year, many companies begin gradually to reduce the various allowances and premiums on the ground that there is no longer much of a sacrifice for the expatriate family unit's part because they are presumed to have comfortably settled in. They will have found the most economical places to shop, have determined the best means of transportation, have begun to master the local language, and so on. We will examine more ramifications of longer-term assignments in our discussion of assignment extensions in Chapter 10.

These assignments frequently start out as the normal three-year term, but often begin to be extended because of projects to complete or success with particular clients or customers that makes the departure of this expatriate awkward for the company. If there are no schooling issues, the family can also effectively adapt to the culture, making social friends and gaining acceptance in the community. HR people occasionally write off these people as "having gone native," because they have lost touch with the central nerve center of the company. They are respected for knowing a whole lot about the host country, but just where can that knowledge take them in the pursuit of a broader career?

Both expatriates and managers have a duty, as an assignment gets seriously extended, to sit down and plan the alternatives that will emanate from the extension. What sorts of issues upon repatriation or subsequent overseas posting will there be in light of so much time devoted to one location? What forms of training can be customized for this expatriate so that there will not be developmental needs arising as a result of the extension? Should the mentors be brought in to review what impact on this expatriate's career will be produced by the extension? All of these factors need to be reviewed prior to making the final decision to go forward with the extension, including the time when the next review will be set for a reexamination of the assignment.

Is it fair to reduce or eliminate premiums and allowances in these situations? After all, the expatriate family unit is making an extra sacrifice in being away from their country of origin, and that sacrifice grows, not contracts, with the additional time spent away from home. It is also fair to understand how many of the initial allowances and premiums meant for keeping pace with their former home no longer are that logical; the expat family is not expected back shortly. And they have found all those convenient shortcuts and devices to survive in the host economy. Their shopping and transportation bills inevitably are reduced, and they are able to find a lifestyle that is comfortable for them. Managers are about equally divided as to whether the package ought to be cut back in these situations, even where the policy book contains language that it should happen.

Depending on the value of the expatriate to the organization, the managers and HR may decide to continue the expat on full allowances and premiums. In this day of active competition for good, seasoned expatriates, it would seem the height of folly to reduce the compensation package for an individual who has proven his or her worth. The saying "penny wise, pound foolish" applies to these cases. While the majority of companies continues to opt for the most expensive of housing allowances and continue rich mobility and foreign service premiums to encourage a willingness to go overseas, how can managers justify pulling back compensation from expatriates who have demonstrated their abilities over an extended period of time at the host location?

Now that we've identified the major varieties of compensation packages that are structured for each of the purposes of assignments for expatriates, let's review the individual ingredients that make up those packages.

Elements of the Basic Compensation Package

BASE SALARY

We have already reviewed the need to establish the fairest rate through either home country job evaluation or destination surveys.

SPECIAL INCENTIVE PAYMENTS

Managers need to attract the best performers for overseas work, and often the straight base salary comparison between the candidate's present job and the salary range set for the expatriate position may not accommodate comfortably the proposed new salary (i.e., it may be over the maximum of the salary grade, a definite no-no for all salary administrators). In these cases, imagination can really help. Payments for completing the assignment, or for even starting it can be paid in lump sums.

Another favorite: The candidate can be offered participation in a company profit-sharing or stock option plan. The whole point is that the candidate will look at all the allowances and premiums as just the company's way of keeping him or her even with someone who, given the same base pay, had decided to remain in the home country. The only drawback with these various incentive programs is that they will eventually be circulated among other expats, at which time another chorus of "me, too" begins to resonate in the HR hallway.

FOREIGN SERVICE PREMIUMS

These payments, now coming under close financial scrutiny, are made to compensate the expatriate family for their separation from family, friends, community, social activities, and business associates. They also can be justi-fied by all the angst that goes with settling into a new culture, trying to grapple with the transportation system, finding where and how to shop, and so forth. Because these are all highly intangible factors, there has been a running dialogue between HR and the finance people as to whether these payments, usually a percentage of base pay paid out each pay period, are re-ally required as a carrot anymore.

Critics of this payment point out that the globalization process has con-verted overseas assignments into a "must do" for employees seeking to get ahead in their corporate organizations rather than a "nice to have." If so, they argue, why reward employees for doing something they ought to be do-ing to better their own interests?

MOBILITY PREMIUMS

The justification for this premium is roughly similar to the foreign service premiums. It is paid out as a lump sum at the start and/or the completion of an overseas assignment in recognition of the fact that the expat family was willing to move in the first place. Some companies elect to make this pay-ment only at the start, and others only upon completion, of the assignment.

COMPLETION BONUSES

These payments are targeted to ensure that the posting is completed. One wonders how often that bonus actually fulfills that objective. Managers are fully aware of the high incidence of postings that are not completed to their original terms, and therefore hold this carrot out at the end of the assign-ment in the event that the expat is considering an early departure. While these bonuses may actually retain some good performers who are straddling the issue of departure, they also have the downside effect of creating pressures for holding poorer performers to the end. These expats, the brownouts, might otherwise have left.

So the question arises, in what circumstances will this bonus really benefit the company? Brownouts, the principal benefactors, who probably considered quitting but are continuing on to receive this bonus, are not doing the company any favor by grimly holding on to their jobs. We've all known brownouts during various assignments. They force you to work around them to get things done. The company and other expats and local staff would operate more smoothly if the brownout decided to physically leave rather than sit there but be mentally alert.

The acceptance of employees no longer working hard but collecting their pay is a poor management practice. Moreover, it is a morale destroyer.

HARDSHIP PREMIUMS

This premium is paid out on a regular payday basis for being at a location that has been defined by HR as difficult enough to warrant additional payments. Conditions calling for this extra payment can be heat, cold, unfriendly culture, remoteness, and so on. In some of the smaller oil barracks of the Middle East, the hardship premiums were doubled and even tripled over the standard rate set for a generic hardship location.

The only matter of contention when it comes to evaluating hardship premiums is figuring out who is going to be the fairest judge of what constitutes a hardship. That starts with a clear definition (very difficult) and an impartial observer to apply that definition to the host location.

In order to avoid constant bickering over the relative pain of place A to place B, companies are best advised to seek the aid of knowledgeable third parties to make these decisions. Line managers, don't give that no-win job to HR; they've got it tough enough.

"Hardship" is a concept that comes down to the eye of the beholder.

DANGER PAY

This payment, usually made in lump sums, results from direct exposure to truly hazardous situations. Examples that we can review were camps in southern Sudan that were surrounded by hostile forces, and the artillery bombardments of a Dow-Schlumberger district headquarters in Basra by the Iranian artillery. It is calculated as a percentage of base salary and paid out on each regular payday. Many companies use the U.S. State Department's designation that a specific area is in fact dangerous in order to justify extra pay.

None of these premiums are included in calculations for any benefits or pension plans.

In a revealing survey conducted by PricewaterhouseCoopers (PwC) of Expatriate Tax and Compensation Policies,[13] the participating companies were asked if they provided an incentive premium to employees accepting an overseas assignment. In 1991, 31.5 percent of the companies reported no, and by 1998–1999 that percentage had climbed to 38.1 percent. A further trend was clear; in 1991, 41.9 percent paid the premiums per pay period, but by 1998–1999, that percentage had slipped to 26.7 percent. These kinds of premiums generally run as high as 15 percent of base salary.

COST OF LIVING ALLOWANCES

These were detailed in our exploration of the balance sheet system. They also prevail in all of the various formats except for the host country programs.

MEDICAL INSURANCE PROGRAMS

Benefits managers can make this difficult issue a lot easier for expats by continuing U.S. health care provisions at the host location. However, this is often not feasible, depending on the laws or practices prevalent in some nations. That sends the issue to the host location benefits manager to find a reasonable plan to offer the home country management. The target here is for managers to find the same general level of coverage at the same employee cost as was the case in the home country while ensuring that the employees are receiving reasonable coverage.

SAVINGS AND RETIREMENT PLANS

Again, the benefits manager is the keystone for identifying what kinds of plans can be transported overseas and, if they can apply at the host location, what modifications need to be made to them. Here the goal is to keep the level of plan entitlements equal to what had been in effect in the home country. This ought to optimize expat continued participation in 401(k) and company retirement plans where possible. Government-sponsored benefit programs in the host country are all going to involve extra employee contribution costs without the likelihood of receiving benefits.

RELOCATION COSTS

Virtually all companies will reimburse these regular costs, as spelled out in the overseas manual. However, don't purchase a residence overseas thinking that if you sell it at a loss the company will pick up that loss as a reimbursement. I saw that attempted at NBC, supposedly based on a literal reading of the manual. The only problem was that no one, neither host country manager nor expat, could actually find that clause. Rent instead. It's a lot more fluid when you need to depart the assignment.

TAX AND LEGAL HELP

Most companies will contract with a host location accounting firm with ties to the United States in order to facilitate the tax return process. Legal help is rarely offered through the company unless it is directly associated with another benefit, such as housing.

PERFORMANCE BONUSES

Managers at overseas locations are mindful of the diminishing role that performance pay actually plays in the overall expatriate package. For this reason, those managers ought to make every effort to inject as much performance reward into the package as possible, both through merit and promotional increases to base salary as well as through periodic performance bonuses.

In summary, the programs just listed represent most of the current expatriate rewards systems used by multinationals today. As noted at the beginning of the chapter, expatriate experts are still trying to solve the mystery of a fair yet simple reward system.

The Future? Using Organization Culture and Location Standards to Establish Multiple Reward Systems

Earlier we studied William Sheridan's idea that multinationals could improve their reward systems substantially by linking their compensation systems directly to their stage in the globalization development curve. Mr. Sheridan pointed out how cost-ineffective the present systems are, and that eliminating the costly perks for expats at a given destination where the value of that expat is no longer cost-effective would be a fair way to pay for the expat's real value to that specific location under the requirements of the stage of growth that the corporation has reached globally. This presumes the expat's unique knowledge of technology, finance, and so on is no longer well ahead of local staff skills (i.e., the productivity gap has narrowed so substantially that a local staff person might be able to perform the expat's job).

In this proposal, Mr. Sheridan removes the linkage to the expat's home nation. Instead the link is made to the company's business strategy and its local market. This program will please controllers. It operates within the reality of the company as its own world. The only reference point is back to the actual work location pay rates, governed by the guidelines for that stage of global growth that the corporation has entered.

The proposed system has much logic to it; it succeeds in reducing the traditional line of inequity between expat and local reward for comparable work. Progressive HR people should spend some serious time with that article. The initial drawback, reduced expat rewards, may be in the offing anyway, since many organizations are at last paring down the rich bonuses and premiums systems that accompanied the balance sheet approach like a glove.

George T. Milkovitch, Cornell's M. P. Catherwood Professor, Center for Advanced Human Resource Studies, and Professor Matt Bloom of Notre Dame have come up with a somewhat similar concept to Mr.

Sheridan's. In their 1998 article *Compensation and Benefit Review*[14] Professors Milkovitch and Bloom start their presentation with a review of the traditional contribution of national cultures to present pay systems. They describe how Hofstede's work on national characteristics had shaped the management of international compensation. For example, where a country's character stresses the power-distance dimension (Malaysia and Mexico), the pay structure ought to call for a more hierarchical system, whereas a more individualistic national character (the United States and Australia). An individualistic national character would support more performance-based pay systems.

The authors believe that those national characteristics are no longer relevant, having been supplanted by a wide variety of local cultural characteristics. These, in turn, influenced by political, economic, and other forces, are today's real factors in influencing behavior.

Similar to Mr. Sheridan's proposal, the two professors would link the total compensation so that employee contributions could support organizational goals. They break the total package into three separate pieces:

1. **Core:** Competitive cash, basic benefits, performance-based employability, and work challenges. This piece reflects the corporate global mind-set, and would be consistent throughout the world.

2. **Customize:** This piece assumes there is a business unit or regional management that has discretion to select certain programs that would make the company more competitive in their respective areas. They are base/bonus mix, stock options, and flexible schedules.

3. **Choice:** This piece allows the employees to select their own choices among the following programs: base/bonus mix, benefit choices, tax deferral, assignments, and stock purchases.

This mix permits managers to use strategic flexibility, tailoring the compensation to the location as well as offering the employee a selection of some programs.

A distinct advantage of this proposal is that it would end the one-at-a-time compensation or benefits deal that current systems endure on a daily basis. Comparisons among employees would be academic, given the variety of individual choices that the program would provide. Expats would then be comparing the parts of the package they have chosen, not the dimensions of the package itself.

So, here are two versions of the future. They both pull compensation into the strategy mode, they both do away with home country comparisons, and they both offer real flexibility to local management (and even the employee, in Professor Milkovitch's proposal). They both would produce significant cost savings and offer a degree of fairness that exceeds all other current plans except destination pricing.

These ideas deserve your consideration.

Notes

1. "Linking International Business and Expatriate Compensation Strategies," William R. Sheridan and Paul T. Hansen, *American Compensation Association Journal*, Spring 1996, p. 8.
2. "Compensating Expatriates for the Cost of Living Abroad," J. Frank Gaston and John Napier, *National Industrial Conference Board Studies in Labor Statistics*, No. 14, 1955.
3. *Global Relocation Trends, 1998 Survey Report*, Windham International and the National Foreign Trade Council, June 1998, p. 30.
4. "Understanding the Balance Sheet Approach to Expatriate Compensation," Organization Resources Counselors, p. 4.
5. Ibid., p. 5.
6. "For Expatriate Families, a Home Away from Home," Lisa W. Foderaro, *New York Times*, May 7, 2000. Sec. 14, WE p. 8.
7. "Using an Alternative to the Balance Sheet Approach," Don A. Robins and Robert Buwalda, *GROing Connexions*, Global Remuneration Organization, Vol. 2, No. 2, p. 1.
8. "Beyond the Balance Sheet, Developing Alternate Approaches to International Compensation," Thomas S. Tilghman, *American Compensation Association Journal*, Summer 1994, p. 43.
9. *Pay People Right! Breakthrough Reward Strategies to Create Great Companies*, Patricia K. Zingheim and Jay R. Schuster, San Francisco: Jossey-Bass, 2000, p. 326.
10. "Linking International Business and Expatriate Compensation Strategies," 1996, p. 10.
11. "Expatriate Management: The Search for Best Practices," Reyer A. Swaak, *Global Outlook*, March–April 1995, p. 27.

12. "Expatriate Policy Development," International Human Resources Guide, www.hresource.com/hresources/samplechapters/ihrsSampleChapter-5.htm Nov. 4, 1999.
13. Ibid., p. 2.
14. "Rethinking International Compensation," George T. Milkovitch, M. P. Catherwood Professor, Center for Advanced Human Resource Studies, New York State School of Industrial and Labor Relations, Cornell University, and Matt Bloom, assistant professor, College of Business Administration, University of Notre Dame, reprinted from the *Compensation and Benefits Review*, by the American Management Association, 1998, pp. 4–7.

Illustration by Liz Lomax

What Are the Issues to Consider While the Assignment Is in Progress?

CHAPTER
9

What Are the Issues to Consider
While the Assignment Is in Progress?

"Lead, kindly Light, amid the encircling gloom;
Lead thou me on!
The night is dark and I am far from home;
Lead thou me on!"

> John Henry, Cardinal Newman,
> *The Pillar of Cloud* (1833), "Lead,
> Kindly Light," st. 1

The Jones family unit's arrival at the host country is a partly exciting and partly traumatic event, and very memorable, especially for the children. The predeparture cross-cultural training and the orientation trip should have substantially reduced that trauma. However, most humans, despite the most effective aids, still have some natural trepidation over how a three-year living experience in a totally different cultural environment will work out.

How does John fill out this work permit? What if the apartment that Jane selected on the orientation trip is not ready? Do the children need to visit the school for interviews or registration? How will John and Jane cope with driving around strange streets and neighborhoods? These and a hundred other nagging questions accompany the Jones family just as assuredly as their baggage. And speaking of locating all our stuff in this maze, where's beloved Fang?

Let's review the essentials for furnishing initial support to the Jones family.

Linking Up An Orientation Family

Paris HR can structure the entry process to reduce the inevitable stress by appointing a willing expatriate or local staff family to serve as transitional helpers. That process starts at the airport terminal where their help facilitates the Jones family to navigate the Charles de Gaulle complex facility. Ideally, HR arranged a greeter to help the Jones family during their orientation trip.

The greeter should be able to help locate where the baggage is, and where the family dog can be retrieved, and to arrange transportation to Paris and their new apartment (or more likely, a hotel where they can stay while finding a suitable place).

Security

There is no more fundamental need than the basic knowledge of how to avoid dangerous situations in a new community. In our sample expat assignment case, the Jones family is coming to one of the most civilized cities in the world. Yet like any other major metropolis, Paris has some difficult neighborhoods, particularly after dark, as well as a great many street demonstrations. Again, these basics should have been covered in the original cross-cultural program. But if they were not covered, host country management has a basic responsibility to monitor the risk exposures confronting its expatriate family units.

Almost two-thirds of U.S.-based multinationals have formal security plans in effect at their host locations. Managers ought to see to it that all their locations have such plans, and that those plans are regularly communicated to the staff. But, you ask, as we now have a world devoid of major conflicts, are there still valid reasons to be so concerned about security issues?

The answer is an unqualified yes. Let's look back only a few years to review what events have been occurring that should stimulate serious thinking about personal safety overseas.

For example, the 1998 civil unrest in Indonesia, a country highly populated with expatriates from around the world, caused more than 500 deaths and extensive damage to properties. Much of that violence flared in the capital, Jakarta, where there are several expat living clusters. Among the U.S. multinationals, the U.S. State Department estimated that over half the 9,000 to 15,000 U.S. expats in Indonesia had to be evacuated.

Indeed, managers should construct and communicate contingency relocation plans. Those companies that had such plans performed many of the evacuations in Indonesia. Luckily for those expats working for employers without such plans, most of them were able to hitch transportation away from the rioting. As their manager, how would you have reacted to the challenge of getting your expat out when you had no planned way to do it? Friends of mine were caught in that situation in northern Sumatra and were not appreciative of their employer's oversight.

In fact, the 1999 NFTC survey disclosed that one-third of that study's participating companies had no formal security plans in place.[1] Another 53 percent of them had plans in place but they were limited to only "challenging" locations. Who can predict, considering some of the world's more violence-prone terrorist groups, what location is "nonchallenging"? Is Paris or Rome or New York on that list? Just recall all the car bombings that had pained Paris one summer and the World Trade Center bombing a few years ago in New York City, not to mention the complete closing of the U.S. embassy in Rome following the bomb threats of January 2001.

You managers should also be aware that 60 percent of the Fortune 500 companies carry ransom insurance. Indeed, the Hiscox Group, a London specialty insurer, reported that worldwide kidnappings for ransom in 1999 hit a record 1,789, up 6 percent from 1998.[2]

Another segment of that survey showed that only 24 percent of the responding multinationals gave any form of security training to their overseas assignment people. Managers ought to ensure that their plans are understood and that the training required to activate those plans is furnished to the expats on a regular basis. What steps can you managers take to be forearmed in the event of a security issue?

KPMG consultants William Hibbitt and Timothy Dwyer have proposed the following four security guidelines:

1. Expatriate programs must include contingency planning and crisis management procedures.

2. A company's first step in preparation is to stay informed of potential hot spots by developing a network of information sources, including non-U.S. sources.

3. Cooperating with other multinationals in the country to share resources and information can be an effective way to quickly mobilize an evacuation.

4. Costs of dealing with a country crisis should be assessed and anticipated, including tax implications for expatriates whose foreign residence status may be jeopardized by a removal.[3]

For both managers and expatriates, there is guidance on the World Wide Web for planning techniques through the Overseas Security Advisory Council: http://ds.state.gov. And a final tip for you expats in places such as the Middle East or Africa: You should grow strong relationships with your local staff as to possible violence rumblings; they often will have heard some news that has not yet reached government officials.

I'm reminded of a memorable visit to Havana one New Year's Eve, aboard a British ship. There had been rumors that Fulgencio Batista's government was about to crumble, with Fidel Castro waiting in the mountains to take over. No less than the U.S. ambassador at the time assured us that it would be safe to go ashore that evening. Of course, the late night turned into a violent nightmare, with mobs breaking into shops and shooting at anyone in uniform. Batista had suddenly fled, and there was fighting all over the city. The ambassador had not received accurate information to pass along to us, but all the taxi drivers and shopkeepers at the pier knew, hours ahead, that the city was about to erupt into serious street violence.

You never can tell who really has access to the real possibilities of danger. Have your family understand that when any of them receives word of any impending problem to let you know. Don't wait for the ambassador's alert.

Management owes it to every expat family to spell out the basics in protection. There's a fine line between scaring people about local conditions and instructing them about recommended procedures. Professionals should be able to walk that line.

Housing

Hopefully, the expatriate and spouse, like the Jones family, had been of-fered and accepted a preassignment house-hunting trip that flowered into a final selection of a residence. If not, the first few weeks of the assignment may have to be given over to getting the family unit an appropriate ac-commodation, without which there is the distinct possibility that the ex-pat will be diverted from his or her direct attention from job matters by concern about his or her family's comfort. Relocation services abound globally, and if your company does not have an adequate staff to support the expat and family in this search, it will be worth the investment to sup-ply a trusted realtor to accelerate the house-hunting process. An expatri-ate's initial time at the host country ought to be largely spent with his or her manager and, hopefully, the departing incumbent. If that opportunity has been missed because of house-hunting and school-finding expeditions, the company and the expatriate have lost valuable ground in the process of coming up to speed.

Expatriates, in their quest to find just the right level of housing, should remember that a major factor shall be convenient access to the school of your choice. Consequently, you may want to prioritize your searches. Locate the school of your choice and then start the house hunt within an easy ac-cess radius of it.

Schooling

Here again, the preassignment trip should have revealed which schools would be feasible for the expatriate's children. This concern for appropri-ate education is, similar to housing, so basic that a failure to find a com-fortable school for the kids can be so distracting to the expatriate that the business acclimation process can be delayed or diminished by a prolonged search. In a suitably titled article in *HR World*, "The Parent Trap," writer Karen Taylor writes that "school is the main concern of expatriates; with six stumbling blocks, the key one was education with 93 percent of them showing concern."[4]

Managers can provide much-needed support in this process. The local HR people should maintain files of expatriate children's reactions to their educational institution, so that newcomers will have an opportunity to obtain profiles of what the school experiences are really like at the host location.

Timing is essential. The most desirable international schools have waiting lists and personal interview requirements that can be burdensome as first steps after arrival—still another reason why a thorough pre-assignment orientation trip can be so valuable to the expatriate family unit.

Expat parents should use the school visits to carefully evaluate the teachers, the courses, the facilities, and the track records of those institutions in terms of test scores or subsequent schools or colleges that their graduates attended. There is a wide disparity in the quality of overseas educational opportunities available today, so a smart expat family should keep all schooling alternatives open until they have made a final selection.

Here the Web can be of help prior to departure. There are numerous school web sites now available by host countries that describe the curriculum and the backgrounds of their teachers. Often the law of supply and demand appears to control the quality of teaching. In those desirable locations such as London or Paris, international schools seem to have little problem in recruiting quality teachers. But as one considers the more difficult locations, even increased pay packages appear to have done little to attract effective teachers.

School allowances tend to be on the generous side, usually covering all costs of the international schools and a portion of costs for boarding schools when international schools are not available.

Spouse's Job

We saw earlier from survey data that although more than one-half of expatriate spouses had been employed before the overseas assignment, only 11 percent were able to find a new position at the host location. Host country HR and other managers there should network on behalf of the newly arrived spouse. Consider all the new pressures upon him or her; there is a new residence to move into, a new school to find for the children, a new culture to cope with, and, if all those transitions were not enough, a new lifestyle as a stay-at-home rather than a wage earner. These all add up to a thoroughly stressful situation. It is no wonder, then, that "research shows that expatriate couples are one and one-half times more likely to divorce than those who stay at home."[5] HR and the expats need to network their contacts at the host country energetically to ferret out any openings that may be feasible for the newly arrived expat spouse.

Expatriate spouses should experiment with the Web in obtaining sound advice about the host location. One such site, of several, is called "Partner-2-Partner." Managed by the Living Abroad Resource Center, the site gives access, by country, to other spouses and partners, and has chat rooms and networking information. The same service offers information on visas and immigration. Information about the scope of their services is at: www.livingabroad.com.

The spouse's ability to find another job will be a highly beneficial accomplishment. Now the spouse can return to a normal work routine in a business setting (no more being confined to the home) while contributing additional income to the family chest. I've witnessed numerous shaky relationships turn around after the spouse escaped the home and could begin to focus on work again instead of staring at a TV set.

Just consider the difference in the adjustment transition for spouse Jane if she could locate an interesting administrative assistant's position with a nearby employer. Not only will the Jones family benefit from a second income producer, but Jane will not have to endure staying in the apartment all day while the family is away. That depressing alternative is often a problem for expat families. Returning to the workforce ought to be quite a relief for Jane, and, by implication, for the rest of the Jones family.

Automobiles

Managers have an ample set of alternative arrangements governing expatriate automobiles at the host country location:

- The company owns the car or reimburses the employee, in whole or part, for the car's purchase.
- The company provides a loan to the expatriate to make the purchase.
- The company leases the car to the expatriate.
- The company provides an automobile allowance to the expatriate, and it is up to him or her as to whether to purchase a car.

Cars, often with assigned drivers, are assigned to senior managers, but rarely to mid- and lower-level management. As a general rule, the geographical nature of the assignment (i.e., whether there is safe public transportation available at that location) will often determine whether the company will provide an automobile allowance.

Social/Health Clubs

Most companies make reimbursements to the expatriate for social club memberships where there are legitimate business reasons for the use of such a club. Each location presents its priorities in this regard. The American Club in Tokyo is essential for expatriate contacts, while the Dubai Beach Club is essential to maintain one's sanity in the intense heat of Dubai. Virtually all companies have come to recognize the value of a good health club. The only restriction that management seems to have in this area is that the club should be used as an exercise facility rather than as a purely socializing place.

Vacations

U.S. companies' vacation schedules have traditionally called for less time off than those of European organizations. So if our new expatriate, John, is sent to Paris, the French vacation period (namely, the entire month of August) provides a sharp contrast to the two weeks that John, as an average U.S. employee, had been enjoying. How, then, do multinational companies resolve the vacation entitlement issue for the expatriate?

Table 9.1 summarizes findings of PricewaterhouseCoopers, surveying 266 U.S.-based multinational organizations.[6]

An "Other" category, not further defined, received 4.5 percent. Presumably individual negotiations take over at that point. These consultants further reported that the trend from the 1996 results was for more extended vacation entitlements for the expatriate. Perhaps this movement is the positive side of trying to narrow the differences in two-class expatriate and local staff systems.

Establishment of Mentor Relationships

The departure from home country business associates can mean the beginning of a feeling by the expatriate that those people have put him or her "out of sight, out of mind." Now the new expat is out of the loop as to what is happening at the headquarters. The reverse of that departure also begins to loom as a serious concern. They don't know how well he or she is doing on the job at the host location. This double-edged sword, among all the other new worries created by the relocation, can easily cause sleepless nights.

An effective method of helping alleviate these expat doubts is the appointment of effective mentors both at the home and host country locations. Each mentor should act as an adviser to the expat. The home

Table 9.1 Does Vacation Entitlement of Expatriates Change As a Result of the Overseas Assignment?

Company Responses, 1998	Percent of Companies
No	43.3%
Yes—expatriate vacation increased to a minimum of 20.8 workdays	27.7%
Yes—expatriate vacation increased by a minimum of 7.4 workdays	3.4%
Yes—expatriates receive full host country vacation entitlement	11.6%
Yes—expatriates receive the better of the host or home country vacation entitlement	9.4%

Data Source: PricewaterhouseCoopers, 1999 Survey of Expatriate Tax and Compensation Policies.

mentor also serves as a conduit of information about recent job changes, reorganizations, strategy shifts, and so on back at headquarters while conveying whatever messages the expat wants to transmit to the people working in the home country. This communication link can be especially helpful in reminding the assignment people to look out for possible job openings for the expat, either back home as a repatriate or on another overseas posting.

For you expatriates, the home leave provision in your policy manual should be actively used to the maximum. That leave provides you with the opportunity to return to your home business associates and make the eye contact required to remind them of your continuing existence and contributions on behalf of the company. There has been some tendency by expatriates to take the money allocated for home leave and use that fund for vacations instead. For the sake of effective career pursuits, that time away from the host country operation is far better spent back at home headquarters, seeking out your functional counterparts, your expatriate program manager, the manager of training/development, and the management succession people, to find out the latest developments, relay pertinent tidbits of data from your host country operation, and, in general, remind them that you still exist.

The emphasis for the host country mentor is more on acting as a guide as to how the host operation and culture really work. These coaches can point out who are the really effective business associates, both expatriates and local staff, and, conversely, which of those staff people are to be avoided. Host country mentors can also serve as introducers to the family units that can, in turn, give informal advice to each member of the family—schoolteachers who are particularly effective, food shops that sell produce of good quality, the best of the local physicians and dentists, and so on.

Establishing Performance Goals

As the assignment begins to get organized, all of the major distractions need to be rapidly dispatched by both the manager and the new expat before clarifying the specific objectives of what that manager wants to achieve over the course of the performance year. They should review the job description and agree as to the various priorities and timetables for the recurring and project work. They need to agree on periodic informal evaluations of performance, so that any early snags may be identified and rectified. Finally, they need to agree how performance will be judged, who will do the judging, and how the performance will be rewarded.

These steps, if undertaken in a straightforward manner, will save the relationship much in the way of misunderstandings and ineffective communications. There is a natural reluctance to review problems that most managers turn into a general reluctance to approach them directly. No one is truly comfortable informing a subordinate that he or she is not performing up to standard. It is due to this general feeling by managers that the corporate world has witnessed a trend by most performance appraisers to rate the bulk of their people in better-than-average categories (e.g., 4 in a 1 to 5 range for outstanding ratings) instead of positioning the bell-shaped curve around 3, the rating for average performance.

Performance Appraisal Training for Managers

Both managers and expatriates are well aware of the psychological issue of effectively conducting fair, efficient performance appraisals. The best way a company can deal with traditional problems with this is to offer training guidance to the manager. That training requires professional staff people to conduct it effectively, and if there are not enough good in-house people available through the company's own training area, this kind of instruction can be contracted for with a variety of consultants. What are some of the pitfalls that sound training will seek to target? Here is an all-too-brief list of eight "deadly sins" of performance appraisals, courtesy of *HR Matters* magazine,[7] which states, "Training managers to perform effective and consistent evaluations is essential, since both managers and employees often are uncomfortable discussing performance. The training should include warning supervisors to refrain from the following eight common errors that can distort or even invalidate the evaluation process."

1. "Basing the evaluation on the employee's most recent behavior, instead of evaluating the whole performance period." Here we can add that guiding the manager to take copious notes during the entire performance

year is an effective method of bringing back to mind those early performance triumphs and tragedies. Secondly, when the manager sets up periodic performance review meetings monthly, say, the two perceptions of
how the job is going can be fully exchanged without the pressure of a
merit increase or a bonus eligibility hanging over the manager and the
rated employee.

2. "Allowing irrelevant or non-job-related factors to influence the
evaluation, such as physical appearance, social standing, participation in
employee assistance programs, or excused time off for leaves of absence."
Whether you are an expat or a manager of one, if you are located in a
confined or remote host location, these factors inevitably do take on importance. You'll soon appreciate that the nine-to-five aspect of home
country jobs does not apply to many overseas locations, where one winds
up socializing with company associates and their families on a regular basis. Indeed, in some remote locations, the expatriate families can't wait to
break out of the compound and meet someone not from the employing
company. The net of this is that these feelings often serve to influence the
manager's general feelings, and in turn, may be reflected in more specific
job ratings.

3. "Failing to include unfavorable comments on the evaluation, even
when justified." This observation goes to the heart of avoiding an unpleasant confrontation. There should be no surprises in any evaluations,
but if there have been no prior reviews, the manager has no choice but to
tell it like it is. The expatriate, in this case, also has the right to ask why
prior discussions about the subpar performance were not held so that he
or she could have taken action to improve. A good performance appraisal form should have ample room for the rated employee to write
such comments.

4. "Rating all subordinates at about the same point in the scale, usually
in the middle." The scale, if the traditional 1 to 5, works against more fi-
nite gradings because the terminology is so broad that almost any employee could well fit within category 3 or 4. The requirements for
outstanding (5) and subaverage (2) are more specific and require the
manager to make a strong decision to use them. This is especially true
with a 5, which is usually a rating that is required to be specifically substantiated in a backup letter attached to the appraisal form. Most managers shy away from that rigorous requirement and are probably guilty of

underrating some really outstanding expatriates who ought to have, in all fairness, received that rating.

At the other end of the 1 to 5 scale, managers generally give 2 only to employees who have performed so badly that they may be terminated. The 1 rating simply does not exist anymore. Usually the descriptive wording calling for that numerical rating likens the poorly performing expat to a se-rial killer.

5. "Allowing one characteristic of the employee or aspect of the job performance to distort the rest of the rating process." Here is another dif-ficult psychological hurdle for a good manager to overcome. Human na-ture generally guides us to take an outstanding characteristic and apply the judgment of that trait or skill to all the other facets of the job we know much less about. So if an expatriate has unusually fine language skills, it may work to his or her credit when the manager is then asked to evaluate how well he or she gets along with clients, customers, local staff, and others.

6. "Judging all the employees too leniently or too strictly." In these cases the manager has a perception issue, which may best be handled by meeting with his or her own manager to review how high the performance bar ought to be set. We've all had the experience of easy- and difficult-grading teach-ers during our educational careers. In those days we needed to be assured that the comparative rankings were genuinely fair. It is a far more serious situation in the global corporate community, where performance ratings follow expats over the globe, and could come back to either unduly hurt or help the expat in a subsequent assignment or promotion decision. Man-agers ought to verify that their own direct reports are all using essentially the same standards in rating their subordinates.

7. "Allowing one very good or very bad rating to affect all other ratings of the employee." As an important part of the review process, all managers must review the expat's prior performance appraisals before they sit down with the expatriate and review the current evaluation. As the years accrue and a few appraisals turn into larger numbers, the effect of a single good or bad review ought to stand out like a sore thumb. If, on the other hand, there are just a few appraisals in the file of a new employee, the prudent manager ought to review the ratings and the rationales for those ratings carefully. If necessary, that manager may want to reach the original rater to ask further questions about a prior rating.

8. "Permitting personal feelings to bias the evaluation process." This is a problem related to number 2. Managers in remote or small locations have to adjust their professional mind-sets in concentrating on the performance of the job and only those nonjob traits that affect performance.

There is one notable tendency of rating managers that somehow didn't make the list. After years of observing this trait in action, I feel compelled to add another universal poor practice to the list. I refer you the subtle practice of back-ending the final performance appraisal rating to position the rated employee for compensation consideration. Managers will do this either for a merit increase to base salary or for eligibility for a bonus pool payout. In both cases, managers may protest, but this abuse of the appraisal process has to be widespread.

Here's how it thrives. Most salary administration plans revolve around obtaining final performance appraisal ratings and creating a matrix that would then translate that rating into a percentage increase. For example, if a 4 is entitled to a 4 percent to 6 percent merit increase, and a 3 would receive consideration for only a 3 percent to 5 percent raise, a manager could be influenced to raise the rating for employee X from 3 to 4 in order to secure the 6 percent increase that he or she is seeking for that employee. There are all kinds of other factors that are considered when salary review time rolls around annually, but at heart it is that adjustment that creates issues. That manager is given a merit allowable pool, and if he or she has decided to "borrow" some raise money from that pool, there will be someone else who may turn out to have lost the difference in his or her merit increase.

Back-ending also thrives at bonus time. Each company manages its own ground rules for bonus eligibility, sometimes based on title, base compensation level, grade level, and even performance ratings. This, of course, will include an employee with an outstanding rating of 5, if the management has structured a bonus cutoff using the rating as the final cutoff.

These practices do not produce fair results. They demonstrate that the rating system, clearly not a science to begin with, can be manipulated by managers who want to achieve specific compensation objectives through this management tool.

This list of don'ts is not intended to be comprehensive, but a good manager can turn these factors around for dos that should provide some sound guidance in fairly appraising performance.

Who Should Do the Performance Appraisals?

Just who should do performance appraisals is a continuing question for domestic jobs in the United States, and even more difficult for expatriate positions. Long gone are the days when the only reviewer was the direct supervisor. Then his or her manager would have a small space to concur or disagree and sign. For all the historical reasons we have just reviewed, the process was seen by most thinking managers as flawed. How can we get around all the traits issues to find a better cross section of ratings that would round out the performance profile of the rated employee?

The answer comes in the form of employing multiple reviewers. These other associates may not be as directly familiar with the work of the rated employee, but they could add perspectives from various viewpoints: peers, subordinates, even customers or clients. Called the 360-degree process, this methodology has gained considerable support as to jobs in the United States, despite drawbacks in terms of costs and the longer time periods required to complete the process.

When we turn our attention to overseas work, the multiple reviewer process gets even messier. Now we have associates of the rated employee who are located miles and time zones away, but who nevertheless come into contact with the rated expatriate's work and could feasibly render a valuable evaluation of how he or she is performing. Many expatriate jobs have direct ties back to the home country or other operations in the host country region. This multiple network of periodic contacts is then supplemented by regular visits from home country staff and line employees, all on missions to find out how well the host country operation is really doing, and, in particular how John is progressing in his new marketing job in Paris. Who could rate his performance?

Here are a few of the candidates: his immediate manager, the Director of Sales and Marketing; the Country Manager, France; the HR Director, Paris; the Marketing Director, Europe region; the Corporate head of Marketing; his expatriate and Paris staff peers, including the Manager of Sales, France; the entire team of subordinates in the Paris operation working for his function; as well as selected clients and customers in the French market. Each of these people will see John's performance in a slightly different light, but then the challenge is to give fair weighting to each of their observations and ratings.

Despite the complexity of such multiple ratings, this methodology would appear to be a sound investment for any global company trying to get a handle on its more important executives, whether they are assigned in their own country of origin or are on assignment in another country.

Let's examine what the major players are doing about expatriate performance ratings today (respondents provided multiple answers):[8]

Performance review in host country	71%
Performance review in home country	56%
Regular expatriate visits to home office	44%
Regular manager visits to host office	39%
Annual expatriate surveys	19%

The survey sponsors noted that companies with fewer than 100 expatriates favored home country reviews, while companies having more than 100 expats favored host country appraisals. Apparently once the evaluation structure is firmly in place at the host locations, it is more beneficial to delegate these appraisal duties to the employees working there who are qualified to handle them. A significant number of home country reviews may be connected to the increasingly shorter assignments, management development assignments and, very importantly, those project-driven assignments where often the host management may not be able to put the completed project into perspective, while corporate staff in the home country may have had ample other projects in other countries to compare the results in country X with similar work performed in other overseas locations.

Another study adds the element of self-evaluations,[9] listing no less than 10 different candidates for the performance evaluation of an expatriate. (See Table 9.2.)

The same study found that on average an expatriate is evaluated by three individuals, while the same companies that participated in that study re-

Table 9.2 Raters of Expat Performance

Percent of Surveyed Companies Using Raters from Inside the Host Country	*Percent of Surveyed Companies Using Raters from Outside the Host Country*
Supervisor (75%)	Supervisor (41%)
Self (39%)	Regional executive (23%)
HR professionals (12%)	Corporate HR (17%)
Peers (10%)	Sponsor (7%)
Subordinates (7%)	
Customers (1%)	

Note: The percent is the average percentage in which each type of rater is involved in evaluations.
Data Source: Globalizing People through International Assignments, J. Stewart Black et al., Reading, MA: Addison-Wesley, 1999, p. 167.

ported an average of six raters for their home country positions. Another interesting statistic is that inside raters are local staff nationals for one-third of all expat evaluations taking place there.

What Is the Quality of These Appraisals?

If we can believe self-assessments, the same companies taking part in the study just discussed were asked to evaluate the effectiveness of their performance appraisal programs overseas. More than one-half the organizations (53 percent) admitted that the programs were only "average or below average," this assessment coming from the very same managers responsible for those programs. In contrast, those same managers indicated that their programs work much more effectively domestically.

What are the reasons for these overseas problems?

First, the statistics show that only half as many raters are being used overseas as in the home country. This is despite the facts that overseas jobs tend to be broader in scope than their domestic counterparts and the managers come in contact with many more professional associates.

Second, there is an abysmal lack of training given to these raters, both in the home and host country areas.

Third, only 42 percent of the companies in the 1999 NFTC study used clear performance objectives[10] as criteria for assignment success. Unless there are specific goals set out at the inception of the overseas assignment, how can the expatriate be fairly evaluated?

Fourth, the ratings formats do not accurately measure the skills required for success. Most companies use standard evaluation formats that are applied to each location, often the same form as for domestic evaluations, despite the patent fact that overseas jobs require different skills, and those skills in turn can be sharply contrasting from city to city. Management needs to give local managers flexibility in proposing customized changes in the forms and procedures that will be used for their locations. A fine source for obtaining data is to interview former expatriates from each location in order to draw up a composite of what skills are deemed important enough to be used as measuring standards for the appraisal process. As indicated earlier, many organizations really use the appraisal process as a compensation tool, but even that use is virtually irrelevant in most overseas situations where allowances and premiums have grown more important than the core base salary.

The appraisals ought to be used as guidelines for training and development of the expatriate, and should be followed up with a revised set of objectives that are mutually comfortable to the manager and the overseas assignee. A well-done appraisal can also be of help to the management succession manager as well as the functional head. Both can begin to plan ahead for future roles for the expatriate if the appraisal accurately evaluated the pertinent skills and traits required in the present job.

Even the so-called hard standards of sales, net profits, and so on can be affected by currency devaluations, inflation spirals, outside economic market conditions, and other factors over which the expatriate will have little or no control. Each host nation, down to individual city or even work site, should be examined as a different place to work, each with its own unique skill and trait demands.

A smart expat will sit down with each of his or her raters at the beginning of the evaluation period to review the standards his or her performance will be measured against. The form should be reviewed together, and they must reach a mutual understanding of what the terms mean and what the company is really after in measuring performance. Then as the assignment proceeds, they should meet periodically to ensure that they are still looking at the form and the job performance it measures in a consistent fashion.

Productivity Gap

The dreaded productivity gap prevails in all new jobs for each of us; the only issue is how to shorten the start-up period. The key difference between productivity gaps in overseas assignments and those that prevail in domestic jobs is the unique combination of distracting and challenging additional obstacles that face the newly arrived expatriate and family. Just think of the following transitions as you try to focus on a new job overseas:

- You had to pull up stakes and depart from your home, friends, and business associates.

- You had to convince your spouse and children that the relocation would be good for them.

- You had to make a farewell round of meetings and parties with coemployees and neighbors—"No day at the beach!"

- You had to sell or rent your residence, move out all your furniture, store most of it, and ship some household goods to the host location—and they're not here yet.

- You are living in 30-day temporary quarters, a hotel, while waiting for your new residence to become available.

- Your spouse has no job but wants one badly.

- Your children bemoan the fact they were pulled away from their school friends and aren't so keen about invading a new school in a very different place.

- You haven't selected a school yet because they require an interview with the prospective student.

- You will need to prep the kids on how best to answer the questions and ask a few smart ones themselves.

- You and family have definitely not mastered the local language yet, causing all kinds of embarrassment in shops and restaurants.

- You have not fully engaged each member of the local staff who will be working with you, and you will need their help immediately. But who to ask and trust?

- You have no idea which of your home country banks are here and whether you can transfer funds directly, and the bills are already piling up.
- You need to locate good physicians, a dentist, and the nearest good hospital, and master the local transit system.

Is it any wonder, with these thoughts buzzing around the new expat's head, that getting down to the business of business is viewed with foreboding? Sure, you can reach out to your boss, HR rep, and mentor for advice, but you don't want to be seen as overdoing it. So you need to work out each of these challenges one at a time. And that takes time.

Statistics as to the time needed to begin to be productive are fuzzy at best, since who can ever clearly define what is the acceptable level of productivity for any given position except the job's manager? Unlike doing piecework in a factory setting, overseas management jobs require various sets of skills, and both technical and human traits, to tackle various cross-cultural business issues.

Please read this from the consultants at Windham and the experts at National Foreign Trade Council:

> On average, respondents (177 companies with 51,000 expatriates) estimate that expatriates require nine weeks to return to full productivity after moving from one location to another. . . . Based on individual surveys conducted with the expatriates, we believe that the nine-week estimate is low and that expatriates require another three or four weeks just to manage their move—bringing the total to 12 weeks.[11]

Faced with this productivity gap, what are management's alternatives in dealing with it? We asked that question of an experienced international HR executive, Marianne Ruggiero. She has logged outstanding years with American Express, ING Barings, Salomon Brothers, Citibank, and J. Crew, both managing overseas assignment programs and being an expatriate herself.

Marianne offered two related mentoring concepts that seem to make sense and are worthy of your consideration, both as managers and expatriates.

Marianne's first recommendation is to "think 360 degrees about the new expat with the help of a local mentor." She goes on to advise that management should "match the new expat with your best administrative assistant—his/her suggestions will enhance the executive's ability to fit in quickly and easily."[12]

She also supports the concept of adopting a senior mentor at the host location, ideally from another department or division, who can observe the expat on site. This local mentor and the home country mentor should share information to facilitate the new expatriate's contributions locally and ensure that his or her efforts are visible back at the home location as well. Let's follow up on what kinds of mentor communications can be most meaningful.

The home country mentor should consider communicating to the expat:

- Any corporate shifts in strategies, area goals, or policies that might affect the expatriate now or in the foreseeable future.
- Any turnovers in management personnel that might affect the expatriate.
- All communications sent by senior management to all corporate or domestic employees.
- Any job fills or departures in positions that might be appropriate for repatriation for this expatriate.
- Any technology changes being implemented in the headquarters operation that would impact this expatriate either during the assignment or on return.
- Any organization restructuring that might impact this expatriate upon return or could affect his or her contact status with the home country operation now.
- All human resources policy changes, particularly any additions or amendments to the overseas assignment policy.
- Any public relations or public newspaper accounts of company activities that could be of value to the expatriate.

With what sorts of communications back to the home country mentor should the expatriate be concerned?

- How performance on the job is progressing in terms of results, both positive and negative, at the host location.

- Any acquisition of new skills, such as new contacts in the host country that might be important for the corporate functional people to know about, language skills or cross-cultural lessons.

- Any perceived market opportunities that the corporation might be interested in, although this subject should always be raised with the expatriate's direct report first.

The concept is to establish a close relationship with the coach so that the line between official and personal thoughts will be well recognized and respected. The mentor should not be positioned as an individual who is used to go around direct management at the host location. The process, whether involving a mentor from the host country as well or not, should be carefully utilized. The expatriate should think carefully before using this effective communications tool. And as management changes (remember, people are now typically leaving after slightly over three years for another company, not just another job within the same organization) the expatriate needs to maintain as strong a link as possible back to that home country mentor, because upon return that expatriate will find a brand-new set of players in a different organizational structure.

At this point we should also ask, what can a good HR area do to support the overseas assignment program?

The first issue is to obtain a senior management consensus as to who should be managing the expatriate program. The possessor of that responsibility (ideally the HR function) should then form a team with the major corporate functions to assure the program is being managed the way senior management intended.

The second issue is to determine how that organizational setup can be clearly communicated to expatriates in the workforce, so they know to whom they should address their concerns.

- Construct and implement a system whereby expatriate job openings can be reviewed with host country management to ensure that the local staff candidates are fully screened prior to putting the opening into the expatriate system.

- Review the expatriate program results on no less than an annual basis so that weaknesses can be identified and properly dealt with.

- Identify what sorts of program benefits are possible for future consideration (usually in light of one-off arrangements that have been grudgingly negotiated over the past year).

- Review the present orientation program in light of what the expatriates actually had to say about it. Their feedback should be captured immediately after they have been through the orientation process and then no less than six months into their assignments to retrieve their second thoughts about the value of the program, now seen from a more practical perspective.

- Review the spouse assistance program in light of assignment rejections. What were the requirements that those expatriate candidates were seeking for their spouses?

- Review the repatriation process, ensuring that this program starts upon the expatriate's departure, and then follow up with senior management and the management succession people to verify that effective planning is being done with the expatriate.

- Review the entire performance appraisal process. Has it proved to be an accurate predictor of employee success or failure?

- Audit the evaluation forms against the subsequent assignments and performances by the expatriates.

- Establish formal training programs for the appraisers and follow up to determine whether they learned from the program.

- Review the entire expatriate package to determine whether it conforms to the strategy that the company has decided on.

- Explore whether the allowances and premiums are still necessary to attract and retain good people.

The purpose of this HR laundry list is to maintain the big picture of long-term goals on the HR screen. Expatriate management today has taken on the ugly characteristic of fire-fighting individual problem cases to the point where an overall examination of the major issues is forgotten in the heat of battling fires (finding suitable replacements in a hurry). In this bigger picture effort, HR will have to address senior management to determine what their directions are, particularly for global or host country strategies, then to fit the HR strategies to support those corporate objectives.

As the expatriate assignment proceeds, HR must keep an active managerial role in monitoring what is happening to the entire expatriate family unit, and needs assistance from the host country HR person to gain an understanding of what is happening and, if necessary, coordinate strategies to remedy problems. One of these ongoing programs should be continuing training for the expatriate on assignment, especially with cross-cultural courses.

Postarrival training, particularly cross-cultural sessions for the entire family, can be especially effective. Most companies appear to drop their regard for cross-cultural development at the time of the expatriate family's departure from the home country. That is a mistake. Once the family has been exposed to the host country culture for two or more months, they will have gained enough surface knowledge about their surroundings to begin to ask the right questions. Many consulting firms such as ITAP, Prudential, and Cendant specialize in customizing these kinds of programs to the company's perceived needs. Spouse support groups can become a valuable networking and learning operation; these exist in every major city and can easily be reached through web sites even before departure from home.

Notes

1. *Global Relocation Trends, 1999 Survey Report*, Windham International, National Foreign Trade Council, and Institute for International Human Resources, May 9, 1999, p. 54.
2. "Keeping Expatriates Out of Danger," William J. Hibbitt and Timothy Dwyer, *International Human Resources Journal*, Fall 1998, p. 40.
3. Ibid.
4. "The Parent Trap," Karen Taylor, *HR World*, Jan.–Feb. 2000, p. 35.

5. Ibid.
6. PricewaterhouseCoopers, 1999 Survey of Expatriate Tax and Compensation Policies.
7. *HR Matters*, July 2000, p. 6.
8. *Global Relocation Trends, 1998 Survey Report*, Windham International, and National Foreign Trade Council, June 1998, p. 31.
9. "Globalizing People through International Assignments," J. Stewart Black, Hal B. Gregersen, Mark E. Mendenhall, and Linda K. Stroh, Reading, MA: Addison-Wesley, 1999, p. 167.
10. *Global Relocation Trends, 1999 Survey Report*, p. 34.
11. *Global Relocation Trends, 1998 Survey Report*, p. 7.
12. Letter from Marianne Ruggiero, New York, NY, Sept. 11, 2000.

What Are the Issues in Adjusting the Length of the Assignment?

What Are the Issues in Adjusting the Length of the Assignment?

"Now this is not the end. It is not even the beginning of the end.
But it is, perhaps, the end of the beginning."
Winston S. Churchill, Speech,
Nov. 10, 1942

We've set out statistics indicating a trend toward shorter overseas postings. For both the manager and the expatriate there are significant benefits and drawbacks in changing the length of the overseas posting.

Shortening the Assignment

Why is the average overseas assignment getting shorter?

Could it be due to the sizable number of assignments that are cut short by quits or involuntary terminations? Possibly, but we don't have any hard data that would lead us to that conclusion.

It could be due to the increasing number of project and developmental postings. By their nature, those objectives do not require a three-year term to succeed. Wise managers should continue to maximize those forms of assignments in the future. They open doors of opportunities for the expatriates while giving the host location the expertise of the project manager on the one hand and serving to broaden the global understanding of an employee on the other.

Although we cannot at present extract assignment duration trends for each of the basic types of expatriate assignments described earlier, there could be very good or very bad news depending on which group is stimulating these contractions. If we could break out the averages for each—ongoing replacement, project, or developmental postings—those facts would be most helpful to us in gauging what the multinationals are doing in repositioning their overseas postings. For example, are they shortening the traditional three-year term? If so, is that because they now expect the expat to train a local staff replacement?

If managers are in fact accelerating the pace of moving local staff into formerly expat roles, that would certainly be a clear indicator that true globalization of employee assignments is moving ahead. That should reflect the growing populations of trained local nationals who can, and should, fill many of these roles effectively. There should also be a similar trend for more extensive use of third-country nationals for the same reason. But as we saw from the 1999 NFTC/Windham survey, the expatriate population continues to grow, with 66 percent of the respondents estimating that it would continue to expand in 2000.[1] This could mean that there are new companies and/or new positions that are developing, and the expats are the first group to "hit the beach," with managers intending to follow up their work with even more handovers to local staff.

This strange dichotomy between shortening assignment spans and additional expatriates on assignment could be due to the changeover from regular operational replacements to more developmental and project-oriented work. If either of those factors is basically responsible for the shorter terms, then we can understand that there are different motivations driving today's managers. As to the possibility that more organizations are using developmental assignments, either for fresh university graduates or for the middle level of managers such as we saw in the Daimler-Chrysler transfers, such a trend would demonstrate that senior managers have, at last, begun to fully appreciate the value of this overseas experience in promoting the broader growth of the employee. That recognition should produce greater promotional and developmental opportunities for this group of expatriates.

Then there is the possibility that there are increasing numbers of project assignments for expatriates. If this is the main factor in shorter assignments, then we should explore whether the nature of those projects is a one-time phenomenon or represents a series of continuing projects. If we are viewing a phase of projects, such as systems installation, then there could well be a decline in project work for expatriates in the future. However, if those projects involve continuing functions at the host location, then we'll realize that there will be a longer-term beneficial effect. In that event, there is not so much a need to "fix it now" as there is a requirement to develop employees at the host location, whether other expats or local staff, to learn the professional techniques that are required by the nature of the project. Again, that would be good news for managers seeking to globalize their workforces more effectively.

Another major factor in this lowered average could very well be the high incidence of failed assignments and quits. Both of these continuing problems require managers to decide how to fill the new vacancy. Most managers' knee-jerk reaction: "Get me another expat, quick!" Those high rates of early terminations continue to plague managers and will not start to diminish until those managers begin to screen, train, select, and prepare their candidates more effectively. Since senior managers are rewarded handsomely for exercising patience in many business matters, shouldn't they begin to demand that their subordinates restructure the expatriate process to halt the slide of money out the company's doors?

Let's start with expat quits. You managers have an obligation to find out what factors caused an expatriate to leave if your company is ever going to take real steps to reduce the velocity of the revolving door. How do you start?

You trigger that process through exit interviews with the appropriate line manager or human resources, preferably both. There is likely to be a difference in the straightforwardness of the departing expat as he or she speaks with the manager versus HR. The latter may be perceived as more experienced in dealing with departees and would probably not have been connected with any management issues that would inhibit the departing expat in the interview with the manager. After their interviews, the manager and HR meet to discuss the reasons offered by the expatriate. They evaluate those issues and make their recommendations to senior management accordingly. Table 10.1 looks at the top four reasons that

Table 10.1   Top Four Reasons Employees Quit Domestically

Reasons	Percent of Companies Reporting
Better career opportunities	78%
Dissatisfaction over salary/benefits	65%
Poor management	21%
Moving to follow relocating spouse	18%

Data Source: SHRM 2000 Retention Practices Survey.

employees quit domestically through the SHRM 2000 Retention Practices Survey.[2]

The vast majority of participants (87 percent) obtained this information through exit interviews. Over half of the participating organizations indicated that they made changes based on the information that had been obtained during the interview. We should analyze exit interviews with some grains of salt. Many departing employees do not want to burn their bridges; hence they may resort to better compensation at the new job rather than state that their bosses were intolerable. They know that future reference checks on subsequent job searches could come back to haunt them if they left stirring up controversy.

When we consider that U.S. companies with a population of 5,000 or more employees experience a domestic annual turnover rate of 26 percent, managers of the expatriate populations ought to take into account that their overseas assignees will likewise be predisposed to leave more often than their predecessors of just a decade ago. In fact, all the difficulties inherent in overseas work ought to drive up the annual departure rates even higher than those just listed for U.S. domestic work.

For example, the highest proportion of departures was to work for another company. It is logical to believe that this is also happening with expatriates. However, the next highest reason, dissatisfaction over pay and benefits, which a whopping 65 percent of companies reported as a factor, would likely be minimal for overseas jobs. On the other hand, expats would undoubtedly put strains on the family as a leading factor, with some lesser percentages for better career opportunities and poor management.

We suspect that the contraction of overseas assignment durations may also be due in part to expat spouse and family problems—both for families that did accompany the expat and encountered serious issues at the host location and those who stayed behind and created a whole different set of problems. We saw that almost one-quarter of all married expats were not able to work out suitable arrangements to have their spouses and family units join them overseas. Indeed, almost 40 percent of the children who were eligible to accompany the expat did not do so.

Common sense ought to enter at this point. We should be able to infer that a split family for a long period of time is going to produce real problems for one, if not all, of the family members. Again, we have no separate data as to what percentage of the early assignment endings are due to this factor, but common sense should dictate that many lonesome expats learn to appreciate more deeply the value of their families' company and want to regain that earlier than originally expected.

We should also look to corporate costs as another reason that the posting durations are shrinking. We've already seen a variety of very high estimates of how much these assignments can cost. Senior managers must be reviewing plans for turning over work formerly done by expats to local staff with barely concealed glee. They can see those savings loom larger every day.

Well, how does that contrast with putting a local manager to work instead?

All companies have ample financial reasons for transferring what have been exclusively the job domains of their expatriates to local nationals and third-country nationals (TCNs). In the Bartlett and Ghoshal book *Managing Across Borders*, the authors estimate that maintaining an expatriate manager costs 2 to 10 times as much as hiring a local manager for the same position.[3] (See Table 10.2.)

That same study went on to ask those companies, "What would you estimate to be the cost of a failed assignment?"—including replacement costs

Table 10.2 Costs of Expatriate Assignments by Region (1994)

Region	Average Incremental Cost of an Expatriate Assignment
Africa	$514,000
Asia	$428,000
Europe	$293,000
Pacific	$255,000
Middle East	$218,000

Data Source: Managing Across Borders, Christopher Bartlett and Sumantra Ghoshal, Boston: Harvard Business School Press, 1998.

(identify, train, prepare), reduced operational efficiency, and so on.[4] (See Table 10.3.)

But despite costs, many companies still believe that they are getting value from the expatriate programs. The optimistic news for managers is that they believe their companies' return on investment (ROI) on expatriate programs is, according to the 1999 NFTC study:[5]

Good to excellent	34%
Average	48%
Fair/poor	18%

The bad news is that the same survey could produce no general agreement by the responding HR managers as to what standards should be used in setting their return on investment calculations. Perhaps this is because, as human resources people, they are injecting into the return the quality of services being rendered by those expatriates—an intangible value if there ever was one. And in terms of quality, how could we estimate how a qualified local staff person would have performed in the same job? There would be less headquarters expertise contributed by a local national, but think of the goodwill and the deeper knowledge of the customs, culture, and business traditions that a local staffer would bring.

The Windham International consultants recently offered some insights as to how they would recommend that managers maximize their return on expatriate investments. Here is how they describe their approach:[6]

Table 10.3 Cost of Failed Assignments

Estimated Cost	Percent of Companies
Under $250,000	42%
$250,000 to $500,000	37%
Over $500,000	24%

Data Source: Managing Across Borders, Christopher Bartlett and Sumantra Ghoshal, Boston: Harvard Business School Press, 1998.

- View expatriates as investments.

- Ask why we are making that investment and how to manage risk while on assignment to protect the investment's value.

- Define the criteria for the investment.

- Determine expectations such as the payout period, performance targets, and milestones.

- Capture all costs.

- Agree on assignment objectives (strategic or tactical).

- Decide what form the return will take—increased revenues, enhanced working environment, greater corporate visibility, preparation for the next assignment.

Windham does point out the inherent problems with the ROI approach. On the one hand the costs become immediately identifiable, while on the other hand the benefits often take considerable periods of time to surface. They emphasize the need for efficient performance appraisals to identify the contributions of the expatriate on the job as a stepping-stone in comparing the cost for obtaining those contributions.

If you managers need to review the value of the expatriate program with your senior management, you may want to consider employing this quantifiable approach to measuring the value of these assignments to them. At least it provides you with a common ground of verifiable numbers from which to work.

Until companies can focus better on effective spousal aid programs, this worrisome problem will continue to force the couple to decide between doing the assignment on a nonaccompanied basis or, as is more likely, turning down the overseas opportunity altogether because they recognize the difficulty of trying to find a suitable position for the spouse at the host location.

There are difficult psychological reactions that can come into play if the termination of an expat is not properly planned. There could be a negative impact on the other expatriates and local staff, not to mention severe emotional strains on the expatriate, spouse, and children. Unless the family has been openly hostile (a rare but not unheard-of event in difficult locations), an abrupt end to the assignment brings with it thoughts of professional or social failure. Peers, neighbors, local staff, and other expatriates will all be presumed, in the mind of the expat, to view him or her as a failure. The embarrassment also spreads to the company, for the second-guessers will question the screening and selection processes that were used, or worse than that, suspect that the managers made a poor decision.

Managers need to do a sensitive job of presenting the early departure in the best light possible. For example, to preserve the expat's career possibilities, HR can agree with the departing expat to term the termination as one of mutual consent. The main element in all these cases is the need to have maintained open communication between the expat and manager about what was the major problem. If the termination comes as a bolt out of the blue, with no chance for the expat to even try to mend his or her ways, that kind of poor management will be talked about by all concerned—other expats, the local staff, the neighbors (usually other expat families from other companies), the home country corporate staff, and all the former colleagues of the returned expatriate. No one wins in these situations.

Managers ought to realize that there will be additional unwelcome fallout in the aftermath of early departures, whether they were for voluntary or involuntary reasons. Anytime an expat quits or is terminated, the other expatriates and the local staff immediately begin to set about unearthing the reasons for the termination. Performance issues? Chemistry problems? Higher pay? Better benefits? Longer vacations? Unsatisfactory working/living conditions at the host location? All of these questions, and lots more, spread through the expatriate and local staff communities as soon as word of the departure is announced. Expat families will seek out those answers quickly, and they nearly always succeed in doing so.

For example, the oil industry is often geographically structured such that the major companies find their expatriates closely clustered together in remote locations around the globe. Companies that are aggressive competitors have expats who become good neighbors and close social friends. These continuous close social contacts, wherever they evolve, bring the entire expat family units together so often that this frequently leads to extensive trading of expatriate package information. Consequently, when one of the multinationals introduces a new or improved benefit, the other expat members of the community will immediately be aware of the new development. They will invariably ask their own employers to match or better the latest expat program.

This is why HR people need to stay close to the regular surveys; their employees are always learning about the latest changes to policies and comparing those with their own program.

The expatriate with an offer in hand from a competing company has a choice: Do you accept it now or do you take that offer to your own company and see if you can elicit a counteroffer? The answer will depend on how greatly you value your career with your present company, and whether staying on would be a better choice in the long run for you. But even if you do elicit a counteroffer, and you accept it, you will never be perceived in the same way again by your company's management. Experienced managers know that once an employee has entertained the notion that another employer would be seriously appropriate to work for, loyalty to the first employer is perceived as substantially reduced.

Now you expats may rightly claim that there are no more social contracts with employers anymore (the traditional "womb-to-tomb" practice), so why would an employee's willingness to depart create negativity among management's ranks? There are three general reactions to the counterproposal acceptance.

First, some managers tend to view the negotiating employee as a mercenary, an employee willing to forgo all the benefits of working in a good company and with business associates such as themselves. (Remember, the expat's intent to depart causes them some sense of rejection as well.)

Second, managers will anticipate that it will be only a matter of a little more time before the expat leaves, since he or she has already passed over the threshold issue of being comfortable with a departure. When managers have this natural reaction, they become hesitant to discuss long-term projects or competitive strategies with the stayer, knowing that the expat might soon be out of the door on the way to work for a competitor.

Third, once the manager has agreed to make a counteroffer, that new package will almost always present a compensation equity problem for HR. The enhanced package contents will receive widespread publicity. The remaining expats and local staff will then be equipped with leverage for their own requirements, and will be encouraged by the new package to go out into the labor marketplace and search for offers.

For you expats, the best advice is to refrain from the temptation of sounding out your present organization for their counteroffer. Unless you really believe that in your case managers will not react to your remaining on in the ways they normally do, you'll gain nothing by probing for a counteroffer to entice you to stay.

Some firms do not make counteroffers as a matter of policy. They recognize the employee has all but departed—if not in body, certainly in mind. Others will counter just to keep the expatriate on the job a little longer while they are contacting HR to start the replacement process.

As the manager of the expat with an offer, you should follow the old rule; don't make the counteroffer unless this expat is literally so highly regarded that his or her loss will cause irreparable damage to the operation. The manager's counteroffer will generally only postpone the expat's leaving. Often managers know this but go ahead anyway, just to gain some time to commence a search for a replacement. This is a poor practice indeed. Other employees will have invariably found out about the terms of the counteroffer.

As a point of interest for your compensation people, don't forget to elicit as much detail as possible about the new package that the employee is leaving for, so that the compensation people can input that data in their plans for compensation improvements. This is another example of how well planned and well-executed exit interviews can contribute valuable input to your company.

Lengthening the Assignment

There are four reasons that overseas assignments get stretched out:

1. Important projects and goals remain to be completed, or new ones are about to surface, that would create problems for an incoming expatriate without sufficient experience or expertise to wrap up those pieces of business.

2. The job itself, such as country manager, requires extended presence beyond the three-year average, and that was fully understood by both management and the expatriate at the time of departure.

3. The expatriate and family unit have enjoyed the host location job and locality to the point where they request that management consider an extension of the original term.

4. Management has been unable to select an appropriate replacement, and asks the incumbent to stay until one is found, is trained, and can start.

As to the first set of extension circumstances, both management and the expatriate are well advised to review the original employment agreement and discuss how it should be modified in terms of how much longer the assignment will last or, in the alternative, what the specific project or goal is that must be completed for the assignment to terminate. Expat families become a bit itchy toward the end of the original term and begin thinking of their next destination, so extensions for them are often negatively received. Plans for the start of the next assignment must be delayed, not to mention the problems with starting school or the spouse's next job search. For all of these factors, there needs to be closure as to the new departure time.

These situations, which seem to arise frequently, are often caused in part by poor management planning—although there will be notable exceptions such as extensions mandated by unforeseen circumstances. These cases include acquisition or merger with another host country organization and the opening of a new business project. But where management could have done a more comprehensive planning job, the manager should give the expatriate family unit additional recognition for undergoing the slow agonies of having to stay on at the host location. Often, I've seen the expat simply send the family back home, but they need to remain in the last country where the next assignment will be another expatriate tour.

HR people ought to be certain, as assignment terms near completion, that management is carefully observing the workload situation so that the departing expat, and family, will not be unduly delayed by workload issues that could have been anticipated. When the expat family unit encounters delays, that news sends shivers down the backs of other expatriate family units. They will immediately begin to worry that the same sort of problem will occur in their cases. Good managers will avoid these scenarios, in which expat morale at the host location takes a severe beating.

The second reason for extensions concerns certain occupations that, by their nature, require substantial periods to maximize contributions. For example, we can identify occupations such as country manager, government relations specialist, community affairs manager, public relations manager, and visa and passport manager that all demand a thorough knowledge of the host culture and business conditions. In fact, the very nature of the skill requirements of the job goes to the heart of understanding the host country and developing the appropriate relationships with local community contacts. These jobs call for a thorough knowledge of the customs, language, and traditions of the nation or city in which the company does business. Unlike many of their staff counterparts who are doing essentially what they would do in any location, the location becomes the very focal point of these occupations.

Multinationals dearly covet these individuals. They are virtually not replaceable for significant periods of time. That translates into a rich competitive market for their services. That, in turn, provokes an active piracy trade. Competitors like nothing better than to capitalize on a long-term expat's unique acceptability at a host location while also receiving his or her debriefing about the company's strategies. They receive full value from these kinds of people. As they gain the community's respect, the company's stature also grows, providing many varieties of business and social opportunities that would not be accessible to a new corporate arrival.

As examples, IBM, American Express, RCA, and Fairchild all had U.S. expatriates in Japan in the 1970s and 1980s who had been there for 10 years or more. They all had been well accepted by the Tokyo community, which made their advice to our team at Schlumberger insightful. A fascinating part of their characters was that all of them, to some degree, had begun to think in the Japanese manner. All had become fluent in the language and fully comfortable with the culture.

Examples of this phenomenon with expats coming to the United States also stand out. Yoshio "Terry" Terasawa of Nomura and Young Man Kim of the SK Group had come to the United States as expatriates many years ago and stayed on in New York to become unofficial ambassadors of Japan's and Korea's respective business communities there. In each case they had put in more than 15 years of high-visibility work and in many respects, had become Americanized.

Long-term assignments eventually pose a dilemma for management. The value to the company of these people's employment continues to grow as each year passes, yet they originally came on full expatriate packages, which are essentially constructed to protect the expatriate for a shorter period of time (back to that three years again). Consequently, managers face the question of whether they should continue to apply the full package or begin the process of gradual integration into the local economic standards.

Windham and the National Foreign Trade Council call this process "localization," and have done some survey work that reveals some strange corporate practices for these valued people. In 1999, for the first time in the history of their venerable expatriate practices survey, they asked what the companies were doing about "localizing" their long-staying overseas assignees. A surprising 40 percent of the 264 U.S.-based multinationals replied that they did localize. The question did not go further to ask whether some or all of their longer-term expats were reduced in terms of their expatriate packages over the course of time. The sponsors concluded, "This is a way to control assignment costs and a way to ensure the long-term success of international operations by developing local talent."[7]

The survey went on to ask at what year of service in the host country the localization process started for the 40 percent who were localized. The average was 4.2 years. The localization process (i.e., the reduction and eventual elimination of the expatriate package) was complete for these expatriates after an average of another 2.4 years. It will be interesting, in light of the continued global expansion trends, to see whether these current practices will be made permanent at the very time that companies are still aggressively competing for overseas markets. Managers know that you can compete effectively only if you have well-regarded expatriates working on your behalf. There is a time for cost shaving, but this is not the time or group of people that would be ideal to target as expendable as the new decade begins; they simply represent greater value to their companies than the savings to those employers brought about by their repatriations.

Let's turn the long-term assignment around and observe it from the perspective of the expatriates. Their first issue is whether they have reduced or destroyed their own career opportunities back at the home headquarters by staying overseas. There comes a time in each employee's career when the management succession people decide that either the experience the employee has gained is sufficient to warrant moving up the corporate ladder or that there has been such a long detour gaining knowledge of just one host country that there are no viable career avenues left to consider. The longer the expat is away, the more likely that others with broader exposures will be considered for high management positions. The long-term expatriate then has only narrow repatriation opportunities in his or her future. He or she may be forced to focus on a few jobs such as in-house consultant, helping the major corporate functions understand how their strategies impact the host country. There will be relatively few familiar business associates left at headquarters if our long-term assignee has been away for 10 years or more. Allies would have departed and strangers now sit in their chairs.

Expats should establish and maintain a protective home country mentor relationship and bolster communications ties with regular home leaves. The expat's visit to headquarters must include a talk not only with his or her functional boss, but also with the manager of management succession. These officials need to realistically review with the expat whether the overseas assignment has removed the expat from serious career consideration at home headquarters (if in fact the expat wants to return at all).

Consider what sacrifices the long-term expat has made for the company. The spouse and family have become enmeshed in the local culture, having established enough long-term friends and associations that they are unlikely to be that pleased to return "home." They may no longer have ties to their old community.

Long-termers tend to localize themselves socially to the extent that they do not need the expensive clustering cost-of-living, shelter, and other allowances. But if they are in responsible positions, which is true in most of their cases, they also have special social obligations that make them truly representatives of their companies. As such, if companies are intent on shaving costs by taking away their expatriate packages, they need to substitute a substantial local compensation program that will enable these employees to present an impressive image to the local community.

This category of extended-assignment expatriates calls for lots of tender care by management. These individuals grow to be virtually irreplaceable. Many of their host country contacts will be difficult for their replacements to cultivate and gain the immediate confidence of. As these individuals mature, there will be significant interest by other expatriates and local nationals as to how well the company will treat the extended assignment person. Much good or bad can come to the company by virtue of its generosity in managing the compensation and, if necessary, retirement of the expat.

The next group of extended assignees consists of those expats who, for either business or social reasons (often both) would like to stay on at the host country beyond the original term of their employment agreement. Since the company is under no legal obligation to honor this request, management is facing the practical decision as to whether it makes business sense for the current expatriate to continue or revert to the original schedule of assignment terms, which would call for a replacement at the end of that term. This expat decision can stem from various factors, such as how well did the expat enjoy and succeed on the job or how well the family unit has entrenched themselves in the host nation. These factors that weigh toward staying need to be balanced against the likely results of repatriating. For those contingencies, the expat needs the input from HR, the corporate functional people, and the home country mentor. The expat needs to get a picture of how he or she is currently perceived by home country decision makers and whether staying away for a period of additional months or years makes sense. The expat should ask what the next assignment might have been and whether there is another expat candidate waiting in the wings.

Corporate HR gathers data to recommend to senior management whether the expat's request should be accepted, and if so, for how long. If management denies the request, they will have to consider the effects on the morale of the other expats and local staff at the host country. In these cases the host HR manager can also provide some guidance by finding out what the specifics for staying really are, and then reviewing those reasons with corporate HR. They need to remember that virtually one-off deals can come back to haunt the company.

How much does a particular host nation affect these extended assignment requests? The United States, United Kingdom, and France have traditionally led the list of countries where expatriate family units have asked to stay on. While it may be the spouse driving the request to extend, the expat needs assurance in the form of a career-planning meeting that extending will not adversely affect his or her career. Career planning meetings, incidentally, do not appear as a regular practice by most of the multinational firms. If your company does not offer them on a regular basis, you the expatriate ought to request one, no less than once per year. And this does include periods when you are on overseas assignment.

For you managers, these career-planning sessions offer fine opportunities to find out the mental state of the expat. They can often reveal potential issues before they surface. Consequently, they should be a part of your standard operating procedure. Since HR normally conducts these reviews, the possibility of a problem with an expat's direct manager could come out in this discussion. HR then needs to be ready as to how to process that kind of sensitive information.

The last category of assignment extensions involves the case of the delayed replacement. Corporate HR is entrusted with the responsibility of moving candidates through the assignment process on a timely basis. Similar to an airport controller, the expat assignment manager daily balances takeoffs and landings. When an expat is ready to depart, he or she is mentally on the runway with engines running, and in no mood to return to the hangar because the replacement craft has not even departed yet. The decision in the control tower is difficult. The host country cannot afford a total vacancy, and the new manager in the home country wants to start with the new repatriate. A tug-of-war will ensue, good for no one.

There is a message of neglect when this occurs. Employees view the lack of a screened, waiting, replacement as an indicator that management had essentially forgotten about this assignment and only awoke to the task when contacted by host country HR for profiles of the candidates. At least 12 months prior to the expiration of the employment agreement, the wheels of screening need to be turning. That same deadline needs to cause the manager of management succession to explore that career alternatives for the incumbent expatriate. We will revisit that key trigger in our discussion of the next assignment.

Let's take the most typical assignment extension scenario brought about by the "missing" replacement scenario. Suppose John has been quite successful in adapting to the Paris office's staff and culture. As he is well into his third, and final, year of his contract term, the company, Dot.com, belatedly discovers that there is no viable expat successor in the pipeline. While John and family have been generally pleased by the Paris posting, they are all looking forward to their repatriation to the United States.

John's boss is sympathetic but makes clear that the Paris operation cannot afford a vacancy in John's accounting position. It would be too destructive to the ongoing Paris operation.

Consequently John is asked to stay over the contract term for an indefinite period until a suitable replacement is found. John can hardly afford, careerwise, to risk his corporate future with Dot.com by insisting on departing Paris as scheduled.

Of course, if John had already been offered and accepted another position back at Dot.com headquarters, he could try to move the decision making to his current and new managers. However, the repatriation job process is seldom complete while expats are still on assignment, so John will not have the luxury of letting the bosses duke it out. It's all up to John.

Consequently he must confront Jane and family with the choice of staying over with him, or returning to the United States to begin the repatriation process. This is, for the Jones family, a lose-lose dilemma. If spouse Jane, children and dog depart—perhaps because of school or job considerations—they are really in a state of limbo. They may choose to relocate to their prior community, but are still not really sure where John's next Dot.com work location will be. Their departure would leave John as a lonely leftover in Paris, counting the days until repatriation.

The alternative for Jane and the children—staying over in Paris—is also a problem. Do the children sign up for another school term? Does Jane indicate to her manager that she will be sort of a temporary, ready to depart as soon as John's replacement arrives?

No one, neither the company nor the Jones family, wins.

Notes

1. *Global Relocation Trends, 1999 Survey Report*, Windham International, National Foreign Trade Council, and Institute for International Human Resources, May 9, 1999, p. 8.
2. Society for Human Resource Management.
3. *Managing Across Borders*, Christopher Bartlett and Sumantra Ghoshal, Boston: Harvard Business School Press, 1998, p. 180.
4. Ibid.
5. *Global Relocation Trends, 1999 Survey Report*, p. 48.
6. Ibid., p. 15.
7. Ibid., pp. 36–37.

Illustration by Liz Lomax

What Are the Issues in the Next Assignment Process?

CHAPTER 11

What Are the Issues in the Next Assignment Process?

"So it's home again, and home again,
America for me.
My heart is turning home again, and
there I long to be."

Henry Van Dyke (1852–1933),
"America for Me," st. 2

L et's explore the two types of future assignments for the expatriate: repatriation to the home country and another expatriate assignment.

Repatriations

What can be so challenging about going home? After all, don't we really know friends, places, and customs so well that all that is needed is the plane ticket?

Hardly true. Not only has "home" changed while expats like John were away on assignment, but John and all the members of his family have also changed—perhaps imperceptibly to them; but changed they are, in a very real cultural sense. Their experiences living in a culture such as Paris will color the way each of the family perceives life.

Let's turn to another film classic, Ingmar Bergman's *The Seventh Seal*, for a vivid portrayal of repatriation difficulties. The Knight has just returned to Sweden after years on a crusade to the Holy Land. Here is the difficult conversation as he encounters his wife, Karin, after years away:

> Karin: "I heard from people who came from the crusade that you were on your way home. I've been waiting for you here."
> The Knight is silent. He looks at her.
> Karin: "Don't you recognize me anymore?"
> The Knight nods, silent . . .
> Karin: "Now I can see that it's you. Somewhere in your eyes, somewhere in your face, but hidden and frightened, is that boy who went away so many years ago."[1]

Both managers and expatriates tend to underestimate the repatriation challenges but both parties to the expat contract can take appropriate steps to surmount those challenges.

Managers generally put off planning the next posting for an expatriate until so late in the assignment that meaningful coordination in finding an appropriate opening is all but impossible. In our hunt for best practices, we advocated earlier that the subject of the next assignment, including repatriation prospects, should be reviewed by management with the potential expatriate before he or she ever departs for the overseas posting. No matter how large or small the multinationals are, they put this planning out of sight because three years away is apparently too far off to commence meaningful planning. Let's review current next assignment planning practices.[2] (See Table 11.1.)

It is unfortunate that in the survey there was not a further breakdown

Table 11.1 Next Assignment Planning Practices

When Repatriation Is Addressed	Percent of Respondent Companies
Before departure	17%
Six months or more before return	27%
Under six months before return	46%
Not discussed	10%

Data Source: Global Relocation Trends, 1999 Survey Report, Windham/ NFTC/IIHR, p. 39.

of when, within the six months just prior to return, the next assignment discussions happened. My own experience with a half dozen multinationals leads me to hazard a guess that these strategy-setting talks are generally scheduled in the final month, and, more accurately, the final week of the overseas posting.

These numbers reflect important practices and bear our closer scrutiny.

We'll start with the obvious. The most opportune time in the entire expatriate assignment process is to review, prior to the expat's departure for the overseas posting, what plans will be in effect for that expat's next assignment. The benefits of starting the planning process go both to the expat and management. They have a common stake in trying to maximize the benefits of the expatriate experience for this employee's own best career pursuits and the company's long-term management succession plan. Both of these positive objectives are thwarted when the company or the expat does not move to have this first planning session prior to the start of the assignment.

So what do these survey numbers tell us about what these two parties are doing about that mutually beneficial kick-off session?

We learn that only 17 percent of the companies participating in this survey have this first planning session before the overseas trip is begun. The remaining 83 percent of companies have lost a golden opportunity to remind the new expat of their support and to express a genuine interest in his or her career.

Predeparture Career Interview

Usually HR, the expat's functional head, and the manager of succession planning are all feasible candidates, in any combination, to sit down with the departing expat and exchange perspectives about what kinds of jobs would make sense after completing this posting overseas.

For the expat's view we'll return to John. This meeting forces him to focus on what kinds of work he would really want to do in the future, and also where he would want to perform that sort of job. He gets the advantage of being in an important role. He has been duly screened, trained, assessed, and selected, and is receiving postselection preparation. That all adds up to a significant company investment in John, so he has some important leverage in talking about his next job or next training cycle. He also has the ear of the three important career people in the company. He should act quickly enough to get on their calendars before leaving for assignment—for once he's on the assignment and not in front of their faces, it will be progressively more difficult with every passing day for John to capture the attention of any one of this trio.

John ought to be prepared to listen to what company representatives have to say about the alternative career paths the managers believe would be beneficial for him to take, and what steps they would see as appropriate for John to take to hit those targets. As his input is requested, John ought to be prepared to state what his own aspirations are and how he would proceed to pursue them.

After the two mini-presentations, both John and the company representative (HR for short) discuss what kinds of management development and training would appear to be appropriate for the job(s) he is ultimately seeking. Potential training and development courses will be identified and later scheduled.

John is curious about the alternative of moving on to another expat assignment after this one has been concluded. HR promises to keep John informed about possible openings, both at the home headquarters and at other locations. John is also curious about where the organization sees his new role in the context of its larger strategy.

Both John and HR want to keep their options open and agree to periodic contacts, either directly or with the help of John's new chosen mentor.

This is no time to insist on a specific job. But if HR, based on their long-term scheduling, sees an opportunity for John, he should seek as much information as he can still get about it before departure. Some companies would guarantee that there will be *a* job to which an expat can return. Management gives a guarantee that the job will be at a minimum salary or corporate hierarchy level. John promises to give HR feedback as to his perception of all the pieces of the expatriate package.

This discussion was certainly not a day at the dentist. Both the company and the expat have begun to think of what each could do in the next three years to bring the expat back into the corporate mainstream where his new experiences can be utilized. The parties have agreed to open and maintain an active communications link so that if any significant changes in direction occur, the other will be promptly notified.

John's profile goes to the manager of management succession, along with expected date of repatriation.

This simple scenario will be most helpful to both John, who has the feeling that management knows who he is and what he'd like to do, and to HR, who at this early juncture has a clear picture of John and how he might best fit into the organization on his return. It's fortunate that John is with a company within the 17 percent of organizations that carry out such procedures for their expats before departure. As planning progresses overseas, please refer to the 12-step best practices set forth later in this chapter, which can also apply to others received later planning overtures from the company.

Postdeparture Career Planning

For the not so fortunate 83 percent of organizations that do not start the planning for the next post prior to the expat's departure, you've certainly made it difficult for yourselves and your expatriates. You had the chance to convene all the managers who will be ultimately responsible for the repatriation with the departing expat to determine what your respective tentative plans are, exchange those ideas, and think about what further steps will need to be taken over the course of the assignment.

As to you managers and expats who are working for companies with policies providing for at least a six month time frame before the end of the assignment to plan repatriation (27 percent), you have the time, but not the convenience, of arranging all those discussions that John had at home headquarters before he left for Paris. You do have the time to e-mail, fax, and telephone, and should start as soon as the company policy permits it.

Those of you in the 46 percent group who wait for less than six months (let's be truthful, more like a few weeks) you are going to have difficulties in getting to all the key decision makers with what you want to do and where you want to do it. Once you finally find them, the next challenge is the short lead time to actually make it to the candidate list for jobs opening up around the time of your return. Our recommendation is to take the home leave and follow the same procedure we outlined for John. You'll just have more difficulty getting to see everyone you need to see in the limited time of your visit, so try to have HR arrange the set of interviews for you.

Those of you working for firms, whether as a manager or an expatriate, that have no planning for repatriation assignments (10 percent), it would be interesting to view your expat and repat turnover statistics. That lack of attention to an essential element of commonsense planning sends a really negative message to the expatriate population. Could it be that these organizations are all in the first stage of globalization, and therefore still don't attach much importance to the overseas workforce to begin with?

All you repatriates can do on return is to try to see everyone that we set out in John's case as soon as possible and hope for the best. The one comfort you have is the knowledge that you're not alone. Let's look at your company:

According to a recent newspaper article titled "A Study Sees a Downside to Going Overseas as an Executive,"[3]

"It's very perplexing—companies in general are just not doing a good job of planning global human resource needs and development," says William Best, a vice president in A. T. Kearney's international consulting business.

For its study, the Conference Board canvassed 152 companies whose 1994 sales ranged from $3 million to $75 million—two-thirds of them based in the United States and the rest in Europe and Asia.

It found that only 38 percent of the American respondents guarantee expatriates a position on their return, compared with 47 percent of the European companies that answered the survey. And 87 percent of the American companies said that most repatriated executives were not promoted when they returned.

Often, companies leave executives in limbo until their tour of duty is nearly up. Four months before repatriation, at 60 percent of the American companies surveyed, fewer than a quarter of the expatriates knew their assignments.

The new survey shows that little has changed of late, despite the new international emphasis. A 1990 study, for example, found that 80 percent of the United States expatriates felt that their companies did not value their overseas service. Two years later, another study found that 77 percent of Americans sent overseas returned to jobs with less responsibility than the positions they held abroad. Up to half of them quit within three years of their return.

This statistical nightmare was updated in a January–February 2000 article in *HR World*, in which J. Stewart Black writes: "One quarter of U.S. employees who return from successful international assignments leave their firm within a year of repatriation."[4]

Dr. Black goes on to predict that the majority of those people are going to the competition. If one puts this 25 percent alongside the estimated 20 percent who had failed assignments and another 20 percent who wound up as brownouts, the net long-term success rate for expatriate assignees would appear to be less than one-half.

Table 11.2 presents some of Dr. Black's research data regarding planning for repatriation.

If it's any relief, at least we know that U.S. multinational managers are not alone among global competitors as to the inability to plan out the assignments for their expatriates for their return. Strategizing of careers appears to be anathema to the Dutch and Finnish as well. The Japanese managerial system does not usually call for this kind of advance planning in the first place, so it is pleasantly surprising to note that a third of Japanese repatriates now are furnished with an idea of what they are going to do in advance of their repatriation.

Dr. Black also explored the reverse cultural shock that many repatriates feel upon their return. (See Table 11.3.)

What lies at the heart of reverse cultural shock? Reasonable observers, and apparently most corporate managers, would view the process of going home as a renewal of a lifestyle in which expats had lived comfortably for several years prior to departure. How does being away from the culture kindle a shock upon reentry?

Table 11.2 Planning for Repatriation

Nationalities of Repatriates	*Percent Not Informed of Their New Position Just Before Repatriation*
Dutch	63%
Finnish	62%
Japanese	66%
American	68%

Data Source: "Coming Home," J. Stewart Black, *HR World*, Jan.–Feb. 2000.

Table 11.3   Reverse Culture Shock

Nationalities of Repatriates	Percent Reporting Reverse Culture Shock
Dutch	64%
Finnish	71%
Japanese	80%
American	60%

Data Source: "Coming Home," J. Stewart Black, *HR World*, Jan.–Feb. 2000.

The major reason appears to be that the expat family unit is unprepared for the cultural change. *HR World* quotes one U.S expatriate who stated: "Be mentally prepared for enormous change when coming home. Expect repatriation shock to surpass the culture shock you might have experienced when you went overseas."[5]

The expat and family on assignment are adapting every day to a different culture whether knowingly or not. As they settle into the process of gaining new cultural traits they are losing the traits needed to comfortably mesh with their prior culture. When they are asked to return to that prior culture, those years of adaptation cannot be abruptly dismissed. As Hofstede would have predicted, the more severe the contrasts are between the two cultures, the greater the shock upon reentry. The shock impacts both the expat and the family.

As an example, we can turn to Japanese expats returning to Japan. Here are some snapshots taken by *New York Times* reporter Howard French in Tokyo:[6]

> Strikingly, many overseas Japanese say that the adjustment required to fit back into their society is often more traumatic than the adaptations required in moving abroad.

And as for the changes at work:

> Even managers sent overseas by their companies are routinely assigned to back-office jobs until their superiors can be sure that their foreign ways have dissipated. "When I first returned, after eight years in the United

States, my boss would tell me flatly that America had spoiled me, and kept me in a position where I would have really limited contact with customers," said Toyokazu Matsumoto, 51, a manager with a major Japanese corporation.

The reverse of the repatriations between the United States and Japan is consistent with the Tokyo article. Nomura sent a steady stream of three or four U.S. nationals on assignment to the Tokyo operation. We found that the longer they stayed on assignment there, the greater was the likelihood that they had adapted Japanese approaches to solving issues. This was especially true in their increased patience and their need to review possible solutions with a variety of managers prior to implementation.

Managers should appreciate the fact that their repatriates don't normally expect the shock. They need some preparation for it, particularly since most of them have unrealistically high expectations of the level of work they will be performing on return. When they are finally informed as to the nature of the new job (invariably less than what they had hoped for), that deep disappointment then gets combined with the realization that their home culture isn't really that comfortable anymore.

You managers can alleviate much of these expat family unit negative feelings by providing meaningful preparation for the move back. Deborah Conlan, writing in *Mobility*, quotes the following summary of the 1998 Employee Relocation Council (ERC) survey of multinational firms.[7]

According to ERC's most recent international survey:
Twenty-two percent of the participating organizations provided formal repatriation programs. The types of assistance most often provided to U.S. expatriates include employee career counseling (73%), spouse career counseling, and family reverse culture shock counseling (62%).

If less than one-quarter of the multinationals have recognized the significance of this problem, you managers need to do some planning to implement such programs from the ground up. Once again, there is no lack of good consultants working in this area. Managers can either use them on a continuous basis (costly) or learn the process and bring the programs in-house.

We just made reference to expat expectations on reentry. Managers need to sufficiently lower those expectations in those instances when a repatriation position has not yet been identified, or the return job is not as responsible as the expatriate position was. In fact, this will often be the case because the very nature of expatriate positions, as stated earlier, will generally be broader than their home country counterparts. The operations overseas tend to be smaller, creating jack-of-all-trades types of positions as opposed to the more specialized job structures that are in place at the home operation.

The next step in a nonplanned repatriation is to trace what actually happens to the former expat. Once again, we can refer to another *New York Times* piece. In a May 2000 feature, article writer Jobert Abueva sets forth more discomforting statistics relating to the assignments in which these repatriates found themselves back home.[8]

Percent of repatriates reporting their companies did not communicate clearly about what they would face at home	60%
Percent of repatriates still filling temporary assignments three months after returning to work in the United States	33%
Percent of repatriates who reported that their permanent position upon returning home was a demotion	75%
Percent of repatriates who reported they lacked opportunities to put their foreign service to work	61%
Percent of repatriates who left the company within a year of returning from assignments abroad	25%

One striking feature about all these practices is how closely they relate to each other. Certainly the foundation for repatriations appears to be set in sand because there is so little effective planning that is being devoted to the process. All five of these practices can be significantly improved upon, given managers' serious attention to the overall repatriation process.

You repatriates need to take note of the managerial practice and take appropriate steps to obtain corporate help in your own relocation process—even if there are no formal corporate programs providing for the help. You'll need to address directly the issues of the appropriateness of the next job and the help your family unit will require in trying to readapt to the home country culture.

Both managers and expats can learn valuable lessons by reviewing this survey. If managers of the participating companies had taken the first step of exploring what positions made sense to consider as alternatives for the repatriate, there might have been mutual agreement as to appropriate jobs for the repatriate. Since there had been no search by managers on the expat's behalf, there will be no such discussions. This critical omission converts what should be a procedure into a lottery. Managers are left with little choice but to offer whatever positions seem remotely appropriate or offer a temporary holding position as the alternative.

Managers should be especially concerned about the answers to the last survey question. The participating companies reported that one-quarter of all repatriates had quit the company within just one year of their return. This is the payoff from poor practices. Repatriates are uniquely attractive search candidates for other organizations, and particularly direct competitors. Headhunters are fast to recognize dissatisfaction. From that basis, they can move on to exploring the expatriate experience, with emphasis on what was learned abroad. They focus on technical knowledge, business contacts in the host country, and the repatriate's success in adapting to the host country culture. If the repatriate does sign on with a competitor, it is frequently to return to the original host county to capitalize on the knowledge the repatriate gained there.

For you managers, the darkest part of these multiple tragedies is the recognition that these many repatriate scenarios could have been avoided by directing the staff to make the time and effort to search efficiently for attractive job alternatives.

As to the propensity for repatriates to quit, *New York Times* reporter Abueva quotes Dr. J. Stewart Black, who states that the 25 percent quitting rate by repatriates in one year is "double the proportion of departures by those who never go abroad . . . and they typically leave to go to the competition."[9]

Further, that article went on to point out one case where an organization lost every single one of its 25 repatriates over a two-year stretch. Black summed it up: "The company might just as well have written a check for $50 million and tossed it to the winds."

You HR managers cannot afford to permit your company to hemorrhage that badly. You would be hard put to explain to the company controller how 100 percent of repatriates decided to leave. Controllers are very sensitive to replacement costs and will demand an explanation why these people voted with their feet. Your only choice is to put in place a sound repatriate program.

You HR people have been entrusted with the marketing responsibility for the expatriate program. As with any product, you'll need to examine its strengths and weaknesses in order to make it more attractive to your potential consumers—your potential expats. You will be asked by those candidates as to the career status implications of accepting the overseas assignment. Can your organization truthfully assert that such postings will be beneficial for employee careers?

Try this comparison. Take your own company's statistics and match them against the 1999 NFTC survey findings regarding the impact of the overseas assignment on repatriates' careers shown in Table 11.4.[10]

Here the payoff is no payoff. The one category that an expatriate assignment observer and an HR professional would hope should predominate, faster promotions (i.e., recognition), actually occurs in only one-fifth of the repatriation cases. Note that fully one-half of the companies were not really certain about their actual results. This fact is not a good omen. Repatriate career success is clearly vital to track carefully, and one-half of the survey participants are simply not doing that.

In the face of these onerous statistics and their human casualties, not to mention the precious company funds being "tossed to the winds," can we offer you, the manager, and you, the expatriate, best practice recommendations? Yes! And, what's more, both of you can read from the same page to understand mutually how you can get there. What's more, you'll be able to fully appreciate what the other party to this expatriate contract must do to make your repatriation process work successfully.

Table 11.4   Overseas Assignment Impact on Careers

Impact on Expatriate's Career	Percent of Companies Reporting
Faster promotion	21%
Caused change of employers more often	20%
Easier to obtain new position in company	19%
Not sure	50%
Other	10%

Data Source: Global Relocation Trends, 1999 Survey Report, Windham/NFTC/IIHR.

Best Repatriate Practices

PRERETURN TRAINING

We briefly discussed the fact that at the core of the repatriate challenge is the general misunderstanding that it is easier to return to a place you thoroughly know than it is to venture overseas to a new culture. This natural misconception is especially easy to come by for first-time expatriates. They need professional-level counseling to convert that delusion to more realistic thinking.

Our best practice was the scenario set out for the firm that took the time to conduct the assignment planning before departure. But if your firm is part of the over 80 percent that waits until the expat has departed for overseas, we'll address these recommendations to you.

TRAINING/COUNSELING

This training/counseling needs to start no less than 12 months prior to the end of the assignment. The entire expatriate family should attend. At this stage of the overseas posting, managers will not as yet have a clear signal from corporate HR as to the next assignment. In consequence, the training is structured more generically than a customized program designed to cover just a specific home or host location.

The training should focus on reverse culture shock and if, luckily, a new position has been identified at the home country, there should be a customized piece to target the particular location of that job. For example, if the position is in New York City, there will be different adjustments required than if the Jones family opts for the Moose Jaw, Canada, opportunity.

MANAGEMENT SEARCH FOR ALTERNATIVE OPPORTUNITIES

At a time around 12 months from the expected end of the expat's assignment, HR should contact the expat's functional head (in John's case, the corporate head of marketing), notifying that manager that the expatriate's assignment will be finishing up in less than a year. HR will ask whether there are any possible openings that could be identified at this early stage to red circle as appropriate for the expat? The management succession person needs to participate actively in these conversations. The director of employment and director of training should also be brought in at this stage to obtain their views as to possible job alternatives and development for John in that process.

The assignment search will be greatly facilitated if the expatriate submits a self-assessment. This is particularly valuable if that assessment includes the new skills acquired while overseas. The direct manager and the two mentors should be asked for their input as well to round out the expat's profile. The broader portrait will give the HR people a more accurate and updated standard to work with in their search for potential job fits.

REVIEW OF ASPIRATIONS WITH EXPAT

At the optimum, the mentors that were selected and have been working with the expat on a continuous basis will already have homed in on a few areas of key interest to the expat and have made preliminary inquiries as to whether HR believes it will be worth pursuing those avenues. The corporate functional head (in John's case, the corporate marketing director) will review John's background for a preliminary determination of what kinds of jobs will make sense upon repatriation. They then contact the soon-to-be repatriate to elicit his desire or wish list, to compare it with the positions that they have tentatively identified as plausible ones for further consideration.

The expat should at this stage schedule his or her last home leave so that the various managers with input, including the home country mentor, will be available for sit-down meetings during that leave. If there has been some preliminary paring down of opportunities, the expat can use that home leave for interviewing opportunities. The spouse should be authorized to accompany the expatriate on this trip.

If the repatriate location has been identified, that home leave should also be used as a house-hunting and school-finding trip. The expat needs to show his or her face around the corporate offices to remind those managers (many of whom were not even there when the expat left). Network, network, network. The expat should know that HR employment does not do all the placements in any organization. The returning expat needs to be somewhat of a salesperson, the commodity being himself or herself. Without effective sale techniques the expat may not receive serious management consideration.

EVALUATION OF EXPAT IN TERMS OF NEXT ALTERNATIVES

As a best practice, the company can send a positive signal of management's genuine concern to its expatriate workforce by assigning a senior team to review the profiles of returning expatriates in order to recommend where that employee should be reassigned. Monsanto, among other progressive organizations, has experienced success with this approach.

The senior staffers review the self-assessment, discuss the potential openings with HR, and interview the expatriate during the home leave. They make their observations and specific recommendations known to HR for inclusion in the database used for the final placement decision.

EXPAT REVIEW AND UPDATE OF JOB DESCRIPTION

Almost invariably this key element of ensuring that the organization clearly understands the nature of the duties being performed by its employees is omitted in the procedure of positioning the repatriation. But all jobs change in content, especially where the responsibilities tend to be so flexible and broad as they normally are for overseas positions. This review by the expat should be done with the direct manager and the HR people at the host location and transmitted to corporate HR so that the home office has a clear picture of what the overseas assignee has actually been doing. In addition to what skills are required in performing that job, the performance appraisals should also be sent back to corporate HR to show how well those job requirements were actually fulfilled by the expatriate.

The completed appraisals should be reviewed carefully by HR to follow up to see whether or not the goals that had been agreed upon as job objectives were successfully tackled. HR needs to pay particular attention to the employee comments section of the appraisal form. This section provides management with a window of observation of the expat's thoughts about the job and the host location. Are the reactions to the various appraisal items positive or defensive? Are there ideas and recommendations emanating from the expatriate that indicate a strong willingness to develop further? Experienced HR people can extract vital signs of an employee's mental outlook from this portion of the form.

The other side of performance appraisal advice is to the expatriate. At the time you are completing your segment of the form, remember that management may be carefully reading over your remarks, so that the simple "I agree with the appraisal" furnishes HR with no clue as to your real frame of mind. This can be especially helpful when promotions as well as repatriation assignments are being considered.

COMMUNICATION AND DECISION MAKING

Once appropriate repatriate opportunities are identified, the communication and decision-making processes begin.

Hopefully there will be more than one opportunity that can be offered to the returning expatriate. As soon as these job openings are known, the updated job descriptions for them should be forwarded to the expat so that he or she can review actual job content in order to make a decision. Even if there is only one such position available, that description will play an enormous role in clarifying the extent of the job responsibilities back home.

Most expatriates carry unreasonable expectations that their current level of autonomy and the wide breadth of job functions will also apply to home country positions. As we discussed earlier, this is rarely the case unless the job identified is a substantial promotion (which is the optimal alternative for both management and the repatriate, except that it rarely occurs). The expatriate will be less prone to disappointment over narrower job breadth if he or she already understands that through reading over the position description. It will be far more difficult to ferret out how much autonomy goes with the job, but the general rule of thumb that domestic positions are more directly managed than overseas assignments is usually correct.

If there are no suitable permanent positions found by the management, as is often the case, the repatriate should exercise some patience and limit the status inquiries to once per week.

First, the usual tack of assigning people in these cases is to find the holding pen we mentioned earlier. Rather than becoming depressed by temporary work, repatriates can further their career interests by exploring jobs that might branch out from what they had always perceived as their only path. In John's case, management might choose to see if he would be interested in a training role, working with potential expats. Here, the balance that John should weigh involves the possibilities of new marketing positions opening up at headquarters or investigating whether he has a genuine liking, and possesses the required skills for training. Repatriate John will need to seek HR, management development, and mentor advice in working through the alternatives. If spouse Jane can find a job more easily at the headquarters location than in Moose Jaw, that kind of factor should be considered, along with school quality, housing, and other factors.

So the ultimate best practice for you repatriates: keep all your options open, including outside opportunities if the temporary position stretches beyond your comfort level.

JOB OFFER(S)

Once suitable positions have been found, HR sets up appropriate interviews for the repatriate with each of the respective home country hiring managers. Home country manager and corporate functional managers are alerted to the final choice and are asked for their input to the repatriate, if he or she so desires that counsel.

The compensation component will have been calculated by corporate compensation, using only the expatriate's base pay component of the expatriate package as the basis for making the new base salary adjustment.

POST-RETURN TRAINING AND REVERSE CULTURAL SHOCK SESSIONS

The training people need to review the repatriate's record and the input from management succession to position the right kind of technical training that will develop the employee's skills along the career path lines that were previously identified. These recommendations ought to be shared with the repatriate's new manager so that there is a basic understanding of how the company is strategizing his or her career path.

Concurrently, the home country training people should organize reverse cultural shock sessions for the entire family, preferably as soon as they have returned, or in the alternative, while still at the host country, if sufficiently professional counselors are available there.

HOME COUNTRY NETWORKING

For both expatriate and spouse it is never too early to commence networking once the site of the repatriation position has been selected. For the returning expat, he or she should begin to establish a regular communications avenue with the home country manager. The expat needs to get a grasp of what objectives the home country manager has in mind, as well as some idea of how deeply into the management of those requirements that manager will involve himself or herself.

For a further exploration into that new position, the repatriate ought to reach out to the current incumbent to review present objectives that are expected to continue through the repatriate's assuming the reins. The repatriate should ask the incumbent about management style issues, other work associates, and any tips that the current incumbent believes would be helpful in settling into that position. During this entire process, the repatriate ought to be in touch with the home country mentor to exchange views as to the most effective method to start the new job. What corporate contacts will be most helpful? Which ones, if any, would be better avoided? Should the mentor relationship continue?

For the spouse, the same issues regarding housing, job, and school that confronted him or her on the cusp of the expatriate assignment are again looming at the start of the repatriation process. If the family is returning to the same work location that they left, much of the necessary networking on these subjects can be accelerated, but with caution. So much change can accompany the passage of time that the place they thought they thoroughly knew as home may be a different place when they return to it. Therefore, the family unit is better positioned mentally if all members are prepared to return to a new environment. The family benefits by taking this mental set in that they will not be assuming that they are already well versed in every aspect of the settling-in scenario.

Consequently, the expat family unit needs to contact realtors, school administrators, and any friends who might be living in their target residence area for advice as to the wisest choices for the expat family. If the expat has a financial/tax adviser, this is the time to reach out for advice as to the ramifications of looking for purchase or rental properties in the target location. Also, the first year back from an overseas assignment is usually a tax nightmare for repatriates, and the company's tax support ought to continue until the first tax year back in the home country has been properly accounted for to both host country and home country tax authorities.

The spouse ought to contact his or her last employer, if that was a comfortable fit, to see if there are any opportunities there. In addition, the network of search people and friends ought to be reinvigorated with calls/e-mails, followed up with an updated resume. Effective searches average anywhere from six to nine months, so the more lead time on this process the spouse can be provided, the better off the family unit will be financially.

EXIT INTERVIEW

Well-managed companies are keenly interested in how the expatriate really felt about the job, the management, and the coemployees, both other expatriates and local staff at the host location. The expat's host country manager or HR sets up an exit interview to obtain the expatriate's thoughts, either formally or informally. Managers try to gain feedback from the expat under the assumption that departing expatriates generally will be open in their evaluations. They will not be around to view any beneficial or detrimental fallout on fellow staff members.

Managers can derive valuable information during these exit interviews. The expat is transferring back under mutually agreeable terms. Consequently, he or she should be in a mental framework to evaluate people and programs fairly. Both managers and repatriates should be prepared to handle the issue of the confidentiality of the information gleaned from this discussion.

For departing repatriates, you should keep in mind the balance between being totally open with your host country manager and relating evaluations that may ultimately come back to haunt you. You are still an employee of the same company, and individuals who may be severely hurt by your assessments may still be employees years later when your paths cross again.

So host country compensation people want to know the level of new pay, management development people want to know what the employee *really* thought of his or her managers, and so on. Consistent with human nature, the departing expat will not be totally unbiased; there may have been chemistry issues with management, performance problems or the like, that inevitably color the feedback picture for managerial reviews.

POSITIVE REPATRIATION APPROACHES

For a repatriate who has returned to a position that is less than comfortable, that repatriate can take some positive steps while utilizing patience with the continuing search process. What are some of these actions that can help the repatriate and the management?

Consider All Avenues of Potential Contribution

Is repatriate John's only viable alternative as a temporary position holder to sit back, continue the endless inventory of office supplies, and organize the office Super Bowl pool? After all, he's had three years of a Paris expatriate's experience but no one can spare a minute to hear about those overseas adventures. Just track the paper clips, John.

But there are actions that John can take to improve his lot.

He can visit with HR and the training people to see if they would like some input regarding how his own preparation stacked up to what the challenges were in his family unit's transition into the Paris operation and the French culture. This fresh input ought to be readily reviewed by the expatriate management group. John might even find himself on a trainer's platform, outlining to expat candidates what his experiences were in the expatriation process.

John should offer HR his availability as a mentor, not just for future Paris-bound expatriates, but also to any expatriates seeking general help in keeping up with what is going on at the headquarters location. This will provide John with a solid opportunity to remain in the loop so that the mentored expat can be kept current.

John can offer his services to help the assessment team examine possible expatriate pool candidates. He will be able to offer fresh insights into the techniques for successfully grappling with a host country culture, such as the French, which can be unforgiving to expatriates.

John should regularly contact the management succession people to remind them of his eagerness to pursue the career paths that had been agreed upon back at the time of initial repatriation. There may eventually come a time when the succession people will become so exasperated that they will aggressively search through the organization's structure to locate a real fit for John. John should not settle for "don't call us, we'll call you."

Cultivate Networks of Associates and Fellow Repatriates

John should establish and maintain a network of managers who will be able to exchange career opportunity news and render advice.

Conduct Family Financial Audit

John should take this breathing spell to engage in a financial inventory. If he does not have a financial adviser, now is the time to select one. Repatriates, unfortunately, rapidly adjust themselves to levels of spending that are regarded as natural overseas, but can cause monetary woes back in the home country. Overseas, many expatriates are able literally to bank their base salaries and live very comfortably off their allowance, premiums, and special payments. How do these monies get invested? Should there be a family budget, considering the sudden withdrawal of expatriate package rewards? Who will replace those accountants who prepared the multiple tax returns each year? What size mortgage commitment makes sense in sizing up the local housing market?

These and a host of other cost analysis and budgeting exercises are timely and valuable undertakings for any repatriate family unit.

Conduct Benefits Audit

John should take this opportunity to review his family's benefit plans status. Now that they are back in the United States, the Jones family may have to make some careful decisions regarding their cafeteria plan's spectrum of benefits. Should John change the employee contribution portion of his 401(k)? Are there available options for contributing to long-term deferred compensation plans? Do the company's health insurance programs adequately protect his family or should he seek additional coverage? Is long-term care insurance now a viable program for any of the family members? John should first look to Dot.com's own benefits section for help in deciding what programs would be most appropriate for the Jones family.

Expand Family Time

John should also take quality time to renew and grow closer relationships with spouse Jane and children. Overseas jobs generally take more time than the traditional nine-to-five domestic positions. They seem to have more dimensions, more tasks and projects to complete than their domestic counterparts. Now repatriate John is blessed with more hours each week to be a closer husband and dad.

The Jones children face some daunting challenges. Many of their closest friends have moved out of the community. They will also need help in readjusting to the school system. In the three years they've been away, the curriculum, both in breadth and level of intensity, will have begun to diverge from the host country's international school. Dad ought to be around for those initial days when the differences between an international school in Paris and a public school in the United States will become immediately apparent. There may be frequent meetings with teachers to discuss the progress of the children. Both John and spouse Jane ought to be participating in those important discussions.

Solve Spousal Reentry Challenges

Spouse Jane will also have to deal with serious transitions. Many expatriate packages are so rich that the expat and spouse can afford a maid, cook, security person, chauffeur, and other help that add up to a comfortable way to live. On return, Jane faces the sudden disappearance of all these helpers, and if he or she has been away on a long assignment, this transition is a hard one to endure. This element of prereturn training cannot be overemphasized. It just seems that human nature quickly takes such amenities for granted, and once they have been pulled away, the family unit really feels that loss.

By way of illustration, my former hometown Chappaqua, New York, is a small community in northern Westchester County, about 40 miles north of New York City. It is conveniently nestled among major corporate headquarters, including the Reader's Digest, PepsiCo, IBM, and Texaco, not to mention all the New York City corporate headquarters just 50 minutes away by train. As in any bedroom community, many of its residents are employees of those major multinationals, and several families among them have had expatriate experience. It was intriguing to see that those repatriate families who were U.S.-based were generally facing significant adjustment problems in the loss of their expatriate lifestyles. The resulting stress produced some divorces and separations that probably would never have occurred had the couple not been expatriated and then repatriated.

But what made the social impact of relocations even more visible was the lifestyle of the non-U.S. expatriates brought over to the U.S. headquarters for two- or three-year-term assignments. Now once again we could see the household help, the chauffeurs, and the gardeners, in short all the helpers who had been so sorely missed by the repatriate families. When one observed how those sets of repatriates and expatriates mixed socially, one could read the emotional anxieties and longings in the faces of the U.S. repatriates. Their envy was palpable.

Returning families ought to be prepared for this rude awakening because while on the assignment they become so quickly and unconsciously adapted to the new trappings that they can't appreciate the dimensions of life without that help. Sound expert counseling can prepare the family for that shock.

Moving On to Another Overseas Assignment

Earlier we saw that nearly a half of all expatriates currently on assignment had at least one prior overseas assignment. While this percentage may decline gradually because of the trend toward selecting younger expatriate candidates for developmental and project assignments, as well as first-job expatriates (as part of recruiting exposure cycle), the fact remains that companies often select proven veterans over first-timers because of the abysmal overseas assignment completion rates. It is abundantly clear that the lessons learned by expatriates in one host country can be reapplied, almost generically, to any other host county. The challenge for the veteran expatriate is to give sufficient time and effort to appreciate sufficiently the customs and culture of the new host location.

For example, if you have just completed a three-year assignment in Tokyo and are now advised that your next location will be Seoul, you will have learned many necessary lessons in the process of adjusting to the Japanese culture. You will have mastered the patient listening process and the ability to work with consensus building, among many other cultural practices that may or may not be reapplied by cultural conversion to the Korean ways of doing things. Expats are generally tempted to apply those techniques that proved successful in the first location to the second, particularly if some of the outward cultural clues resemble each other.

This would be a very big mistake in the case of Tokyo and Seoul because the two cultures contain sharply contrasting customs and mores that still persist, even in the face of rapidly advancing acceptance of many Western mores by both nationalities.

Having worked with both cultures for a number of years, I can only pass along the general advice that they are more different than alike, and the further one gains contact with both, the more those differences, at first hardly discernible, become more readily apparent. A good expatriate needs to appreciate this, and the best way to achieve their appreciation is another set of cultural and training sessions for the entire family prior to departure from the first host location.

By way of example, if our expat John had been assigned to Seoul, not Paris, and had become familiar with the fast-moving decision-making process that most *chaebols* (Korean corporate families) encourage of their employees (and indeed, the multinationals tend to follow the same processes), he would have a difficult initiation period in Tokyo. The Japanese local staff would back away from such a direct approach to resolving business problems, preferring more time to review and more people involved to do that reviewing. John's employer could have avoided such errors by providing sound, experienced, counseling before John ever left Seoul.

When management gives a second successive overseas assignment to an expatriate, that employee must raise some concerns to management.

The expat must appreciate that he or she will be removed from the home country operations center for another significant period. Although the assignee will now be exposed to another business environment and culture (thereby increasing the expat's subsequent marketability and value to the firm), the downside from his or her perspective is the shrinking career horizon as viewed from home headquarters. In this regard, all of the factors we referred to in the discussion of lengthening assignments also directly apply here. If there is a six-year, not a three-year, absence from the power base of the corporate decision makers, there will be an even greater mountain to climb if the expat is interested in climbing it. If internal promotion to a top corporate chair on that mountain is not what the expat really wants out of life, then a second successive overseas tour can open the way for a series of expatriate opportunities, à la the Schlumberger International Staff, in which the expat family gradually loses the link to the home country.

As we saw in the Dubai portrait of Trevor and family, this sort of career and lifestyle can become attractive (and, indeed, addictive) because of its ever-changing, ever-challenging nature. There are many such inveterate expatriates on assignment today who would staunchly resist a repatriation assignment because that old lifestyle and management process are no longer appealing to them, and simply not challenging enough for their tastes.

These second (and third, and so on) host country assignees must consider the long-term impact on family. Virtually all of these expats I've encountered had talked through the sacrifices inherent in loosening ties to their country of origin and had come to terms with the decision that it would be a better lifestyle to continue the expatriate career path. The spouse in these families is called upon to decide whether seeking a new job every time there is another reassignment is in his or her best interest. Some occupations are more transportable across national boundaries, including teaching at an international or local school.

The expat needs to consider the pluses and minuses on the academic well-being of the children continually changing schools every three years or so. Certainly they will benefit from the sheer variety of cultural exposures, but will the varying quality levels of instruction and the disjointed course progressions translate into choosing a private school to ensure a steadier academic process?

Critical family considerations such as that schooling dilemma or the spouse's own career will continue to challenge the managers of overseas programs to come up with serious programs and policies that will produce the net effect of maintaining the family unit at the host locations.

Assignment Refusals

There is precious little literature describing how assignment rejections actually impact employees. In the case of multiple overseas postings that we just reviewed, suppose an expat would prefer to renew his or her link with the home operation, or has a spouse unwilling to try another posting without a job, or children whose education would appear to be at risk if another overseas tour were to be undertaken. All of these reasonable factors could enter into the expatriate family's decision—hopefully unanimous—that turning down the next overseas assignment, or turning down the repatriation assignment in favor of another overseas posting, would be in their best interests.

Most reasonable managers will professionally work through the benefits and detriments in the rejection of the overseas opportunity with the candidate. Unless the organization has a specific and crucial need for this expatriate, the only reasonable alternative is for the company to withdraw the offer and find him or her a suitable position in the country of choice. Managers will appreciate that sending a family against their wishes will likely result in a failed assignment anyway, so why even take that chance?

But for you candidates who have already rejected one assignment, be very careful that you have bona fide reasons for turning down a subsequent assignment offer made after a reasonable interval from the first offer. Experience tells us not to reject that second or third posting offer unless you happen to be the CEO's closest personal friend or relative. Employees who become immobile in a mobile employee population will lose credibility as loyal, trustworthy, long-term players, barring some understandable obstacles such as ill health of a loved one. In today's world of revering the term "globalization" and all that it stands for, an employee who persists in rejecting overseas opportunities will sooner or later be dropped from the list of high-potential employees.

But then again, not every employee dreams of getting on that list; they often have other priorities, and that is perfectly fine as long as their self-assessments are thorough.

Notes

1. *Four Screenplays of Ingmar Bergman*, Ingmar Bergman, New York: Simon & Schuster 1960, p. 160.
2. *Global Relocation Trends, 1999 Survey Report*, Windham International, National Foreign Trade Council, and Institute for International Human Resources, May 9, 1999, p. 39.
3. "A Study Sees a Downside to Going Overseas as an Executive," Judith H. Dobrzynski, *New York Times*, Aug. 3, 1998.
4. "Coming Home," J. Stewart Black, *HR World*, Jan.–Feb. 2000, p. 30.
5. Ibid.
6. "Japan Unsettles Returnees, Who Yearn to Leave Again," Howard W. French, *New York Times*, May 3, 2000, p. A14.
7. "Repatriation Planning," Deborah Conlan, *Mobility*, Sept. 1998, p. 22.
8. "Return of the Native: Costly Transitions," Jobert E. Abueva, *New York Times*, May 17, 2000, p. C8.
9. Ibid.
10. *Global Relocation Trends, 1999 Survey Report*, p. 38.

Illustration by Liz Lomax

Expatriate Assignments: Future Directions

Expatriate Assignments: Future Directions

"I have but one lamp by which my feet are guided and that is the lamp of experience. I know no way of judging of the future but by the past."
Patrick Henry, Speech in Virginia
Convention, 1775

And so our modern revolution of the computer, not the musket, continues its frantic pace. Patriots Paine and Henry would be fascinated with this struggle's sheer velocity and faceless leadership. Their revolution took years to foment and was led by extremely well known patriots. Our current globalization momentum springs from hundreds of corporate boardrooms occupied by thousands of corporate executives deciding on global strategy and dispatching their corporate troops—in the form of expatriates—to engage the corporate competition on foreign battlegrounds.

Many of those senior managers, the generals in this conflict, are operating under a severe handicap; they developed through home headquarters operations and have no expatriate experience. They are familiar with overseas locations and cultures, but as hotel guests, not as residents. As such, they continue to perceive that all of these foreign marketplaces can be somehow lumped together as "globalized," and therefore merit one-size-fits-all solutions.

A truly thought-provoking book on senior management's strategic overseas staffing choices is *Managing Across Borders*, by Christopher Bartlett and Sumantra Ghoshal.[1] They describe an often-used approach and present a viable alternative:

> For many companies, developing such a portfolio of roles and the interdependent relationships to link them has been a difficult task. Awash in the waves of the so-called globalization of industries and competition, the top management of many worldwide companies has instead launched extensive and expensive programs for "globalizing" all their managers. No company invested more in this effort than ITT, which took all managers responsible for the telecommunications business through a large-scale educational process in one of Europe's premier business schools, with the explicit objective of transforming national specialists into global generalists. The investment ceased only when the business was sold after years of struggle. . . . The reality is that in a volatile world of the transnational corporation, there is no such thing as a universal global manager.

Are they saying that general international exposure for selected employees such as the executive educations programs described earlier are wasteful?

Not at all. The participants are selected by their managers with specific strategies, whether offensive or defensive, prompting their attendance. ITT was taking the tack that every single telecommunications employee was going to receive extensive international training exposure, regardless of the particular strategy of his or her own department, or, for that matter, their corporation.

The authors propose another structuring, three groups of specialists, business managers, country managers, and functional managers. They set distinctly separate roles for each. The business manager needs to understand thoroughly how to make transactions across national borders; the country manager needs to understand the needs of the host nation; and the functional manager serves as the cross-pollinator. They report to a corporate manager, whose roles are those of global visionary and a talent scout.

This concept could well be the kind of model your senior management could start with in its analysis of how to delegate overseas responsibilities effectively. It certainly smacks of a sound needs analysis approach, which, unfortunately, does not appear to be the current practice of senior management when it comes to organizing a smoothly coordinated overseas postings process. In any event, this book ought to be especially valuable reading for corporate organization design gurus in their perpetual quest to find the right combination of overseas responsibilities.

The future of expatriate assignments is unclear because two conflicting forces that are at work now will continue, in all likelihood, in the foreseeable future. On the positive side, the galloping global economy continues to demand ever more skilled and cultural adept people to advance those strategies planned out in the boardrooms. Without these effective performers, the weaker organizations are going to be swallowed whole by the stronger companies.

The "marriage" of Daimler and Chrysler is playing out as proof of this trend. It will continue as a living case study—World 101, for senior management. The Daimler organization was planning for international growth and had staffed its organization with employees who were ready to learn, to go overseas, and to contribute knowledge to the organization. By contrast, Chrysler had not encouraged expatriate activity, apparently believing that it could somehow survive in the auto industry wars by staying home.

On the darker side of the expatriate process is senior management's puzzling reluctance to put real effort into effective programs of planning and compensation. One theory is plausible: Senior managers today, Mr. Daft being a rarity, have not been expatriates themselves. They would be more sensitive to the various needs of their overseas assignees had they experienced the cultural, economic, and reward inequities firsthand. The vast majority of so-called multinationals continue to staff the corner room with headquarters homegrown executives. That's the way intracorporate politics usually work. But when one backs away to look at the future, they would be far better positioned bringing in the more seasoned overseas managers, whether local staff or expatriates, to give some informal executive education to their domestic brethren. Until the corporate boards broaden their field of candidates to include their best overseas managers, their selections for top management will be more of the same domestic-raised executives. General Electric's recent selection of another domestic executive to replace Jack Welch stands out as another example of this history. That promotion was particularly ironic because it followed a clear signal by Mr. Welch just a few years before to the effect that he would be the last GE CEO to have held only domestic positions.

Will management turn this practice around? One would like to think so if the next generation of corporate leaders comes from the ranks of expatriates, such as Coke's Daft. The issue then becomes: Which organizations will come to grips with the problem in the near future, thereby gaining precious competitive advantage in this decade?

Corporate players intent on gaining global markets will have to confront a central issue of structuring their expatriate jobs so their strategies can be fulfilled. On this score we have seen much press on developing all of the company's managers to be globalized.

But there is no reason to extend that globalization process (whether through overseas assignments or education) to all corporate managers. Organization design people ought to be conducting a basic needs analysis to determine which positions are likely to need overseas knowledge and to what extent. Those skill requirements ought to be made known to the training and development people, so they can evaluate the current incumbents in those positions who will need their services.

At this point in time, most senior managers appear to be so focused on the plans to expand market share that they may have failed to pay sufficient attention to assembling the right kinds of people to effectuate those expansion plans. Indeed, no matter how well constructed those expansion plans look on paper, they will not bring success to the company unless the right employees are positioned to carry out those directions.

For that reason, senior managers will have to pause in all that planning for the business in the abstract and start planning for what kinds of employees will be needed to conduct that business effectively.

In this decade we'll soon see what kind of organization and corporate practices will prevail in the hotly contested war over turf. The big picture will continue to be whether management can properly deploy its best expatriates in roles that work together as part of an overall strategy that is clearly communicated to the overseas managers. In the P&G and Coca-Cola cases we saw a common thread of success. Companies can expand all over the globe, but being successful means the company must understand each of its marketplaces and modify its products and presence to fit comfortably into that local culture. And companies can do that only with the help of individuals who understand the corporate mind-set and can make the right adaptations to an overseas location—in short, expatriates.

Today's expatriates and the managers of their programs will gain nothing by waiting for an enlightened ex-expatriate to gallop into the boardroom and set overseas processes straight. Apparently that could be a very, very long wait. Expatriates, their managers, and the managers of the assignment programs can take the initiative in planning and implementing the improvements for which these programs call. Perhaps this is a time when real reform can work its way up the company structure rather than coming down from the senior ranks.

There is every reason to believe that senior management will take notice and action when they observe an improvement in successful assignment rates, a slowdown in the departures of repatriates, and, so vital to the company, a distinct improvement in overseas performance because the best people were selected, trained, and cared for by empowered company managers.

You managers and expatriates have a voice in determining your future success, and your joint efforts at bringing sound practices to a process that cries out for improvement will help your company's future in the new decade as well as your own.

In writing this book, I set out to show the problems that have arisen in the expatriate process that have generated an adversarial relationship between manager and expatriate. The purpose in setting out each of the problem practices was not to place blame on either party to the overseas contract; rather it was to show the steps that each can take to go forward in a more effective relationship—bringing more bottom-line results to the company while ensuring that the assignment is a challenging and enjoyable process to the expat.

If corporate managers are sometimes portrayed in today's press as the villains solely responsible for the current failed assignments debacle, that criticism ought to be shared, to a lesser extent, by the expatriates themselves, who could and should be more proactive in bringing forth their suggestions as to appropriate steps to take in improving the overall process.

This book, then, ought to serve as a guide for both manager and expatriate in converting what has been a master/servant mentality into a genuine planning partnership.

And that process, I earnestly submit, is a combination of understanding what steps are mutually beneficial, agreeing to them, and following up with regular communications that ensure that the agreement—and any new modifications to it—are being properly followed. I've attempted to set out each of those steps as "best practices," probably an overworked label today but nonetheless appropriate for this expatriate process application.

What the book cannot spell out is the best method of specific communication. That is a matter for the manager and expatriate to work out for each assignment. Since human beings tend to be so unpredictable in their interrelationships, I leave those individual chemistry solutions to the manager and expatriate. Both will need a great deal of time and effort to make those communications truly effective.

Good luck to the both of you!

Note

1. *Managing Across Borders*, by Christopher Bartlett and Sumantra Ghoshal, Boston: Harvard Business School Press, 1998, p. 232.

Index

Abueva, Jobert, 284–285
Acquisitions, cross-border, 2
Adaptability, 32, 85, 109, 113
Adaptation, cultural, 172
Adjustment:
  cultural, 42
  family, 86
  to length of assignment, *see* Length of
    assignment
  reverse cultural shock, 281–283, 291–292
Age Discrimination in Employment Act
    (ADEA), 31
Alliance Capital, 21
Allowance:
  compensation package, 54–55, 96
  cost of living, 209, 224
  incremental compensation, 211
  mobility, 209
Alternative opportunities, management
    search, 287–288

American Compensation Association Journal,
    209, 211–212
American Express, 38, 69, 268
American Graduate School of
    Management, Thunderbird
    International Consortia, 147–150,
    155
Amoco, 21
Analysis:
  of company/target employer, 117–122
  self-, 110–116
Annual reports, 5
Antiglobalization movement, 2
Antitrust, 3
Aon Associates, 95, 185
Aspirations, review of, 288–289
Assessment:
  background checks, 144–145
  corporate practices, 135–136
  personal circumstances review, 143

309

Assessment (*Continued*)
  recommended management practices,
    136–137
  self-assessment tools for candidate,
    140–142
  structured interview, 142–143
  testing, 143–144
  tools for management, 137–140
Assignment duration, 50. *See also* Length of
    assignment
Assignment objectives:
  demand-driven, 49–72
  developmental-driven, 72–77
  generally, 31, 47–48, 101
  types of, 48
Assignment/project extensions, 66, 220,
    266–270
Assignment refusal/rejection, 163,
    300–301
Assistance programs:
  employee, 242
  family, 86
  legal, 225
  spousal, 87, 164, 253, 263
  tax, 225
Associates for International Research
    (AIRINC), 201
Atlantic Richfield (ARCO), 21
Atlas Van Lines, 85
Authority, delegation of, 168
Automobiles, 55, 237–238
Autonomy, 13
AXA, 21

Background checks, 144–145
Balance sheet approach:
  base salary and, 201–203
  components of, 34–35, 96,
    201–202
  goods and services, 204–205
  housing, 203–204, 221
  reserve, 205
  strengths of, 206–208
  taxes, 205–206
  trend in, 218
  weakness of, 208–212
Barrett, Edgar, 136

Bartlett, Christopher, 304
Base salary, 201, 221
Beckett, Francis, 155
Benefits audit, 295–296
Bennett, Rita, 141–142
Bennett Associates, 141
Bing, Cass Mercer, 186
Black, Dr. J. Stewart, 97–98, 143, 281, 285
Bloom, Matt, 226–227
Bolles, Richard Nelson, 122
Bonuses:
  completion, 222–223
  generally, 53, 70, 176, 244
  performance, 225
Book list, information resources, 122–126
Briefings, outreach campaigns, 107
Brookes, Michael, 113–114
Brownouts, 91, 98, 223
Buck Consultants, 201
Burns, Patrick, 51, 142
Business Week, 154
By the window, 71

Candidate(s), *see* Potential
    candidates/expatriates
  evaluation of candidates, 108–109
  local staff, 174–175
  notification of candidates, 109–110
  outreach campaign, 107–108
  pool review, 175
  potential candidate list, 106–107
  self-assessment tools, 140–142
  training for, *see* Training programs
Career development:
  educational programs, 17
  importance of, 129, 271–272
  opportunities, 13
Career management/planning, 57–58, 114
Career Mosaic, 123
Career path, in employment contract,
    57–58
Career planning, postdeparture, 279–286
Cendant, 254
Chevron, 65
Children, of expatriates, 14, 40–42, 112,
    162, 261, 296
Citigroup, 75

Club membership, 55, 238
Coaching, 180, 192, 252. *See also* Mentor(s)
COBRA, 59
Coca-Cola, 7–9, 305–306
Communications, 44, 101, 106, 169–171, 240, 290–291
Compaq, 21
Compensation:
  expatriate, 53, 109
  history of, 176
  package components, *see* Compensation package
  reward programs, 121
  senior management, 97
Compensation package:
  base salary, 201–203, 221
  case illustration, 213–214
  choices in, 227
  completion bonuses, 222–223
  core, 227
  cost of living allowances, 209, 224
  customized, 227
  danger pay, 223–224
  extended assignments, 270–271
  foreign service premiums, 222
  generally, 177
  hardship premiums, 223
  legal assistance, 225
  medical insurance programs, 224
  mobility premiums, 222
  performance bonuses, 225
  relocation costs, 225
  retirement plans, 224–225
  savings plans, 224–225
  special incentive payments, 221–222
  tax assistance, 225
Competition, dealing with, 265, 281
Completion bonuses, 222–223
Conference Board, 198
Conlan, Deborah, 283
Consensus building, 169
Consortium, 146–149
Consulting firms, 97
Consumer Price Index (CPI), 205
Cook, Thomas, 19

Cornell University, 154
Corporate challenges, critical, 87–88
Corporate cross-border growth stages:
  case illustration, 120–121
  companies encouraging full coordination between overseas locations, 119–120
  companies operating businesses on purely global basis, 120
  companies operating complete businesses in each country, 118–120
  domestic companies using overseas locations for sales, 117–118
Corporate headquarters, location of, 118–120
Corporate philosophy, 31, 114
Corporations, assessment practices, 135–136
Cost of expatriate programs:
  average, 99, 175
  balance sheet approach, 208–209
  compensation, *see* Compensation; Compensation package; Reward systems
  failed assignments, 100, 262
  out-of-corporate-pocket expenditures, 97–98
  lifestyle issues, 96–97
Cost of living allowances, 209, 224
Counteroffers, 265–266
Cover letters, 128
Cranfield University School of Management, 37
Cross-border projects, 107
Cross-cultural experiences, 19
Cross-cultural programs, 183–188
Cross-cultural training:
  customized, 187–188
  duration of, 186
  importance of, 184–185
  sample agenda, 187
  utilization of, 185–186
Cross-functional teams, 100, 165
Cultural shock:
  dealing with, 187
  reverse, 281–283, 291–292
Cultural training, 160

Culture issues, 13–14, 168–174
Currency exchange, 96, 217

Daft, Douglas, 7–8, 305–306
Daimler-Chrysler, 9–12, 67, 258, 305
Daiwa Securities America, 19
Danger pay, 223–224
Day-to-day operations, 48, 72–73
Decision makers, in selection process,
    164–166
Decision making, next assignment process,
    290–291
Delayed replacements, 272–273
Delegation, 168, 304
Demand-driven assignments:
    case illustration, 68–72
    defined, 48–49
    developmental-driven assignments
        distinguished from, 72–73
    employment contracts, 52–61
    project assignments, 65–67
    regular operational functions, 49–52
    rotational assignments, 63–65
    role of prior incumbent, 61–63
Destination pricing, 203, 216–217
Developmental-driven assignments:
    case illustration, 73–75
    defined, 49
    employment contracts, 75
    experienced manager, 72–75
    for recent university graduates, 75–77
DHR International, 19
Digest of Education Statistics, 37
Digital Equipment Corporation (DEC), 21
Directory of Jobs and Careers Abroad, 128
Distance learning programs:
    combined with classroom sessions,
        154–155
    components of, 153–154
Diversity:
    age, 37
    gender, 36–38
    racial, 37
Driscoll, Jack, 127
Drug screening, 94, 145
Due diligence, 144
Dwyer, Timothy, 233–234

Education, see Training programs
    career development programs, 17
    expatriate children, 12, 42, 65, 112, 123,
        162, 299
    information resources, 123–124
    transcripts, 191
    university training programs geared to
        international careers, 155–156
Elders, treatment of, 44
Empathy, importance of, 172
Employee assistance programs, 242
Employment ads, 128
Employment contract provisions:
    allowance, 54–55
    car, 55
    club, 55
    compensation, 53
    health benefits, 55
    home leave, 55
    housing, 54
    international assignment manual,
        references to, 60–61
    job duration, 52
    job location, 52
    mentors, 60
    negotiations, 178–179
    next assignment, 57–58, 75–76
    payment method, 53
    pension, 55–56
    premiums, 54–55
    preparation programs, 57
    relocation arrangements, 53–54
    schooling, 55
    Social Security programs, 55
    taxes, 56
    termination, 59–60
    training programs, 57
    vacations, 55
Employment Relocation Council,
    85
Escape Artist, 123
Euro, 16
European Union, 3
Evaluation process, of candidates,
    108–109
Executive search firms, 19, 32,
    126–127

Executive training programs:
  case illustrations, 147–149, 151–153
  consortia, 146–147
  customized, 150–153
  distance learning, 153–155
  importance of, 145
  virtual classrooms, 155
Expat Exchange, 123
Expatriate families, managerial concerns,
  84–91. *See also* Family issues/concerns
Expatriate Moms, 123
Expatriate's Handbook, The (Twinn/Burns),
  51–52
Expatriates, generally:
  candidate pool, review of, 175
  diversity and, 35–38
  fairness, perceptions of, 206–207
  family issues, 11–12, 14, 38–43, 84–91,
    109, 111
  generic trait requirements, 167–174
  lifestyle of, 96
  nonfamily, treatment of, 43–44
  potential, *see* Potential
    candidates/expatriates
  profile of, 29–44
  sources of, 32–36
  trait requirements, 168–174
  turnover rate, 99, 280

Failed assignments:
  cost of, 262
  rate of, 135
  reasons for, 84, 86, 91, 98, 100, 134,
    262–264
Fairchild, 268
Family issues/concerns:
  assistance programs, 86
  challenges, generally, 85
  children, 14, 40–43, 112, 162, 261,
    299
  divorce, 84
  extended assignments, 71
  family profile, 176
  financial audit, 295
  impact on, generally, 11–12, 14, 109,
    111–113, 299
  in selection process, 93–94

  self-analysis and, 111–113
  spousal employment, 71, 163, 178,
    236–237
Family visitation, 66
Federation of American Women's Clubs
  Overseas, 123
Financial audit, 295
Financial issues/concerns, *see* Bonuses;
  Compensation; Compensation
  package; Reward systems
Flexibility, importance of, 172–173
Forbes, 14–16, 21
Fordham University, 154–156
Foreign service premiums, 209, 222
Fortune, 5, 14–15, 18
401(k) plans, 56, 295
Frazee, Valerie, 85
French, Howard, 282
Full expatriate package, 177

General Electric, 305
Ghoshal, Sumantra, 304
Giant Food, 21
Global Assignment Preparedness Survey
  (G-A-P-S), 143–144
Global firms, listing of, 14–15
Global HR Leaders' Agenda Survey,
  36–37
Globalization, *see also specific corporations*
  benefits of, 13–14
  family, impact on, 11–12, 14, 40–43
  future directions, 305–306
  information resources, generally,
    17–18
  movement, development of, 2–3, 12, 136
  trends in, 17
*Globalizing People through International
  Assignments* (Black), 97, 143
Global Relocation Trends, 1999 Survey Report
  (NFTC), 17, 31, 36, 48, 82–83, 87–88,
    101, 161, 163–164, 183, 196, 233, 247,
    262, 286
Global Resume and CV Guide, The, 128
Global transition process, 8–9
Global WorkForce, 85
Goal-setting, 240–241
Golzen, Godfrey, 36

Government web sites, as information
    resource, 124
Gregersen, Hal, 98
Group Carso, 21
Grundling, Dr. Ernest, 167–168, 173
GTE, 199

Hansen, Paul, 196, 212
Hardship premiums, 223
Hayes, Samuel, III, 25
Health benefits, 55. *See also* Medical
    insurance programs
Health clubs, 238
Hibbitt, William, 233–234
Hiring manager, functions of, *see* Selection
    process; Selection process model
Hiscox Group, 233
Hofstede, Geert, 152–153, 170, 172, 227,
    282
Home country:
    compensation standards, 200–201,
        212–215, 217–219
    mentor, 251, 270, 292
    networking, 292–293
    return to, *see* Repatriation
Home leave, 55, 70, 279, 288–289
Host country:
    compensation standards, 200–201, 203,
        215–219
    local staff, 174–175, 188–189
    mentor, 192
Housing, 54, 162, 181–182, 192, 221,
    235
Hubbard, Phillip, 25
Human resources (HR):
    functions of, *see* Screening
        procedures/techniques; Selection
        process; Selection process model
    job description updates,
        166–167
    potential expatriates, concerns of,
        116
Hymowitz, Carol, 146–147

IBM, 69, 127, 268, 297
Incentive payments, 221–222. *See also*
    Bonuses; Reward systems

Incumbent:
    meeting with, 189–190
    role of, 61–63
Information resources:
    books, 122–126
    Internet, 123–126, 234, 236–237
Ingram, 16
In-house staffing, benefits of, 137
In-progress assignments:
    automobiles, 237–238
    health clubs, 238
    housing, 235
    mentor relationships, 239–240
    orientation family, 232
    performance appraisal, 241–248
    performance goals, establishment of,
        240–241
    productivity gap, 249–254
    schooling, 235–236
    security plans, 232–234
    social clubs, 238
    spouse's job, 236–237
    vacations, 238–239
Institute for International Human
    Resources (IIHR), 17, 130
Insurance, *see* Medical insurance programs
International Assignment Manual,
    references to, 60–61
International schools, 191
Internet, as information resource, 123–126,
    234, 236–237
Interviews:
    behavioral, 141
    exit, 259, 266, 293–294
    importance of, 93, 108, 141–142
    on-site, 176
    personal circumstances review, 143
    predeparture career, 277–279
    structured, 142–143
Involuntary termination, 59, 62,
    166
ITAP, 254
ITT, 304

Japanese companies, 21–22. *See also specific
    corporations*
Job application, 137–138, 176

Job description:
    expatriate review and update of, 289–290
    update, 166–174, 289–290
Job duration, 52, 67. *See also* Length of
    assignment
Job-Hunting on the Internet (Bolles), 122–123
Job location, 52
Job offers, 82–83, 291. *See also*
    Counteroffers
Job postings:
    information resources, 124
    resistance to, 82
Job search, *see* Search for overseas
    assignment
Job Seekers' Guide to Executive Recruiters
    (Hunt/Hanlon), 126
Job summary, 50
Job title, 52, 70
Joint ventures, 2
Jones, Carol, 183
Jones, Stephen C., 8
Judgment:
    informed, 173
    in performance appraisal, 243
Just-in-time managers, 199

Kane, Koichi, 74–75
Kidnappings, 233
Kim, Young Man, 268

Language:
    skills, 109
    training, 182
Legal assistance, 225
Length of assignment, adjustments to:
    delayed replacement, 272–273
    lengthening the assignment, 266–273
    shortening the assignment, 257–266
Letter agreements, 52
Line management, functions of, 88, 165
Line supervision, role of, 105–106
Listening skills, importance of, 169–171
Living Abroad Research Center, 237
Local staff candidates, review of, 174–175
Long-term assignments, 70–72, 199–200
Lucent, 16
Lump-sum payout, 178–179, 210

Management assessment tools, 137–140
Management challenges:
    case illustration, 80–82
    cost of expatriate programs, 96–100
    expatriate families, 84–91
    job offers, 82-83
    lack of management planning,
        100–102
    overview, 79–80
    screening procedures, 83–84
    selection procedures, 83–84
    selection process evaluations, 91
    selection process standards, 91–95
Management planning, lack of, 100–102
Managerial skills, 13
Managing Across Borders (Bartlett/Ghoshal),
    261, 304
Manufacturing industry, 33–34
Medical examinations, 94, 145
Medical insurance programs, 59, 224, 296
Meetings:
    career planning, 271–272
    with host country mentor, 192
    with host location staff, 188–189
    with incumbent, 189–190
    interviews, *see* Interviews
    with other expatriate families, 191
    with real estate broker, 191–192
    with school staff, 190–191
Mentor(s):
    benefits of, 13, 60
    home country, 251, 270, 292
    host country, 192
    initial meeting with, 192
    relationship, establishment of,
        239–240
    repatriate opportunities, 294
    selection, 179–181
    senior, 251
Mergers, cross-border, 2
Milkovitch, George T., 154, 226–228
Mistakes, dealing with, 173–174. *See also*
    Failed assignments
Mobility premiums, 222
Monster.com, 126
Monster International, 123
Moore, Terrence, 80, 82

Morale, 98
Morita, Akio, 22
Multinationals, *see specific corporations*
  antiglobalization movement and, 2
  listing of, 14–15

National Foreign Trade Council, Inc.
    (NFTC), 17, 31, 36, 48–50, 82, 85–86,
    88–89, 99, 250, 258, 269
Negotiations, in selection process,
    178–179
Network for Living Abroad, 123
Networking, 126–128, 237, 288, 292–293,
    295
New branch operations, establishment of,
    67
Next alternatives, evaluation of expatriate,
    289
Next assignment, in employment
    agreement, 57–58
Next assignment process:
  alternative opportunities, management
    search, 287–288
  aspirations, review of, 288–289
  assignment refusals, 300–301
  communications, 290–291
  decision making, 290–291
  exit interview, 293–294
  job description, expatriate review and
    update of, 289–290
  job offers, 291
  networking, home country,
    292–293
  next alternatives, evaluation of
    expatriate, 289
  overseas assignments, 297–300
  positive approaches to,
    294–297
  postdeparture career planning, 279–286
  postreturn training, 291
  predeparture career interview, 277–279
  prereturn training, 287
  repatriations, 275–277
  reverse cultural shock sessions, 291–292
  training/counseling, 287
Nomura Research Institute (NRI),
    151–153, 268

Nomura Securities International, 21,
    23–26, 70, 73–77
Non-U.S.-owned companies:
  acquisitions/mergers, 21
  employment with, 18
  revenues, listing of, 20
Nonverbal cues, 171–172
Notification of candidates, 109–110

Observation, importance of, 171–172
Offer extension, 177–178
Office politics, 168
Ohmae, Kenichi, 26
Oil companies, 33–34
On-site interviews, 176
Operational functions, 49–52
Organization development stages, *see*
    Corporate cross-border growth stages
Organization Resources Counselors (ORC),
    201, 204
Orientation family, 232
Orientation programs, 63, 98,
    253
Orientation trip:
  checklist for, 188–192
  scheduling, 181–182
Outreach campaign, 107–108
Overseas Assignment Inventory,
    140–141
Overseas assignments, potential candidate
    requirements, 23
Overseas Security Advisory Council, 234

Partners, treatment of, 43–44
Partner-2-Partner, 237
Payment method, types of, 53
Pay systems, performance-based, 227. *See
    also* Compensation
Peiffer, Tom, 64
Pension plans, 55–56, 216
PepsiCo, 127, 297
Performance appraisal:
  eight "deadly sins" of, 241–244
  management training, 241–245
  participants in, 245–247
  quality of, 247–248
  self-evaluations, 246

Performance appraisal form, 93, 114, 138–139, 176, 242, 248
Performance bonuses, 225
Performance goals, 240–241
Performance reviews, 53, 114
Persistence, importance of, 173–174
Personal circumstances review, 143
Pets, relocation arrangements, 53, 191
Policy manual, as information resource, 54–55, 178
Politics, impact of, 168
Postselection assessments review, 182
Potential candidates/expatriates:
    analysis of company/target employer, 117–121
    guidelines for, 110–111
    list, 106–107
    self-analysis, 110–116
    training for, 110
Premiums:
    in employment agreement, 54–55, 96
    foreign service, 209, 222
    hardship, 223
    mobility, 222
Preparation programs, 57
PricewaterhouseCoopers (PwC), Expatriate Tax and Compensation Policies, 224
Proactive management, 73
Procter & Gamble, 5–7, 37, 80–82
Procter Way, The, 6
Productivity gap, 249–254
Professional associations, 130
Profit-sharing, 214, 221
Program manager, 114–115
Project assignments:
    case illustration, 68–70
    corporate structure reproducer assignments, 66–67
    longer-term assignments, 70–72
    new branch operations, establishment of, 67
    technical transfers, 65–66
Prudential Relocation Services, 108, 140–141, 201, 254
Pucik, Vladimir, 47–48

Quality of service, 262
Quitting, *see* Voluntary termination

RCA, 268
Reader's Digest, 127, 297
Real estate agents, role of, 182
Real estate broker, initial meeting with, 191–192
Recent graduates, developmental-driven assignments, 75–77
Reference checks, 93, 176
Reimbursements, in employment contract, 53–54
Relocation, generally:
    arrangements, 18, 53–54
    costs, 225
    services, 235
    support services, 188
Repatriation:
    alternatives review, 182–183
    challenges of, 276–277. *See also* Next assignment process
    components of, 13, 16, 71, 179, 273
    planning, 101–102, 183, 276–277
    reverse cultural shock, 281–283, 291–292
Replacement expatriate position:
    allowances, 51
    benefits of, 51
    duration of, 50
    employment agreement, 51–52. *See also* Employment contract provisions
    functions of, 50
    overseas premiums, 51
    salary range, 51
Reproducer assignments, 66–67
Resistance, to overseas postings, 82
Respect, importance of, 168–169
Retirement plans, 224–225
Revenue generation, 15, 19–20
Reward systems:
    background of, 197–199
    balance sheet approach, 201–212
    better of home or host-based systems, 217–219
    calculation methods, 200
    case illustration, 213–214

Reward systems (*Continued*)
  compensation package elements, *see*
    Compensation package
  developmental assignments, 219
  long-term assignments, 199–200,
    219–221
  multiple, 226–228
  short-term assignments, 199
  standards for, 200–201, 212–217
Riordan, Anne, 185
Risk-taking, 109
ROI approach, 263
Rotational assignments, 63–65, 169
Ruggiero, Marianne, 37–38, 250
Runzheimer, 201

Salary, 201, 221. *See also* Compensation
Sanford C. Bernstein, 21
Savings plans, 224–225
Schlumberger, 67–70, 120–121, 172–173,
    213–214
School staff, meeting with, 190–192
Schooling issues/concerns, 12, 42–43, 55,
    62, 181, 235–236, 299
Schremmp, Juergen, 9
Schuster, Jay, 211
Screening procedures/techniques, 83–84,
    92–95, 108
Seagram, 21
Search for overseas assignment:
  information resources, 122–126
  networking, 126–128
Security plans, 232–234
Selection priority, 177
Selection process:
  decision makers, 164–166
  evaluations, 91
  faulty experiences, reasons for,
    162
  model, *see* Selection process model
  procedures, 83–84
  as stand-alone process, 160
  standards, 91–95
  success indicators, 161–164
Selection process model:
  compensation package, 177
  cross-cultural programs, 183–188

expatriate candidate pool, review of,
    175
full expatriate package, 177
job description update, 166–174
local staff candidates, review of,
    174–175
mentor selection, 179–181
negotiations, 178–179
offer extended, 177–178
on-site interviews, 176
orientation trip, 181–192
postselection assessments review,
    182
relocation support services, 188
repatriation alternatives review,
    182–183
selection priority, 177
short-list candidate profile, hiring
    manager review, 175–176
Selection Research International (SRI),
    88–89, 99, 160–161, 164
Self-analysis, 110–117
Self-assessment, 140–142
Self-recognition, importance of, 30
Senior management:
  compensation, 97
  focus of, 110–111, 118
  future directions for, 304–305
  mentoring and, 252
  perceptions of expatriate family, 86–87
  role of, 80, 100, 106, 134–135
Sheridan, William, 59, 196, 212,
    226–227
Short-list candidate profile, hiring manager
    review, 175–176
Short-term assignments, 199
SHRM 2000 Retention Practices Survey,
    260
SK Group, 70, 149, 154, 268
Skills acquisition, 288
Skills development, 29. *See also* Training
    programs
Smith, Adam, 31
Social clubs, 238
Social Security programs, 55
Society for Human Resource Management
    (SHRM), 130

Sony, 21–23
Split-payroll programs, 53
Spousal issues:
    assistance programs, 87, 164, 253, 263
    as success indicator, 162–163
Spouse:
    career/employment concerns, 71, 83, 87,
        163, 178, 236–237
    influence of, 38–40, 86
    meeting with expatriate families,
        191
    reentry challenges, 296–297
    resistance by, 85–86
Status reports, 66
Stern, John, 23
Stock options, 221, 227
Strategic objectives, importance of, 90
Strategic planning, 80
Structured interview, 142–143
Subsidiaries, foreign-owned, 19
Success indicators, 162–163
Succession planning, 57–58, 73, 115, 177,
    269–270
Supervisors, roles of, 88, 93–94
Supply and demand, 31
Swaak, Reyer "Rick", 84, 216
Sweeney, John J., 3

Tabuchi, Yoshihisa, 25
Tale of Three Cities, A (Hayes/Hubbard), 25
Targeting, in overseas assignment search:
    companies, 128
    countries, 128–130
    expatriate assignments by functions,
        130
Taxation:
    deferral, 227
    equalization, 206, 210
    information resources, 123–124
    issues/concerns, 56, 112–113
    planning, 293
    protection programs, 205–206
Taylor, Karen, 84, 235
Teamwork, cross-functional, 100,
    165
Technical skills, 167
Technology transfers, 48, 65–66

Temporary positions, 290–291
Terasawa, Yoshio "Terry," 268
Termination, 59–60
Texaco, 127, 297
Third-country nationals (TCNs), 17,
    34–36, 261
Thompson, Mary Anne, 129
Thunderbird International Consortia,
    147–150
Tilghman, Thomas S., 208–210
Training manager, role of, 134
Training programs:
    case illustration, 149
    consortia, 146–149
    cross-cultural, 90, 94, 115–116,
        183–188
    customized, 150–153
    distance learning combined with
        classroom sessions, 154–155
    distance learning programs, 153–154
    employment contract provision, 57
    executive, *see* Executive training
        programs
    importance of, 134–135
    language, 182
    management, in performance appraisals,
        241–245
    next assignment process, 287
    planning for, 133–134
    postarrival, 254
    postreturn, 291
    for potential expatriates, 110, 115
    prereturn, 287
    university programs geared to
        international careers, 155–156
    virtual classrooms, 155
Trait requirements:
    empathy, 172
    flexibility, 172–173
    informed judgment, 173
    listening, 169–171
    observation, 171–172
    persistence, 173–174
    respect, 168–169
    trust, 168
Trust, importance of, 168
Twinn, Bill, 51, 142

Ujiie, Junichi, 26
U.S. Bureau of Labor Statistics, 36, 39
U.S. State Department, security risk list, 61, 224
University of South Carolina, Darla Moore Graduate School of Business, 17, 23, 156
Unmarried partners, treatment of, 43–44

Vacations, 55, 238–239
Virtual classrooms, 155
Visas, 128–129
Vivendi, 21
Voluntary termination, 62-63, 259–260, 264

Watson-Wyatt, 201
Welch, Jack, 305
What Color Is Your Parachute? (Bolles), 122
Windfalls, 217
Windham International, 17, 82, 85–86, 99, 250, 258, 262, 269
Women, as expatriates, 36–37
Work permits, 128–129, 231
World Trade Organization, 1, 3

Zetsche, Dieter, 11
Zingheim, Patricia, 211